W9-BIW-794

# Steve Jobs

## A Biographic Portrait

Kevin Lynch

# Contents

# Prologue

On 7 June 2011, four months before he passed away, Steve Jobs made what was to be his final public appearance. Standing before the Cupertino City Council he would present Apple's plans for a new corporate headquarters within the district.

Just a day earlier, he'd given an assured performance delivering his final keynote during Apple's Worldwide Developers Conference at the Moscone Center in San Francisco, a swansong which saw him unveil iCloud, the company's new cloud storage service.

Belying the graveness of his now rapidly declining condition, the strident presentation had managed to convince a number of tech commentators to ignore his skeletal appearance and wrongly infer in their write-ups that Jobs was on his way back to good health.

Speaking in front of the twelve-strong committee the next day, Jobs initially cut a starkly different figure under the harsh lighting of the council chamber. Out of breath, his opening pleasantries were delivered in a voice underpinned with uncharacteristic hesitancy.

But as he began to detail how the huge complex would resolve Apple's long-standing issue of housing its soaring workforce numbers, Jobs began to find his footing. Palpably enthused, up went the tempo as he described the planned construction project which had already earned the grandiose nickname of 'The Mothership'.

Where had his new energy come from?

Maybe it was the need to get across his vision for what was ultimately his last big project – the final time he would fulfil his seemingly innate burning need to build something great – an urge that had been a running feature throughout his working life. More likely it was the excitement in relaying the news to those present that his grand plan had finally come together to keep Apple within Cupertino – a short, ten-minute drive from the garage in

Mountain View where he had cofounded the company thirty-five years earlier with Steve Wozniak.

There had been an impasse for some time as Apple struggled to find land within the city sufficient to build an HQ capable of housing 12,000 members of staff. But then a property became available which had particular emotional significance to Jobs, poignantly offering the opportunity to bring his life full circle during one of its final acts.

The land beneath the proposed site was once owned by Hewlett-Packard, a company that had sparked the technological revolution in the area during the late 1930s and, crucially, had given him an early glimpse of the world of computers as a young teen.

> 'So we've got a plan that lets us stay in Cupertino. We went out and we bought some land and this land is kind of special, to me,' Jobs explained during the council meeting.
>
> 'When I was thirteen, Hewlett and Packard were my idols – and I called up Bill Hewlett, 'cause he lived in Palo Alto and there were no unlisted numbers in the phone book. And he picked up the phone and I talked to him and I asked him if he'd give me some spare parts for something I was building called a frequency counter. And he did, but in addition to that, he gave me something way more important – he gave me a job that summer.
>
> 'A summer job at Hewlett-Packard, right here in Santa Clara, right here off 280, the division that built frequency counters.
>
> 'And I was in heaven.'

His recollections of how that summer job had fuelled his interest in electronics and technology made it clear for anyone at the council meeting that the Apple Park project was also serving as a means for Jobs to pay something back. It was a chance for him to leave a final mark on the southern portion of the Bay Area that had shaped his life. He was raised in its free-wheeling culture of experimentation and innovation, its spirit and energy coursing through his veins.

Steve Jobs was a true son of Silicon Valley. The ultimate example.

Chapter One

# To put a ding in the universe

## Steven Paul Jobs was five years old when his family moved from his birthplace of San Francisco to the idyllic suburb of Mountain View, California.

It may have just been a relatively short forty-five-minute drive away from their previous home, but the change from city surroundings was keenly felt. The move to their new cookie-cutter estate house was the final piece in the puzzle for Paul and Clara Jobs, achieving their dream of becoming a stereotypical 1950s American family – something that had once seemed very much out of reach.

The working-class couple married in 1946, but an ectopic pregnancy had ended Clara's hopes of being able to bear children.

The pair were given the opportunity to adopt Steve just a few days after his birth on 24 February 1955. They would go on to further expand the Jobs family three years later when they adopted once again – this time a girl they would name Patty.

Steve had been given up by his birth mother, a graduate student at the University of Wisconsin named Joanna Schieble. A German-Swiss Catholic, Schieble had fallen in love with Abdulfattah Jandali, a Muslim PhD candidate studying political science from Syria who was the son of a self-made millionaire oil magnate. The relationship dismayed Schieble's strict Christian conservative father – unwilling to upset him as he had become terminally ill, and mindful of the prevailing negative attitudes towards unwed mothers at that time, Schieble moved to San Francisco. She separated from Jandali who remained in Wisconsin and reluctantly decided to give up her baby on condition that the adoptive parents be Catholic and college educated.

Neither of the prospective parents were graduates, a detail that prompted Schieble to initially refuse to sign over her child to them. After weeks of negotiating via the doctor, Paul and Clara agreed to guarantee that they would provide a savings account which would eventually fund the boy's college education. It was a significant commitment at that time for a working-class family on a modest income and one that was enough to convince Schieble to relent.

How seriously the Jobs had taken the pledge of ensuring their son's education was illustrated early on when it was time for him to begin elementary school. While looking after her two children as a stay at home mum, Clara had taught Steve to read by the age of just three. This meant by the time he started Monta Loma Elementary he was already far advanced beyond his peers.

While he may not have had the academic background necessary to satisfy Schieble's discerning standards, Paul Jobs also played a full role in encouraging his son's curiosity to learn. Crucially, his love and knowledge of mechanics and craftsmanship would go on to prove a significant influence on his son's later life.

As an adult, Steve would describe his adopted father as a 'genius with his hands', crediting Paul's attention to detail for his own interest in good design and stating that the only thing he wished to pass on to his own children was 'to try to be as good a father to them as my father was to me'.

Paul Jobs had become an engine mechanic after dropping out of high school before signing up to the Coast Guard at the age of nineteen and serving during the Second World War. Thanks to a number of minor misdemeanours he never rose above the low rank of seaman, and he eventually left the guard around the time he married Clara to become a blue-collar machinist. His love and knowledge of automobiles would go on to lead to jobs as a 'repo-man' – retrieving cars from customers unable to make their payments. Paul would top up his income by restoring and selling old cars in his spare time, meaning the family garage was continually in use and a place of fascination for his inquisitive son. Hoping to feed his interest, Paul set aside some space for his young apprentice.

'He had a workbench out in his garage,' Steve recalled once during an interview. 'When I was about five or six, he sectioned off a little piece of it and said, "Steve, this is your workbench now." And he gave me some of his smaller tools and showed me how to use a hammer and saw and how to build things. It really was very good for me. He spent a lot of time with me... teaching me how to build things, how to take things apart, put things back together.' While his father was no expert in the field, the sessions in the garage helping him to rebuild cars as well as household repair projects also exposed Steve to electronics.

The Jobs had landed in Mountain View in 1960 during a period when many young families were flocking to the area. The relocation of Paul's repossession work had prompted their move, but many of the new inhabitants in and around the Santa Clara Valley were engineers, chemists, programmers and physicists who were flooding to the region's booming semiconductor, telecommunications and electronics industries.

Just a mile or two from the Jobs's new home, Shockley Semiconductor Laboratory had become the first company to develop silicon semiconductor devices towards the end of the 1950s. This advancement would prove a major breakthrough for computing but the triumph would be short lived for the company's founder, Nobel Prize–winning physicist William Shockley. His heavy-handed management style brought about a near mutiny of the young, brilliant engineers he had brought to the company. The talented group would soon leave to set up Fairchild Semiconductor, a company that would in turn later birth chip giants such as Intel and AMD.

Hewlett-Packard began in a garage in Palo Alto as far back as the late 1930s and its presence now loomed large over the valley, with the company boasting a 9,000-strong workforce making its technical instruments by the start of the 1960s. Meanwhile Stanford Industrial Park had opened, with the local university leasing portions of its land to companies such as Eastman Kodak, General Electric and Lockheed Corporation, cleverly linking the flourishing tech industry with academic talent from the valley.

The city's population had more than doubled during the preceding decade, with the fruit orchards that had previously characterised the town cleared to make way for highways, new schools and large bases for the host of new tech startups that would shape the area's future. The rapidly changing environment around their home made the Santa Clara Valley area particularly conducive for a young student like Steve to develop an interest in computers.

'It was really the most wonderful place in the world to grow up. There was a man who moved in down the street, maybe about six or seven houses down the block who was new in the neighbourhood with his wife, and it turned out that he was an engineer at Hewlett-Packard and a ham radio operator and really into electronics. What he did to get to know the kids in the block was rather a strange thing: he put out a carbon microphone and a battery and a speaker on his driveway where you could talk into the microphone and your voice would be amplified by the speaker. Kind of strange thing when you move into a neighborhood but that's what he did.'

It would be more than ten years before journalist Don Hoefler would coin the term 'Silicon Valley' in a 1971 newspaper article when describing the region, but at the time of the Jobs family's arrival in town, most residents of Santa Clara Valley would have already been acutely aware that the world's epicentre for technology was already emerging on their doorstep.

# Key Figures

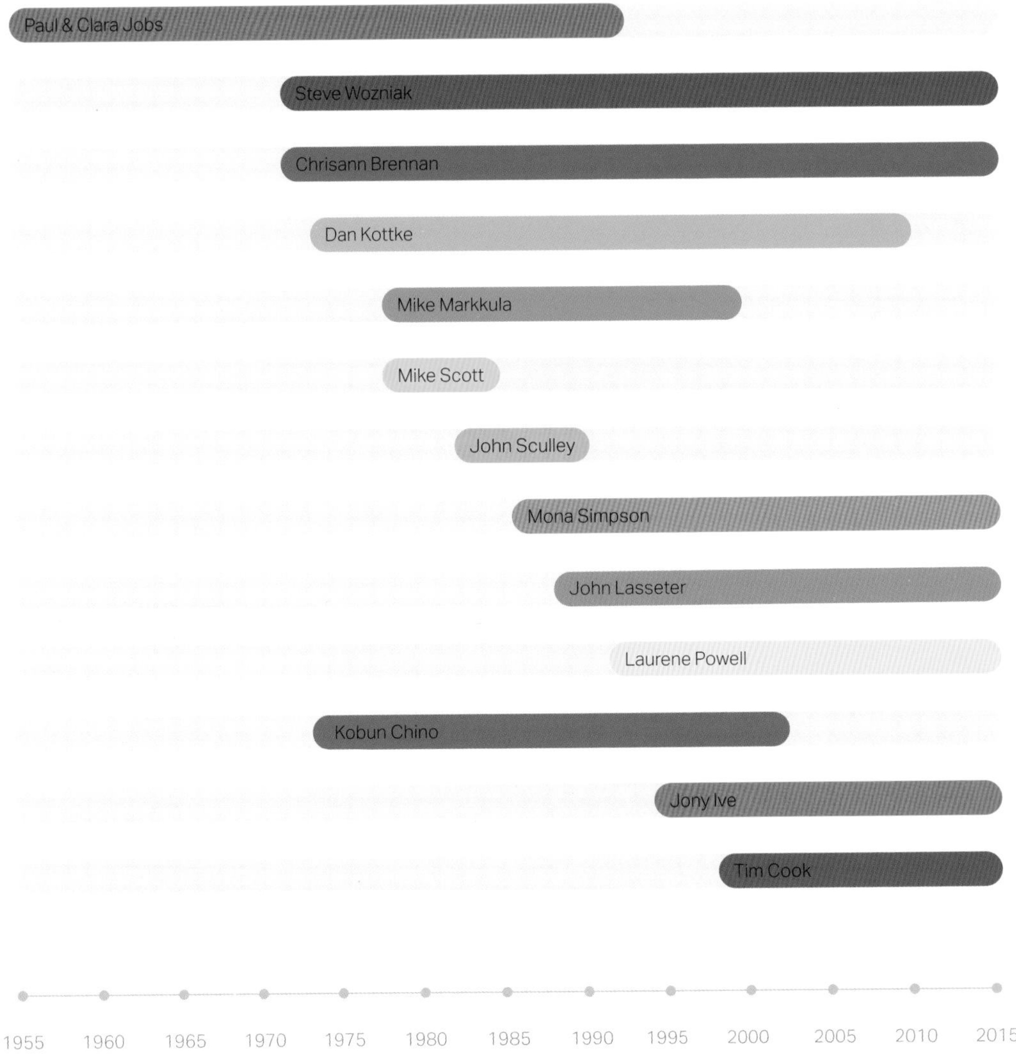

Paul & Clara Jobs
Steve Wozniak
Chrisann Brennan
Dan Kottke
Mike Markkula
Mike Scott
John Sculley
Mona Simpson
John Lasseter
Laurene Powell
Kobun Chino
Jony Ive
Tim Cook
1955
1960
1965
1970
1975
1980
1985
1990
1995
2000
2005
2010
2015

### Paul & Clara Jobs

Adoptive parents. Paul was a machinist for a firm that made lasers in what became Silicon Valley, in Northern California. Clara was the daughter of Armenian immigrants and worked as an accountant.

### Steve Wozniak

Electronics genius who founded Apple with Steve Jobs. Single-handedly developed its launch computer, the Apple I, in 1976.

### Chrisann Brennan

Jobs's high school girlfriend. On and off, often turbulent relationship which didn't improve following the birth of their daughter Lisa.

### Dan Kottke

Steve's college friend and travel companion on visit to India. Went on to become one of Apple's first employees.

### Mike Markkula

Apple's first major investor and employee number three.

### Mike Scott

Apple's first CEO. Brought in by Mike Markkula as Jobs and Wozniak were considered too young and inexperienced to manage a company.

### John Sculley

Brought in from Pepsi to take over as Apple CEO in 1983. Was at the helm when Jobs was kicked out of the company two years later.

### Mona Simpson

Acclaimed author and biological sister of Steve Jobs. Born in 1957, two years after Steve Jobs had been born and adopted and their parents had married. Did not meet her brother until 1986. After being reunited they became very close.

### John Lasseter

CGI animation pioneer and cofounder and CEO of Pixar.

### Laurene Powell

American business executive. Married Steve Jobs in 1991. Together they had three children.

### Kobun Chino

Sōtō Zen master. Became Jobs's spiritual teacher and presided over his wedding to Laurene.

### Jony Ive

British industrial designer. Has headed up Apple's design team since 1986. Was a major figure in the company's resurgence.

### Tim Cook

Originally hired by Jobs in 1998 as Apple's chief operating officer. Eventually took over from Jobs as CEO in August 2011.

# Silicon Valley

## How the epicentre of tech came to be

### 1939

William Hewlett and Dave Packard establish Hewlett-Packard in Palo Alto, with the company initially making oscilloscopes.

### 1956

William Shockley, one of the inventors of the transistor, opens Shockley Semiconductor Labs in Mountain View, California. Employs many graduates from nearby Stanford University and becomes the first company to make transistors out of silicon.

### 1957

Eight former Shockley employees partner with investor and inventor Sherman Fairchild to create Fairchild Semiconductor. Specialising in the manufacturing of transistors, it goes on to make computer components for the Apollo program.

### 1968

Chemist Gordon Moore and physicist Robert Noyce leave Fairchild to found their own company in Santa Clara called Intel. In the years that follow, other former Fairchild employees will go on to found key tech firms such as AMD, Nvidia, and venture fund Kleiner Perkins.

### 1969

Stanford Research Institute becomes one of the four nodes of ARPANET (Advanced Research Projects Agency Network), a government research project that becomes the technical foundation of the Internet.

### 1970

Xerox opens its pioneering PARC lab in Palo Alto. Prototypes developed for a mouse, and a groundbreaking graphical user interface observed by Steve Jobs during a tour of PARC at the end of the decade go on to inspire key features of the Apple Lisa.

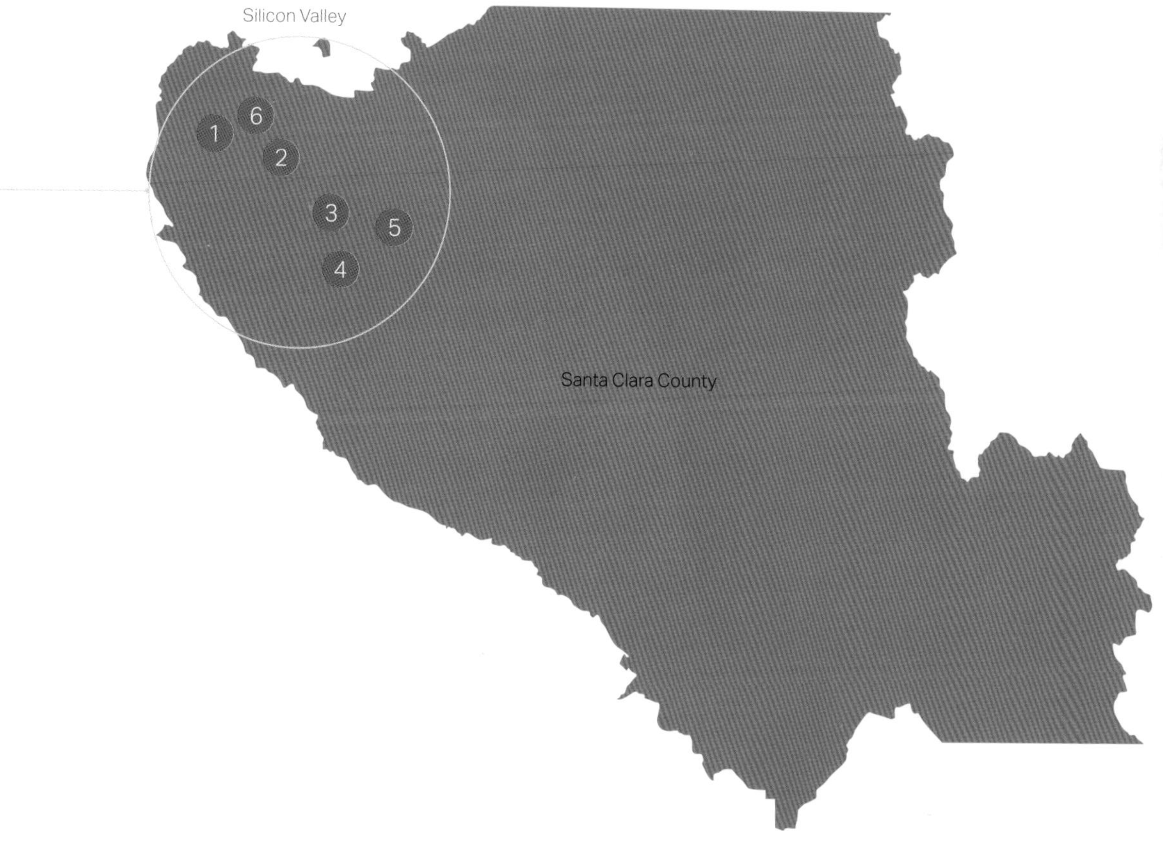
Silicon Valley
1
6
2
3
5
4
Santa Clara County

Chapter Two

# Creativity is just connecting things

2

'So does that mean your real parents didn't want you?' The young Steve Jobs had always known that he was adopted, but these cutting words had sent him into a tailspin.

He was around the age of six or seven when the loaded question was put to him by a young girl who lived across the street.

'Lightning bolts went off in my head,' Jobs vividly recalled some five decades later. 'I remember running into the house, crying. And my parents said, "No, you have to understand." They were very serious and looked me straight in the eye. They said, "We specifically picked you out." Both of my parents said that and repeated it slowly for me. And they put an emphasis on every word in that sentence.'

While it was often levelled at Jobs that some of his quick-tempered behaviour in later life could be explained by a sense of abandonment as a child, Jobs was always quick to dismiss the idea, saying his awareness of his adoption had made him feel more independent, while the love given to him by Paul and Clara allayed any feelings of rejection.

'I've always felt special. My parents made me feel special.' Hyperactive, and often temperamental, parenting their uniquely inquisitive adopted son was not without its challenges. He would often wake early in the morning looking for stimulus, resulting in him being bought a rocking horse and a record player with some Little Richard LPs for him to entertain himself with during those early rises.

Young Steve would also be no stranger to the local hospital, with a dash to the emergency room required on one occasion after he ingested a bottle of ant poison, while his curiosity to discover what would happen if he jammed a hair clip into an electric socket resulted in him being treated for painful burns to the hand.

Keen to fulfil the pledge they had made to his birth mother, Paul and Clara nurtured and indulged their son and did everything they could to ensure he remained set on an academic path. While unquestionably something of a handful, Steve was also exceptionally clever, a fact that both his parents and Steve were acutely aware of at an early point.

Markedly ahead of his peers, he was often unchallenged during lessons at Monta Loma Elementary, causing concern for Paul and Clara when the boredom inevitably turned to mischief-making and a refusal to do the undemanding work he had been set.

Prank-playing would become a feature of Jobs's youth, a trait of his that would first come to the fore as early as the third grade. Finding a like-minded sidekick in his classmate Rick Farentino, on one occasion they left a teacher traumatised after setting explosives off under her desk, while on another they caused chaos by switching the locks on other pupils' bikes after somehow managing to get them to reveal the combinations.

Such high jinks would often result in Steve being sent home, but while Paul Jobs would be firm with his son over his behaviour, he would direct the blame towards the school, asking his teachers to acknowledge that his son was special and that they needed to keep him interested and occupied.

By the fourth grade Steve was separated into another class from Rick, and fell under the wing of Imogene 'Teddy' Hill – the first teacher to truly recognise how bright he was. In later life Jobs would describe her as a saint. 'I learned more from her than any other teacher, and if it hadn't been for her I'm sure I would have gone to jail,' he would acknowledge.

While others saw him as a troublemaker, she worked hard to keep him motivated, initially through the use of bribes, with Teddy offering lollipops and the incentive of a $5 prize if he completed his math workbooks. Eventually the inducements were no longer necessary, with Steve just eager to please his tutor, and he began to flourish.

Encouraged by the progress he had made, Teddy had Steve tested towards the end of fourth grade. The results arrived back with Steve scoring at high school sophomore level, prompting the school to advise he skip two years and go straight into seventh grade. Cautiously Paul and Clara agreed for him to be pushed up a single grade.

While both his teachers and parents saw the move as necessary, the change for Steve was not a smooth one. The leap in grades meant moving to Crittenden Middle, a tough school that had created local headlines for gang fights and the burning of a rival school's bus following a defeat in a wrestling match. Younger, awkward and seemingly wirier than everyone else, he was regularly bullied.

After a year of being put upon, Steve gave his parents an ultimatum. An early display of the strong-willed nature that characterised so many pivotal moments in his later life, he refused to go back to Crittenden after finishing sixth grade and pleaded with his parents to send him to a better school. Such a change would require a move to a new school district and a considerable outlay for the already stretched young family. However, with Paul and Clara having misgivings about sending Patty to schools within the Mountain View, area they opted to up sticks a few miles south to Los Altos.

Situated in a reasonably affluent neighbourhood that had emerged from what had previously been plum orchards, the new Jobs family home at 2066 Crist Drive was on a quiet housing estate and had three bedrooms. Crucially, it came with a garage that would allow Paul to continue fixing up old cars, and would later become the base from which Apple Computers would be birthed.

Steve settled well in the area and soon made fast friends with classmate Bill Fernandez at his new school, Cupertino Junior High. The pair would bond over a shared love of electronics and would work together on science fair projects, with Steve hanging out for hours on end after lessons in his new friend's garage to fix and fiddle with electronic gadgets.

Jobs would also spend free time visiting the house of his old neighbour Larry Lang, a Hewlett-Packard engineer who introduced him to Heathkits – do-it-yourself packs for aspiring engineers which let them build their own oscilloscopes, radios and other electronics. It proved a crucial grounding, as he later admitted:

'You looked at a television set and you would think that, "I haven't built one of those but I could. There's one of those in the Heathkit catalogue and I've built two other Heathkits, so I could build that."

'Things became much more clear that they were the results of human creation, not these magical things that just appeared in one's environment and that one had no knowledge of their interiors.'

Encouraged by Lang, Jobs would further his knowledge by joining the local Explorers Club, a small group of kids who would regularly gather in the company cafeteria at Hewlett-Packard's campus in Palo Alto on Tuesday evenings. There they would be given lessons from HP engineers and set electronics projects.

During a tour of a lab as part of one of those evening sessions, Jobs was given a tantalising glimpse into his future when he was allowed to view a new device HP were developing.

# The inspiration machine

'I fell in love with it,' Jobs once admitted, recalling when he first set eyes on Hewlett-Packard's 9100A as an impressionable youngster at HP's Explorers Club at Homestead High. Described by *Wired* magazine as the first real desktop computer, the 'glorified calculator' proved a massively influential device for Jobs.

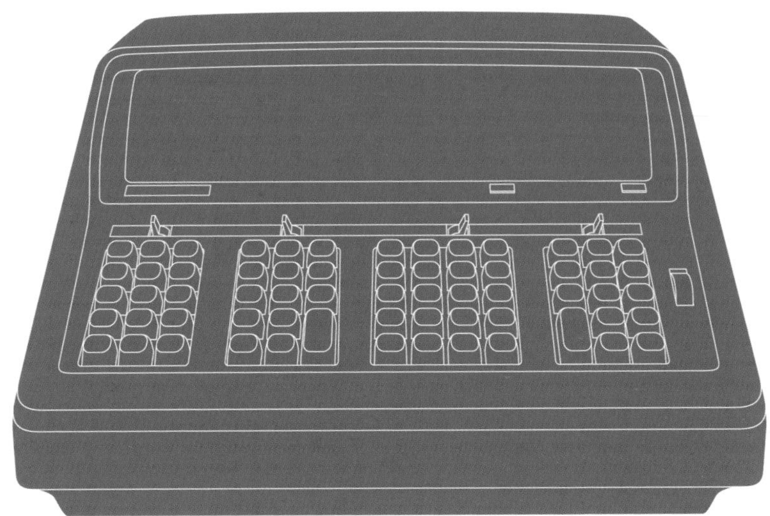

Released

1968

Weight

40lbs (about the size and weight of a professional typewriter at that point)

Price

$5,000
(equivalent to $36,026.93 in 2017)

Display

Three-line CRT readout

Storage

Magnetic card

Hard copies

Optional roll printer

First scientific calculator

The 9100A had trig, log/ln, and exponential functions

> 'I saw my first desktop computer there. It was called the 9100A, and it was a glorified calculator but also really the first desktop computer. It was huge, maybe forty pounds, but it was a beauty of a thing. I fell in love with it.'

Recalling when Bill Hewlett himself had chatted with him for twenty minutes and given him a summer job on the assembly line at Hewlett-Packard, Jobs said he was, 'assembling frequency counters... well, assembling may be too strong. I was putting in screws. It didn't matter.'

'I remember my first day on the assembly line at HP,' he reminisced. 'I was expressing my complete enthusiasm and bliss at being there for the summer to my supervisor, a guy named Chris, telling him that my favorite thing in the whole world was electronics. I asked him what his favorite thing to do was and he looked at me and said, "To f---!" I learned a lot that summer.'

The formative experience was followed by another as Jobs and his friend Fernandez entered Homestead High school in the fall of 1968, amid a backdrop of turmoil across the United States. Anti-Vietnam War riots had broken out on campuses across the country, including the nearby Berkeley and San Francisco State. Lyndon Johnson's grip on power as President was slipping, while Martin Luther King Jr and Bobby Kennedy's assassinations within weeks of each other only served to stoke the idealism of the nation's disaffected youth, pushing many towards the Bay Area's emerging counterculture.

The changing cultural landscape unsurprisingly had an influence on the pubescent Jobs, with his hair growing ever longer over the course of his freshman year at Homestead as he tuned in to the nonconformist spirit of the times. Homestead was a stark, sprawling two-storey complex designed by a prison architect that housed 2,000 students. While Jobs struggled to find friends of his own age there, he found like minds in a group of seniors who shared his curiosity in the nascent hippie movement as well as pranks and, crucially, electronics.

Keen to meet others who were into the emerging electronics scene, around this time Bill Fernandez introduced Jobs to another of his friends. His go-to person when his solder and circuit board projects ran into trouble, Steve Wozniak lived down the street from Fernandez. The son of a engineer at Lockheed, he'd won a number of local electronics fairs and was already beginning to develop a reputation as a local technological wizard. Boasting an IQ of 200, by the age of eleven, Wozniak had produced an electronic noughts and crosses game completely designed around the capability of logic circuits. By his late teens he had a deep knowledge of the scientific programming language FORTRAN.

The meeting with Jobs provided Wozniak the opportunity to show off his latest project. Working over the course of a year in Bill's father's garage, Wozniak had built a computer with Fernandez's assistance using cast-off components gathered from nearby semiconductor companies. Named the 'Cream Soda computer' on account of the industrial amount of Cragmont Cream Soda the pair had consumed during their late-night sessions working on the project, the pair had built what was in effect the first ever hobbyist computer, a full five years before similar devices would appear on the market. Essentially a calculator, programs were entered on the Cream Soda via punched cards with the results displayed using a series of flashing lights. Jobs was blown away by the demonstration and left stunned by how Wozniak's understanding of computing was so far beyond that of his peers.

Despite Jobs being five years younger than Wozniak, the two Steves had plenty of common ground, trading stories about pranks they had pulled and the music they were into – another of Jobs's emerging interests at the time.

Shy, nerdy and somewhat immature, Wozniak's demeanour was in stark contrast to Jobs's articulate and emerging outgoing personality. The energy and enthusiasm of his namesake impressed Wozniak, while Jobs was blown away by Woz's undeniable knowledge and skillset. It made for a dynamic relationship full of potential and one that the pair were fated to harness to near legendary effect.

# The Woz

## Older than Jobs

Steve Wozniak was born in San Jose California, on 11 August 1950, five years before Steve Jobs.

## A precocious talent

Wozniak showed an early interest and aptitude for electronics and computers. In fifth grade he built his own radio transmitter and receiver.The following year he built a machine that played tic-tac-toe.

## A college dropout

Like Jobs, Wozniak didn't finish his degree. He first attended Berkeley in 1971, but ended up taking a break from studying electrical engineering to work on Apple and make money to pay for his fourth year. He would eventually go on to finish the degree in 1986.

## He single-handedly developed the Apple I

He alone designed its hardware, circuit board designs, and operating system in 1976. He also primarily designed its follow up, the Apple II

## He sold most of his Apple stock in the 1980s

Looking to pursue a more engineering-focused role elsewhere, Wozniak decided to quit Apple in 1985, selling most of his stock.

## He survived an airplane crash

He was injured after a premature takeoff from Santa Cruz Sky Park in 1981. He had no recollection of the incident for some time after the crash, but over time he eventually regained his memory.

## A sworn member of the Freemasons

Wozniak says he joined in 1980 in order to spend more time with his then wife Alice.

## Created the first programmable universal remote

The 'CORE' was created in 1987 by CL 9, a startup founded by Wozniak.

## He's in the US National Inventors Hall of Fame

He joined the likes of Henry Ford and George Eastman in 2000 when he was inducted for creating the personal computer.

## Segway sportsman

In his spare time, Woz enjoys playing Segway polo. Similar to the traditional version of the game (played on horseback), Segway polo is now an international sport, governed by the International Segway Polo Association (ISPA).

## He held his own music festival

While on his leave from Apple, Woz took the time to organise a huge three-day event called the US Festival held over the Labor Day weekend in 1982. It featured big name acts including Van Halen, Fleetwood Mac and the Grateful Dead, but it made a huge financial loss.

## Still an Apple employee

Wozniak still receives an annual fixed-sum salary that's estimated to be worth at least $120,000.

## Chapter Three

# Here's to the crazy ones

Like most schools in the area, Homestead High offered students a host of elective classes to complement their mandatory curriculum. While autoshop and woodwork were popular choices, one class in particular sparked the creative interest in Cupertino's kids.

John McCollum was a retired navy pilot, with a passion for nurturing budding computer engineers through his electronics course. A notable star pupil of McCollum's had been Steve Wozniak, who had graduated from Homestead a couple of years prior to Jobs starting there.

An engaging, almost showman-like tutor, McCollum's course mixed theory with a strong practical, product-oriented approach, churning out a long line of fine engineers. Indeed the course would inspire several key future designers of Apple Computer machinery.

McCollum's teaching methods were informed by his military past, with discipline and respect for authority the order of the day. For a well-behaved student like Wozniak, who had been brought up in a conservative, disciplinarian household, this wasn't an issue.

Jobs's rebellious, sometimes arrogant nature, on the other hand, did not sit well in the class. Aloof and often self-isolating during lessons, a flashpoint came when Jobs required a part for a course project. Mirroring his audacious call to Bob Hewlett some months earlier, he made a collect call to a part manufacturer in Detroit, claiming he was designing a new product and wanted to test out the part.

'I was furious. That was not the way I wanted my students to behave,' McCollum said, recalling when he found out about his student's ruse.

> 'And sure enough, in a day or so the parts arrived by airfreight. I didn't like the way he had done it but I had to respect his results.'

Jobs quit the course by the time of his sophomore year, making the realisation, perhaps, that he was more of a tinkerer than a dedicated engineer – a dreamer and a designer rather than a scientist. While he was tiring of the mathematical and systematic aspects of electronic

# *Breakout*!

Jobs and Wozniak took the original bat and ball approach of the classic arcade game *Pong* and added a brand new spin to create *Breakout* for Atari.

### 11,000

Estimated number of *Breakout* cabinets constructed during its production run.

### Home console version

Released in 1978, a version of *Breakout* was among the first cartridges available for Atari's 2600 home console.

### 2

Number of levels - at the time a novel feature for a video game.

### 4

Number of days Wozniak took to complete the prototype.

### Easter egg

A nod to Apple's beginnings, holding down the centre button for a few seconds in the 'About' menu on the original iPod would open a secret version of *Breakout* on the device.

### 1975

Year development began on the game. Jobs was just nineteen years old at the time. It was released in May the following year.

## Single-player gaming

Atari founder Nolan Bushnell wanted a game based on the company's earlier classic *Pong* that didn't require two players.

## Black & white monitor

While the *Breakout* arcade cabinet used a monochrome monitor, the display was treated with an overlay to make the bricks appear coloured.

## 896

Maximum score a player can achieve.

## 44

Number of integrated circuit chips that Wozniak's *Breakout* prototype efficiently required – most games of the time typically needed around 150.

## Space Invaders

Designer Tomohiro Nishikado has admitted his classic shoot 'em up, released in 1978, was hugely inspired by Atari's game and its emphasis on high scores and levels.

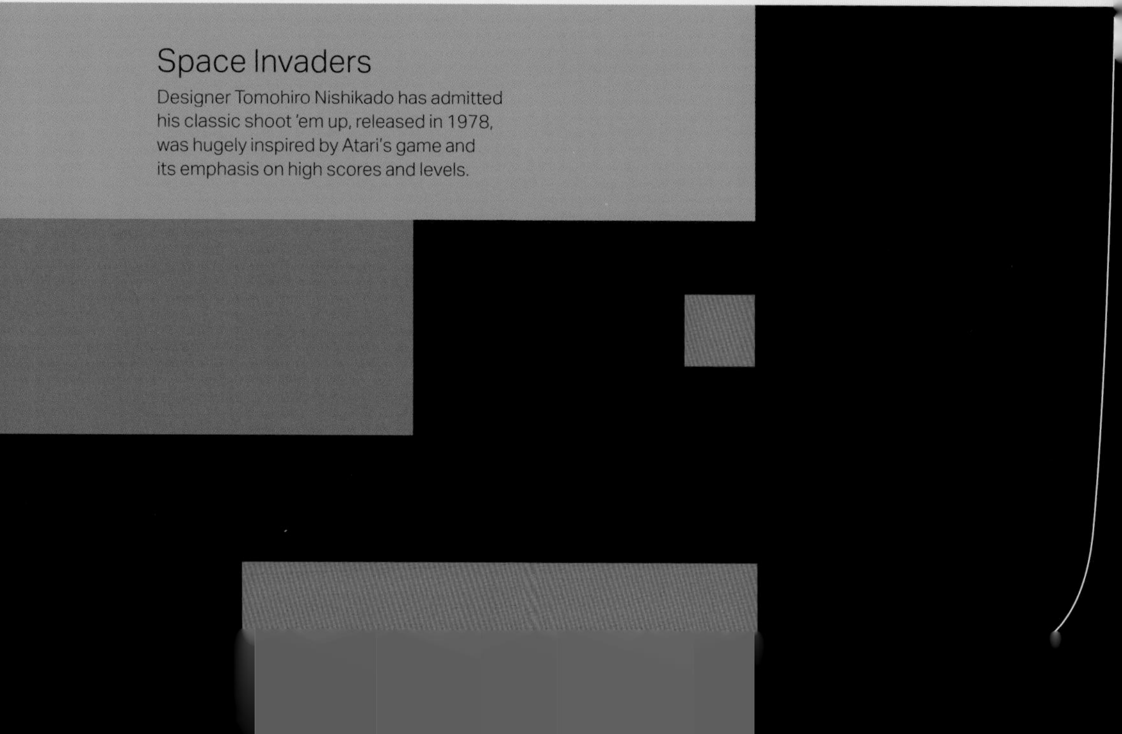

engineering, his fascination with the world of components and parts remained. His attention had turned from the uses of the components to using the components to make him cash. Following a similar path to his father Paul in his haggling and fixing up of broken-down cars, much of Steve's free time after school was spent sourcing computer and hi-fi parts from a junkyard warehouse called Haltek, before selling them on at a higher price or using them to repair equipment at a profit.

During this period, Jobs's friendship with Wozniak began to solidify as they hung out at the Fernandez family garage. Like Jobs, Wozniak had also had to deal with his own academic disappointments. His freshman year at the University of Colorado was beset with poor grades, in part due to his preference to playing bridge and playing pranks rather than studying, with much of his time on site spent using the college's computers to work on his own programs. It would eventually emerge that he had used so much time-share that he had consumed five times the level of the computer science department's annual budget. With his parents unable to afford the high out-of-state tuition fees, Wozniak opted to return to California and instead attend De Anza Community College.

Wozniak would go on to eventually enrol at Berkeley early in 1971, with Jobs making the 40-mile cross-bay journey two or three times a week to see his friend, driving in a red Fiat 850 coupe he had paid for after landing casual work at Haltek.

In addition to their interest in computers, they shared a passion for music, with Wozniak introducing Jobs to Bob Dylan's already rich body of socially conscious folk music. The pair would spend hours on end discussing the singer's linear notes and lyrics of political protest and social commentary while plotting missions to hunt down rare bootleg tapes of their idol. Wozniak explained the fascination as pivotal to shaping the pair's outlook on life:

> 'The Beatles' music was nice and good, but Bob Dylan had words that had meaning to life that you could actually base some of your own philosophies on and that was important to both of us.'

The Dylan obsession was also key in pivoting Jobs's interest further away from science and towards the arts during his junior year in high school, in particular literature and film.

# Hack to the future

Jobs and Wozniak's first business was selling 'Blue Boxes' – simple electronic gadgets that bypassed telephone company billing computers, allowing anyone to make free telephone calls anywhere in the world.

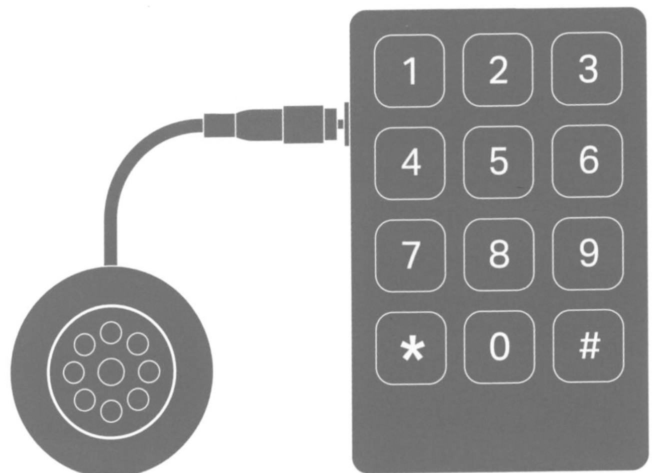


### Library discovery

Jobs and Wozniak began making their first box after stumbling upon an AT&T technical journal at Stanford University's library detailing secret tones for making free calls.

### 2600 Hz

Frequency produced by Blue Box – in sync with the tone used by AT&T to switch long-distance calls.

### Inspired by Captain Crunch

One of the early pioneers of 'phone phreaking' was John Draper, who got his nickname thanks to a free toy whistle in Cap'n Crunch breakfast cereal that could generate a 2600 Hz tone.

### $6,000

Amount reportedly made by Jobs and Wozniak selling Blue Boxes.

### Parts

Jobs and Wozniak's blue box consisted of a set of audio oscillators, a telephone keypad, an audio amplifier and a speaker.

### Prank call tool

Wozniak claims he once was able to prank the Vatican using a Blue Box. Posing as Henry Kissinger, he managed to convince some cardinals but was unable to speak to the Pope who was sleeping.

> 'I got stoned for the first time; I discovered Shakespeare, Dylan Thomas, and all that classic stuff. I read *Moby-Dick* and went back as a junior taking creative writing classes.'

Opting out of the electronics club that had been a big part of his spare time in previous years, Jobs formed a club alongside his friend Steve Echstein which put on laser light shows for experimental jazz concerts that featured a group made up of members of Homestead High's marching band. Named the Buck Fry Club, a scatalogical play on the name of the school's principal Warren Bryld, alongside the concerts the club would also serve as a means for organising pranks. These would graduate from low level antics such as gluing a gold-painted toilet seat onto a flower planter, to far larger-scale stunts such as raising a Volkswagen Beetle onto the roof of the school cafeteria.

Showing his support, Wozniak and his friend Allen Baum, who had both long since graduated from Homestead, joined forces with Jobs, at the end of his junior year, to produce a farewell gesture for the departing seniors. On a big bedsheet Baum had tie-dyed with the school's green and white colours, they painted a huge hand flipping the middle-finger salute along with the words 'Best Wishes' and 'SWAB JOB', the initials of Wozniak and Baum combined with part of Jobs's name. Using a system of ropes and pulleys and perfect timing, the offensive banner was lowered as the graduating class marched past a balcony at the end of the ceremony. The prank earned Jobs a suspension along with a place in the school's folklore.

The thirst for anarchic kicks led Jobs and Wozniak on a trail towards their first commercial venture in the autumn of 1972. Wozniak's mum alerted her son to an article in *Esquire* magazine she thought he would find of particular interest. It detailed an underground group of what would now be commonly referred to as hackers who were building devices called 'blue boxes'. The makeshift gizmos gave out the same sounds that phone companies used to transmit calls. Replicating the tones' exact frequency allowed 'phone phreaks' to catch a phone line and make calls for free anywhere in the world.

With long-distance calls prohibitively expensive and with most people only having one telecoms company available to them, the potential for pulling a fast one over the behemoth phone giants and their monopolies excited Wozniak immensely.

'I was so grabbed by the article,' Wozniak explained, 'I called Steve Jobs before I was halfway through and started reading him passages.'

The next day the pair headed to Stanford Library where they hit gold and found a journal article that listed the little-known frequencies required for spoofing the phone companies' tones.

The pair became obsessed. 'I had a manual typewriter,' Wozniak recalled, 'and I retyped the entire article, every single word, in case I lost the original.' The pair sought out 'Captain Crunch', the most infamous phone phreak profiled in the *Esquire* article who had earned his nickname for his use of a whistle found in Cap'n Crunch cereal boxes that was able to match the 2600 Hertz call-routing tones. 'I imagined him as some suave woman's guy,' Wozniak recalled. 'He showed up and he was much more of a geek. He smelled like he hadn't taken a shower in a while.'

Inspired to improve upon the likes of Captain Crunch's groundwork, Wozniak set about designing his own blue box. Wozniak was well versed in the concept of an oscillator – an electronic device that generates tones – while Jobs had built a frequency counter several years earlier and had worked on assembly lines putting counters together during occasional work at Hewlett-Packard, giving him the know-how for testing Wozniak's designs.

Aiming to create a digital device that was better than any of the amateurish blue boxes circulating within the community, after months of work, Wozniak came up with a working design that cut down on the parts and complexity of what had gone before. The battery-powered unit – Woz's first printed circuit board – featured a keypad tethered to an earpiece. Ingeniously the device did away with an on–off switch, with the box automatically working whenever one of the keys was pressed, prefiguring Apple's disposition for refined innovation.

Inevitably, the pair would use their new creation for prank calls, with Wozniak infamously calling the Vatican, pretending to be Henry Kissinger, before a suspicious bishop called a halt to the stunt by calling the real deal Henry Kissinger, stopping Woz in his tracks before he got to the Pope who had been sleeping at the time.

For Jobs, the device opened his eyes to the potential of the duo's partnership. 'We would give them to our friends and use them ourselves. And you know, you rapidly run out of people you want to call. But it was the magic that two teenagers could build this box for $100 worth of parts and control 100s of billions of dollars of infrastructure in the entire telephone network in the whole world,' he explained.

While Wozniak may have just settled for the glory of having created the device and putting one on 'the Man,' Jobs was quick to recognise an opportunity and came up with a plan to market the blue box to university students in California who were eager to make free phone calls.

The pair hatched a scheme to hawk the very much illegal device on college dormitory hallways, knocking on doors and asking those inside if they were at George's room – a fictional character who happened to be an expert phone phreak. If the discussion triggered an interest, the pair would go into sales person mode and show off what the blue box was capable of. This would often result in a sale, with the pair charging as much as a cool $300 for the illicit gadget.

> 'Experiences like that taught us the power of ideas,'
> Jobs once proudly stated.

The pair made around a hundred blue boxes and had earned around $6,000 for their efforts, before the venture was brought to an abrupt end when the pair were robbed at gunpoint in a Sunnydale pizza parlour. Reminiscing on the hairy encounter, Wozniak told Dan Lyons in 2011: 'Two guys looked like they might be interested [in buying a blue box]. We took them back to a pay phone and made a call to Chicago for them.

> 'They were enamored and wanted the blue box, but they had no money. We got out to the car and they show up with a gun and stick it in Steve's face. We gave them the blue box. But they didn't know how to use it. They gave us a phone number to call so we could tell them how to use it. I came up with this idea of telling them a method that would get them caught by the police, or one that would get them billed. We didn't do it. But, boy, it would have been funny.'

While the whole adventure had come to a somewhat unpleasant end, the blue box project crucially marked out the first time that Jobs had acted as a conductor and conduit of Wozniak's immense talent, creating a platform from which far greater things would eventually evolve.

Indeed, Jobs once unequivocally concurred: 'If we wouldn't have made blue boxes, there would have been no Apple.'

Chapter Four

# OK, let’s get started

4

Apple I

Wozniak was still primarily fixated on the intricacies and possibilities of electronics, but Jobs was now actively seeking out the answers to life's big questions, becoming immersed in the counterculture surrounding the Bay Area.

'This was California. You could get LSD fresh made at Stanford. You could sleep on the beach at night with your girlfriend. California has a sense of experimentation, openness to new possibilities,' Jobs once recalled.

Alongside a growing interest in mind expansion and an underlying search for spiritual meaning, Jobs had also begun what would prove to be a lifelong pursuit of formulating the perfect diet, at this point insisting upon eating only fruits and vegetables.

Earlier in the year he had begun his first serious relationship. Chrisann Brennan was in junior year at Homestead and was working on an animated movie that featured the music of one of the members of the Buck Fry Club band. Petite, artistic and bohemian, Brennan would work on the film outside of class hours in order to avoid scrutiny or supervision from college staff. Such apparent disregard for authority proved attractive to a like-minded contrarian like Jobs. For Brennan, being wooed by the now guitar-strumming, poetry-loving Jobs provided a much-needed escape from difficulties at home in Sunnydale, where her parents were going through a divorce. She saw how Steve was angsty and complicated, but was drawn to his beguiling intellect and romanticism.

By the summer, the teenage romance had developed enough for the couple to rent a cabin along the ridge of the Santa Cruz Mountains, funded in part by Jobs's cut of the blue box proceeds. Steve's father was far from happy about the arrangement, but Jobs's willfulness once again persisted.

Another show of parental defiance would follow. Aiming to make good on their promise made when they adopted their son, Paul and Clara had saved up as best they could, creating a college fund for Steve. To their dismay, he stonewalled any notion of attending an affordable state school such as Berkeley, where Wozniak was; likewise the nearby Stanford where the offer of a scholarship looked likely. Jobs instead demanded he should go to the private and expensive Reed College in Portland, Oregon, the Pacific Northwest's premier liberal arts college.

'Steve said that Reed was the only college he wanted to go to,' recalled Clara, 'and if he couldn't go there he didn't want to go anywhere.' They inevitably caved in to their headstrong son's ultimatum and somehow scraped together more money to fund his academic dream.

There was scant gratitude for his parents' sacrifice evident on the day Steve headed to Reed. After driving him up to Portland, Steve refused to let them come on campus, nor even offer them a goodbye or thanks, an act he admitted to regretting in later life. 'It's one of the things in life I really feel ashamed about,' he told biographer Walter Isaacson. 'I was not very sensitive, and I hurt their feelings. I shouldn't have. They had done so much to make sure I could go there, but I just didn't want them around. I didn't want anyone to know I had parents. I wanted to be like an orphan who had bummed around the country on trains and just arrived out of nowhere, with no roots, no connections, no background.'

To add further insult, Steve's lacklustre attitude towards studying at the end of his time at Homestead High continued at Reed. Having shifted from hallucinogenic experimentation, his new major distraction was a more directed pursuit of spiritual enlightenment via the philosophies of the East. Jobs developed a strong friendship at Reed with a fellow wild-haired student named Dan Kottke who shared his love for the music of Bob Dylan as well as his new-found disdain for shoes. 'I don't think he had any other friends,' said Kottke, 'and so I thought "here is someone I can relate to"'. A dedicated acid- and pothead, Kottke was also interested in raising his spiritual consciousness, and the two helped turn each other on to Zen Buddhism and meditation.

The pair would befriend one of Reed's most notorious characters in Robert Friedland. Friedland had been elected as the college's student body president in their freshman year on the back of a campaign that mainly centred on the legalisation of LSD. Friedland had been arrested and sentenced to several years in prison following an incident a year earlier at San Francisco International airport when he was caught wearing a raincoat lined with 30,000 tabs of acid. He had campaigned for the role as President after he was released and had re-enrolled at Reed in an effort to prove that he was really of good character. Four years older than Jobs, despite being an avowed hippie, the confident and charming Friedland had an exuberant persona and a fast-talking, salesman-like patter. More crucially, he offered further perspective on Eastern spirituality, having travelled to India to meet the renowned Hindu guru Neem Karoli Baba.

According to Kottke, Friedland had a profound influence on Jobs: 'I think Robert taught him a lot about selling, about coming out of his shell, of opening up and taking charge of a situation. Robert was one of those guys who were always the center of attention. He'd walk into a room and you would instantly notice him. Well, Steve was the absolute opposite of that when he came to Reed. After he spent time with Robert some of it started to rub off.'

When Wozniak and Chrisann would come to visit him on campus, Jobs would often moan about the amount of studying required of him at Reed. Increasingly absent from his course, he would prefer dropping in on dance classes and chatting up girls rather than attending his designated lectures.

The resulting outcome was somewhat inevitable. After just one semester beset by poor grades, Steve dropped out and was given a refund on his tuition. Thanks in part to a friendship with the school's Dean of Students along with Reed's liberal attitudes, Jobs managed to remain on campus, getting a real pick-and-mix education as he dropped in on classes that sounded exciting to him, all the while living in dorm rooms vacated by other students. One such course was a calligraphy program. Years later when working on the Apple Macintosh, Jobs would refer back to those classes, using them as the basis for the device's groundbreaking use of fonts and typefaces.

While he was getting no small amount of fulfilment with his somewhat unique situation at Reed, Steve's meditation and Zen was doing little to calm his restless spirit. His interest in unusual diets grew more compulsive, with him at times living for weeks on apples or carrots, the latter causing friends to remark on it changing his complexion to an orange tinge. Believing that the answer to his spiritual hunger lay in the East, he decided on making a pilgrimage of his own to India.

Such an expedition would require money that he didn't have, so, after eighteen months at Reed, Jobs returned home and began a search for regular employment. While flicking through the pages of the *San Jose Mercury News* he saw an ad from Atari offering the opportunity to 'have fun and make money' on their electrical engineering team. Based in the Bay Area, the pioneering video game company had recently released the tennis-inspired arcade machine *Pong* which had caused a massive stir locally in the nascent Silicon Valley area and was now on its way to becoming a worldwide craze.

# The Apple I

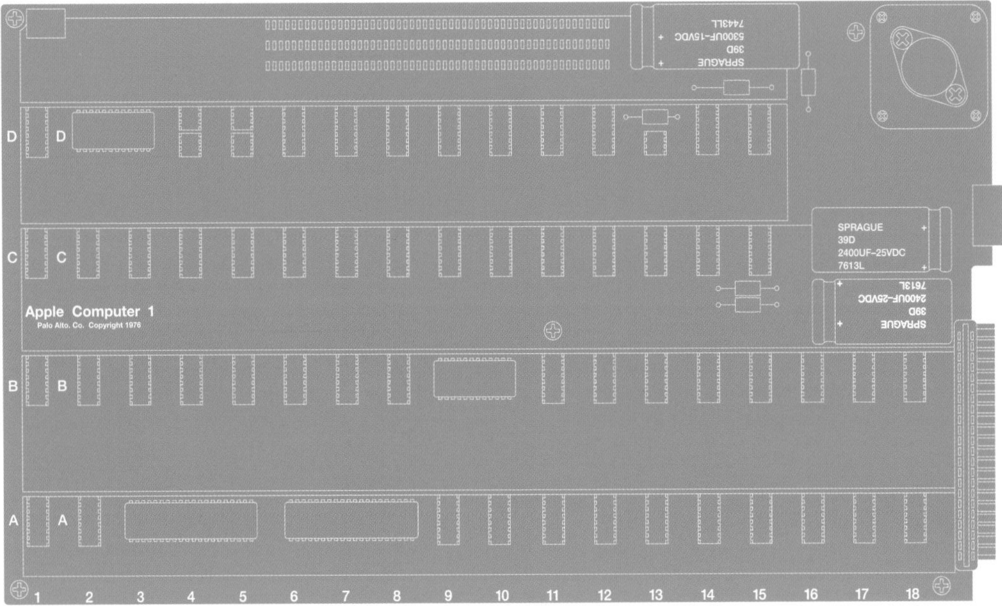


## 6502 processor

Running at just 1.023 MHz, it was 85 % cheaper than the CPU's used on rival computers, helping to bring down the costt.

## Memory

8k RAM, expandable to 65k – a major breakthrough at the time.

## Motherboard

Sold pre-assembled (a novel feature at the time), the single motherboard had around 60 chips attached.

## Monitor

Wozniak included motherboard support for a CRT TV – a unique idea at the time.

## Tape deck

Additional cassette tape interface allowed the user to save program data – a precursor to a floppy disk drive.

## Keyboard

The Apple I was one of the first computers to have a keyboard interface.

## 200

The number of Apple I machines that were built – all by hand.

## 66

The number of remaining Apple I computers in existence according to the online Apple I registry.

Later that same day, wearing sandals and wildly unkempt hair, Jobs boldly walked into the lobby of the company's building, announcing that he wouldn't leave until he was hired. Eventually his persistence earned him an introduction to Atari's chief engineer, Al Alcorn. Despite the nineteen-year-old's strange appearance and behaviour, Alcorn saw something compelling about the college dropout, with Jobs's supreme conviction in his skills convincing Alcorn to offer him a position on his team.

While many on the roster at Atari at that time could have fallen under the stereotype of hippy or, indeed, dropout, Jobs's strong, critical opinions of his colleagues' work, coupled with his poor personal hygiene (a result of his belief that his latest diet of yoghurt and fruit meant he no longer needed to shower regularly) meant he proved a divisive figure in the office, causing his workmates to confront the company's founder Nolan Bushnell. Unwilling to let go of the clearly talented youngster, Bushnell's solution was to move Jobs to the night shift where he could carry out his work away from staff unsettled by his rankling presence and smell.

Within a few months of having settled at Atari, Jobs shocked Alcorn by announcing he was planning to quit to go to India on his much-vaunted spiritual mission to find a guru. Furthermore, he was after financial assistance. Despite Jobs's persuasiveness, Atari not unreasonably wasn't interested in funding his trip. Nevertheless, Alcorn offered to get him part of the way to India. The company was suffering a host of display problems with its arcade machines in Germany that their distributor in the region was unable to put right. As a compromise, the company would send Jobs to work on the problematic displays, and from there he could travel to India.

Upon arriving in Munich, the smartly dressed German managers were left unimpressed by the vagrant-like appearance and general rudeness of the troubleshooter who had been flown in to help. Nevertheless, sorting out the screen problems proved to be a cinch for Jobs. With his work for Atari quickly taken care of, after a quick stop-off in Switzerland he flew out to New Delhi.

The beginning of his quest was a religious festival in the town of Haridwar. There followed a visit to a village called Nainital, situated in the foothills of the Himalayas. Jobs had been told that Nainital was the home of Neem Karoli Baba, the inspirational guru Friedland had spoken so fondly of.

Sadly for the young traveller, upon reaching the village he was told that the guru he was seeking had passed away. Crestfallen, he decided

# The Apple I in Dollars

$2,869.98

Inflation adjusted price today.

$500.00

Wholesale price of the computer.

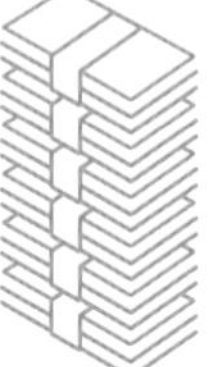

$666.66

The Apple I's original retail price. (according to Steve Wozniak, neither he nor Jobs knew of the figure's religious significance).

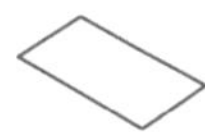

$5.00

The price of *Mini Startrek* game, released for the Apple I in 1977.

$25.00

Cost price of the Motorola MOS 6502 CPU chip used in the Apple I – significantly cheaper than the $175 Motorola 6800 CPU originally intended and used in competing machines.

$905,000.00

Final total after fees paid following a Bonham's auction in New York in 2014 by The Henry Ford American history attraction for one of the first fifty Apple I computers.

# Platform wars

## Desktop PC operating system market share

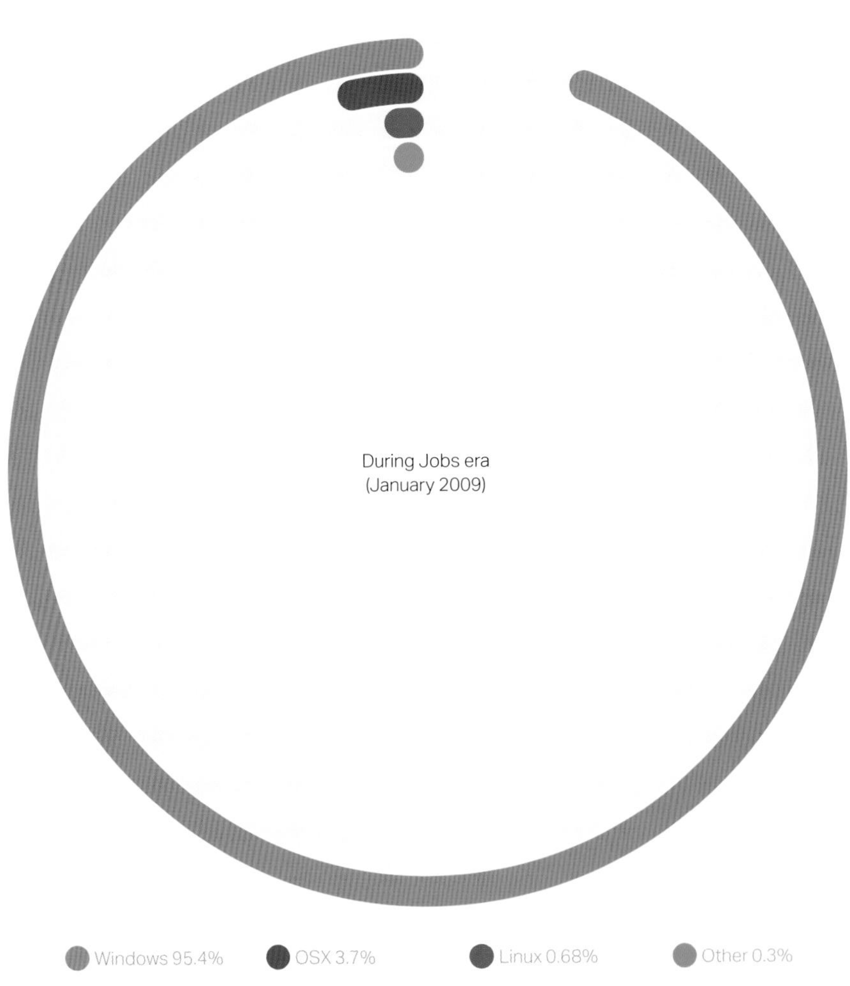

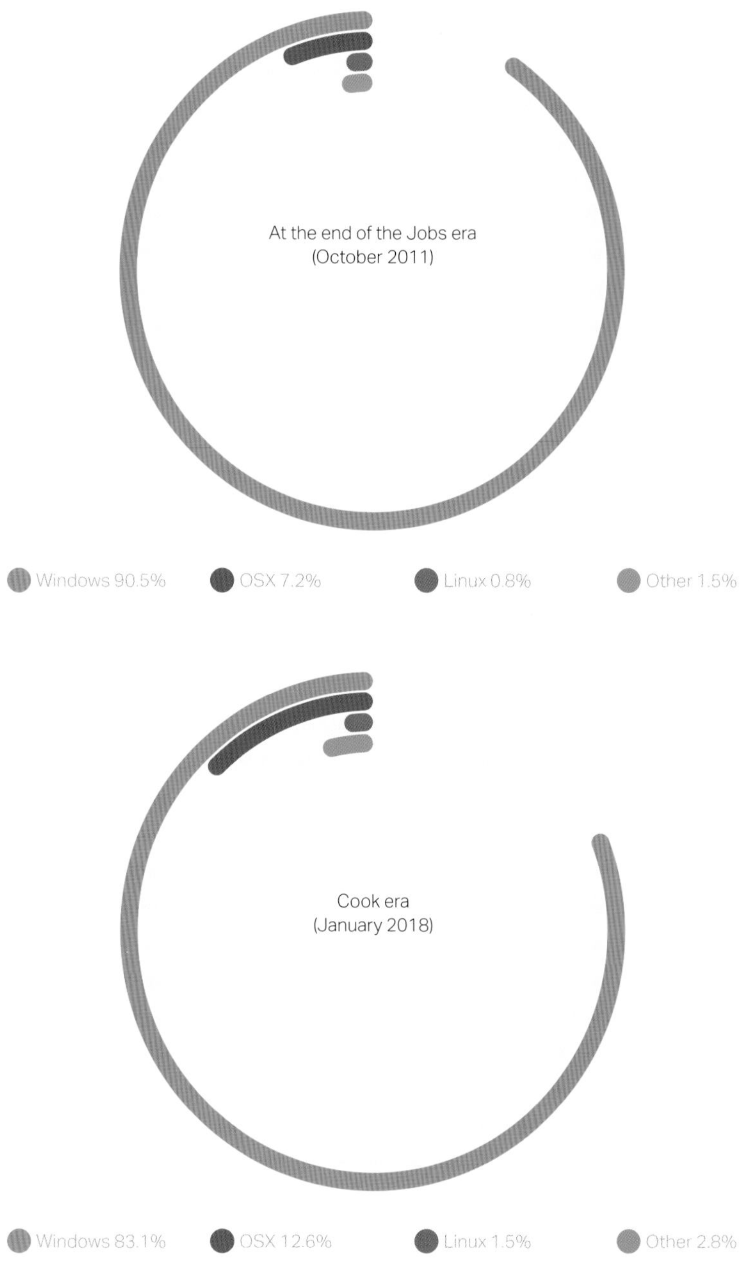
At the end of the Jobs era
(October 2011)
Windows 90.5%
OSX 7.2%
Linux 0.8%
Other 1.5%
Cook era
(January 2018)
Windows 83.1%
OSX 12.6%
Linux 1.5%
Other 2.8%

to explore the surrounding village where he chanced upon a holy man holding court over a large group of followers. Noticing Jobs, who stood out with his Western clothing and long hair, the guru laughed and took him by the arm, leading him up a mountain trail.

Reaching an area with a small pond, the holy man dunked Jobs's head in the water before taking a razor blade to shave off his long locks, insisting that the impromptu haircut would be good for the young man's health.

Some weeks later, Jobs's college compadre Dan Kottke would join him in India and together they roamed the country for several months. While the experience in India had instilled in him 'the power of intuition and experiential wisdom' – a markedly different approach to Western notions of rational thinking – the journey hadn't brought Jobs the inner calm he had desperately longed for.

Steve's appearance had changed so much over the intervening months that his parents failed to recognise him when they went to collect him at the airport. His return to California proved something of a culture shock for Jobs who reverted back down the path of Zen Buddhism, and started to attend meditation retreats at the nearby Los Altos Zen Center with Chrisann. There he met the Zen master Kobun Chino – a figure who would have a guiding influence on the rest of his life. Indeed his management style would be informed by Chino's doctrine of seeking the ability to answer a question with whatever was on one's mind, impulsively – something that would develop into a lifelong habit for Jobs.

Chino's guidance finally provided some answers for Jobs in his pursuit of spiritual truth, so much so that for a while Jobs toyed with the idea of becoming a Buddhist monk at the Eihei-ji temple in Fukui, Japan. However, when consulting Chino on the plan, the response he received wasn't one he was expecting: '[Chino] urged me to stay here. He said there is nothing over there that isn't here, and he was correct. I learned the truth of the Zen saying that if you are willing to travel around the world to meet a teacher, one will appear next door.'

Heeding the advice, in the summer of 1975, Jobs returned to Atari asking for his old job back and was duly offered a role that primarily involved hardware-related troubleshooting. After a while he was placed on a special project by Bushnell to help design a successor to *Pong*. The project would prove to be a huge success for Jobs, but it would be achieved with a bitter betrayal of a good friend.

Think different.

Chapter Five

# A bicycle for the mind

5

COMPUTER MONITOR
DRIVE 2
IN USE
disk II
DRIVE 1
IN USE
disk II
Woz
apple II

Apple II

In essence a table tennis simulator, for all its success, Atari's *Pong* had a glaring limitation for arcade gamers – you needed a human opponent to play it.

Four years after *Pong's* release, its designer and Atari's founder Nolan Bushnell settled on a concept for an updated version of the game that would be named *Breakout*. Rotating the play area through 90 degrees, and replacing the second player's paddle with eight rows of bricks that the player had to smash, crucially the new game would introduce a scoring system, whereby each brick was worth a different number of points.

Jobs had built up a reputation for getting stuff done within the company and so with the game design all but complete, Bushnell handed over the reins to him to work up a prototype.

At a time when microchips were prohibitively expensive, Bushnell offered a further incentive to Jobs, offering him a $100 bonus for every chip he managed to eliminate from the initial concept for the arcade machine. Bushnell also wanted a seemingly unrealistic turnaround of just four days for the prototype.

While Jobs knew the hardware design work involved would be beyond his skills, he accepted the challenge, safe in the knowledge that he could call upon the expertise of his friend to get the project over the line. Having again dropped out of college to earn money, Steve Wozniak had recently landed a plum job working on scientific calculators at Hewlett-Packard. Woz was a huge fan of Atari's early racing game *Gran Trak 10*, and since returning to the company, Jobs had often snuck his pal in the office after hours, letting him play on a staff machine for hours on end.

Despite the narrow timeframe, Wozniak jumped at the chance to get involved, and worked through the night on the game's board design after finishing his day job at Hewlett-Packard. Completing the prototype within the deadline over four sleep-deprived nights, he somehow managed to eliminate 50 extraneous chips from the initial design.

Delighted with the finished result, Bushnell paid Jobs a $750 dollar wage plus a further $5,000 for its remarkably efficient design. Failing to disclose the sizeable bonus, Jobs handed Wozniak just $375 for his vital assistance and used the money to fund a break at the All One apple farm in Oregon where a number of his hippy friends from Reed hung out.

It would be a decade before Wozniak would find out about the bonus after reading about the deal in Scott Cohen's 1984 book on the history of Atari entitled *Zap!* Wozniak admitted the revelation left him in tears – it wasn't so much that he had been short-changed that upset him, but the fact that his friend felt that he had been fair game for manipulation:

> 'It's only one thing in life, but he did tell me that we would get paid 700 bucks, then he wrote me a check for 350 dollars, and he got paid thousands. So, whatever. But he should have told me differently because we were such close friends. The fun of doing it overrides anything like that. Who cares about money? Well, I do care about friendship and honesty,' Wozniak explained in a 2015 interview.

Had Wozniak known about the betrayal at the time, the events of the following months would likely never have happened – events which would see the pair birth a company that would define both their lives.

In January of 1975, the Altair 8800 proudly appeared on the cover of *Popular Electronics* magazine. A build-it-yourself kit computer for hobbyists by Albuquerque-based company MITS, it was a machine that would lay claim to the title of being the first personal computer.

With an at-the-time eye-watering introductory price of $439, it took many days and nights of careful soldering and assembly to hopefully create a working Altair – an endeavour only true hackers would undertake.

Inspired in part by the possibilities of the Altair, two computer enthusiasts from the Silicon Valley area named Fred Moore and Gordon French set up an informal hobbyist meet up. Named the Homebrew Computer Club, the gathering aimed to provide an open exchange of ideas for local enthusiasts, allowing them to trade parts, circuits and know-how for those looking to construct their own computing devices. The first meeting was held in March 1975 in French's garage in Menlo Park, San Mateo County, California, with Steve Wozniak one of the initial thirty tech heads in attendance (in the weeks that followed its membership would expand into the hundreds).

# The Apple II

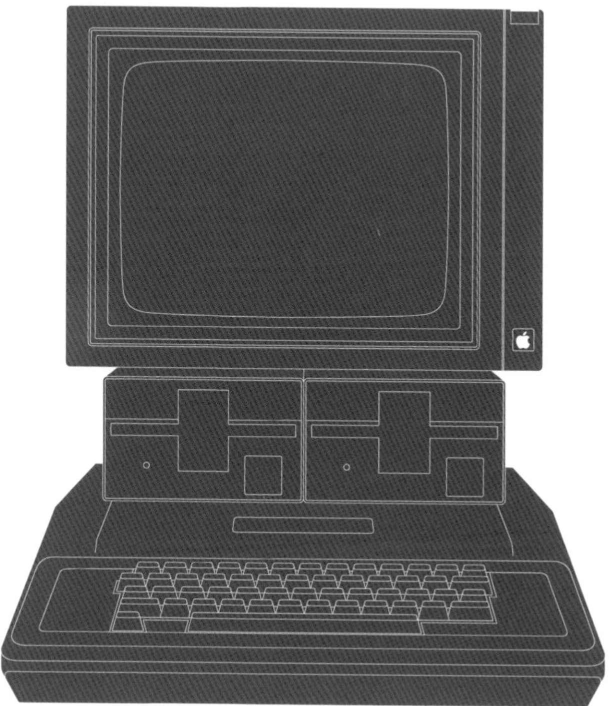

### Plastic casing

The first commercial computer to feature such housing.

### NTSC or PAL video out

Allowed the computer to be connected to a TV for use as a monitor.

### CPU

MOS 6502, 1.0 MHz – the processor that featured in the Apple I.

### Cassette tape

The machine was originally offered with a cassette interface. In 1978 the Disk, a 143k 5¹/₄-inch disk drive, was introduced.

### Memory

4k RAM, expandable to 64k.

### Expansion

8 expansion slots, with the first slot reserved for RAM/ROM upgrades.

### Colours

16 fixed colours at 280x192 (High) resolution, and 16 colours at 40x48 (Low) resolution. Another first in commercial computing technology.

### $1,298

Equivalent to $5,242 in 2017.

### 40,000

Units sold by the time the model was discontinued in 1981.

During the inaugural meeting, Wozniak managed to get his hands on a data sheet that was being shared around for a microprocessor similar to the one used in the Altair that could be programmed to perform many different tasks and functions. It was a revelation for the young electronics wizard as Wozniak recalled in his autobiography:

> 'It was as if my whole life had been leading up to this point. I'd done my minicomputer redesigns, I'd done data on-screen with *Pong* and *Breakout*, and I'd already done a TV terminal. From the Cream Soda Computer and others, I knew how to connect memory and make a working system. I realized that all I needed was this Canadian processor or another processor like it and some memory chips. Then I'd have the computer I'd always wanted! Oh my god. I could build my own computer, a computer I could own and design to do any neat things I wanted to do with it for the rest of my life.'

Inspired to show his peers at the club that an affordable computer could be built, after feverishly working on schematics and hunting down parts, by June Wozniak was proudly able to demonstrate to Jobs a working printed circuit board design that could drive a colour display. Even more uniquely, it used a keyboard as an interface rather than an intuitive bank of switches.

Turning the machine on and testing the concept for the first time was a magical moment. A cursor appeared on the screen – and better still, it reacted correctly to whatever keys Wozniak pressed. 'I typed a few keys on the keyboard and I was shocked!' he recalled in his memoir. It marked the first time in history anyone had typed on a personal computer and seen the results 'show up on their own computer's screen right in front of them.'

Jobs had joined Wozniak in attending a few Homebrew Computer Club meetings after being encouraged by his friend, and would help to carry the large TV screen Woz would use to demonstrate his machine's capabilities.

Wozniak's vision for his machine was led to some degree by altruism – he'd designed the computer with the intention of giving it away for free to other people and was keen to share its schematics with other members of the club. Jobs saw a bigger picture and encouraged Woz not to carry on sharing so much of his great ideas. Arguing that the club's members wouldn't have enough time to build the machines themselves from his schematics, Jobs proposed that they go into business and build the circuit boards themselves, selling them ready-made.

With Wozniak eventually onboard with the plan, the two friends set about the task of blessing their new company with a name. Matrix and Executek were contenders for a while, but were rejected for being too techy. On a return from a stay at the All One Farm in Oregon, Jobs fell upon the idea of naming the company Apple. Jobs worried that the name could be perceived as childlike and that they could also fall foul of The Beatles, what with the now disbanded band's record label sharing the same name. Nevertheless the name resonated in particular with Jobs, who at this time was once again existing on a diet mainly consisting of fruit. The pair liked its simplicity, as well as the fact it would place them alphabetically ahead of Atari in a phone directory, and so the name was decided.

Despite his enthusiasm, Wozniak felt unable to commit full time to Apple, feeling duty-bound to his employer Hewlett-Packard. Indeed Wozniak felt that the honourable thing to do would be to let HP have first refusal on his designs for the machine. Such early uncertainty for the company led Jobs to draft in Ron Wayne, a middle-aged former night shift manager of Jobs's at Atari, as the new venture's 'adult supervision'.

Central to Wayne's role would be the aim of persuading Woz that his board designs should be owned by the Apple partnership. Having argued that all great engineers needed someone with great business drive if they were to be remembered, Wayne's mature negotiating skills convinced Wozniak that the pair did indeed make a great team and a deal was struck.

Wozniak's loyalty to HP still compelled him to let his employers know what he had been working on and offered them an early look at the computer. To his disappointment, the senior managers who witnessed his company demonstration dismissed the prototype as being of only limited appeal outside computer enthusiasts and not something they felt they could develop into a successful product. While the snub came as a blow, it allowed Wozniak to freely enter the partnership with Apple with his conscience clear.

On 1 April 1976, Jobs and Wozniak signed a partnership agreement drawn up by Wayne with an agreed division of shares and profits of

# The Incredible Patents of Steve Jobs

Steve Jobs was a prolific innovator, with his name appearing on around 458 patents - at least 141 of which were credited to him after his death.

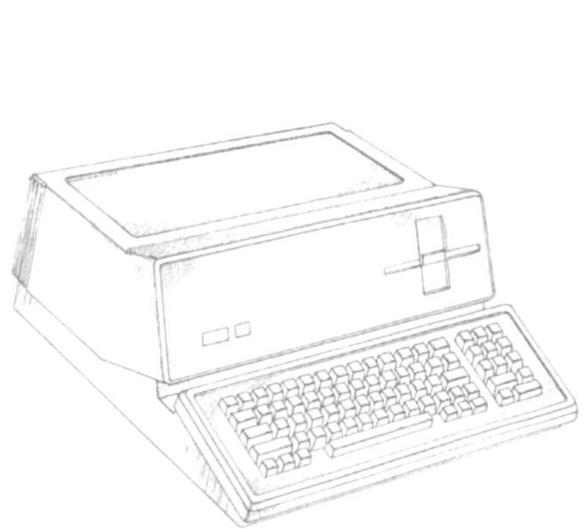

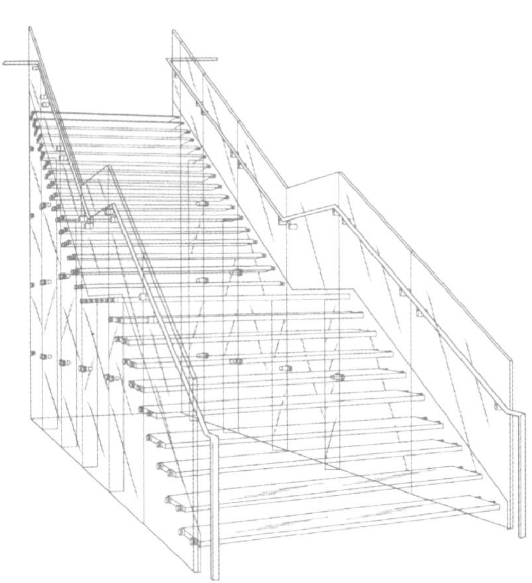

## Personal computer (1980)

Jobs's first patent is arguably his most influential, 'Personal Computer'. Filed in 1980 and approved in 1983, it describes a 'personal computer, substantially as shown', revealing a device similar to the Apple III, launched by the company in 1981 without a monitor.

## Staircase (2002)

Jobs's patents went well beyond product design. This filing illustrates his keen eye for architecture, pertaining to the clear-step staircases you see in flagship Apple Stores and also within Apple's old Cupertino headquarters.

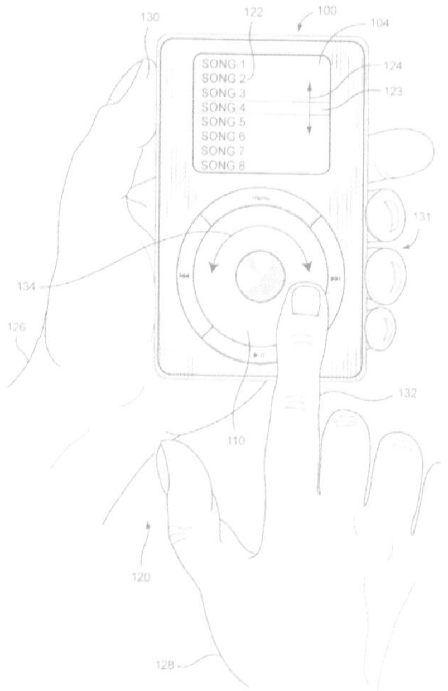


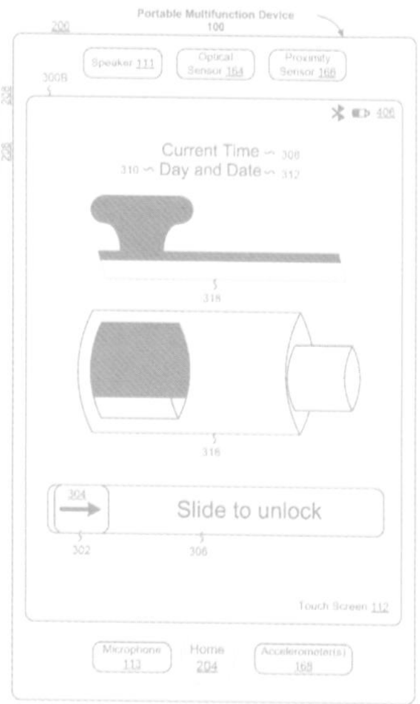


## Method and apparatus for use of rotational user inputs (2002)

This claim for a 'rotational user action supplied by a user' is arguably Apple's most famous user interface feature – the circular action you make with your finger when scrolling using the iPod's Clickwheel.

## Touch screen device, method, and graphical user interface for customising display of content category icons (2008)

Covering scrolling and swiping on a touch screen, the patent has regularly appeared in Apple's numerous patent infringement cases against Motorola, HTC and Nokia, among others.

45%–45%–10%, with Wayne the lesser party in the three-way split. Under the agreed legalese, Wozniak would 'assume both general and major responsibility for the conduct of Electrical Engineering' while Jobs had 'general responsibility for Electrical Engineering and Marketing', leaving Wayne in charge of 'Mechanical Engineering and Documentation' and a remit to be the voice of reason in any disputes.

As well as striking the partnership deal, Wayne offered creative assistance, helping with Wozniak's circuit board schematics as well as creating the company's first logo, with Wayne's finished design featuring a detailed depiction of Isaac Newton under a tree, with a glowing apple overhead. However, just eleven days after signing the agreement, amid concerns over his financial liabilities for any debts in the venture, Wayne withdrew from the partnership. He received $800 for his 10% share, and shortly afterwards $1,500 more. 'As far as I was concerned, it was "found money". So I went ahead and I signed,' Wayne later admitted to the BBC.

With both Jobs and Wozniak satisfied with the partnership agreement, the pair worked to raise capital to get a run of the boards made, with Woz selling his beloved HP 65 electronic calculator for $500, while Jobs sacrificed his Volkswagen bus for the same amount.

It was a modest bankroll to work with, and the reaction during a demonstration of what was now being called the Apple I at the Homebrew Computer Club would have done little to raise morale. The pair had hoped the showcase would generate a flood of sales from within the community, but it was met with a palpable shrug of the shoulders from their peers. One person present during the demonstration, however, did recognise the machine's potential.

Paul Terrell was the owner of the Byte Shop, one of the first computer stores in the area. Impressed by the duo's presentation he introduced himself to Steve and Woz afterwards and expressed an interest in potentially doing business. Eager to jump upon the opportunity, Jobs visited Terrell's store in Mountain View the very next day. After a brief discussion, Terrell, who was acutely aware that there was a huge market for ready-made machines, proposed a deal whereby the newly monikered Apple would be required to deliver fifty fully assembled units. If they could deliver on the deal he would pay them $500 for each computer. Jobs was stunned – this was a figure ten times the asking price the pair had been looking to charge Homebrew Computer Club members for the printed circuit boards alone.

Despite having no access to parts, no space to build the machines, nor indeed any engineers apart from themselves to construct the computers, Jobs agreed to the proposal. 'That was the biggest single episode in all of the company's history,' Wozniak once posited. 'Nothing in subsequent years was so great and so unexpected.'

Apple was now a legitimate business.

Following a string of rejections while touring up and down the Valley, Jobs's persistence and growing wheeler-dealer skills came to the fore when he managed to secure a credit line with Kierulff Electronics, who agreed to act as a supply line for the parts needed for the Apple I. In order to build the machines, Jobs drafted in his sister Patty along with Dan Kottke plus girlfriend Elizabeth Holmes to help solder the boards, while Steve's mum manned a company phone line. Overnight the garage at the Jobs house became an industrial workplace as the makeshift team formed a production line that worked nights and weekends. With a steely focus on delivering the computers on time, Jobs proved to be an unrelenting manager to his friends and family, his temper often rising to the surface when mistakes were inevitably made.

By the year's end, the rough and ready operation had managed to turn out 150 Apple I computers, making the fledgling company $100,000 in revenue. Wozniak had made almost as much from the Apple I as he had from his steady day job at Hewlett-Packard.

Despite this, he showed no intention of giving up his role at HP and was happy with the dual arrangement. While his spare time was at a premium, Wozniak was spurred on to improve upon the Apple I and had already started conceptualising its successor. For Wozniak the next logical step would be to have a computer that could display its results in full colour rather than the monochrome display offered by the original model, while also eking out more power and performance from a motherboard of the same size. The more business-astute Jobs liked what Wozniak was showing him, but knew the Apple II needed to be a more complete package than what they had produced before. Jobs wanted the Apple II to be integrated right down to its software so that it would appeal to anyone who just wanted to plug their machine in and run with it. Jobs vision was now firmly fixed on the mass market.

Chapter Six

# Simple can be harder than complex

'My dream for the Apple II was to sell the first real packaged computer... I got a bug up my rear that I wanted the computer in a plastic case.'

'It was clear to me that for every hardware hobbyist who wanted to assemble his own computer, there were a thousand people who couldn't do that but wanted to mess around with programming... just like I did when I was ten. My dream for the Apple II was to sell the first real packaged computer... I got a bug up my rear that I wanted the computer in a plastic case.'

While the unique selling point for the Apple II was clearly going to be its groundbreaking ability to send colour signals to a television set, Wozniak and Jobs also had a number of other features up their sleeves for their next machine which would redefine the very notion of a personal computer.

Wozniak was intent on adding extra expansion ports. These would let users add cards which could extend the possibilities and uses of the machine, a decision that would in turn open up a secondary industry for peripheral makers, while adding value to its users.

Another fundamental design choice was to include a version of the BASIC programming language built into a chip on its circuit board, allowing users to begin programming straight from boot up. Bill Gates and Paul Allen's Microsoft had provided a version of BASIC for the rival Altair that saw the emergent Seattle startup earn a cool $500 for each machine it was installed on. A deal clinched with Apple for their new machine would make it the most profitable platform for Microsoft until the game-changing IBM PC arrived years later.

Jobs's key interventions in the genesis of the Apple II centred around its aesthetics and general good product design. It would need to be a finished product, not something that resembled a kit. As well as his belief in the importance of a plastic housing with smooth edges incorporating a keyboard which would make the Apple II more desirable as a consumer device, Jobs was keen to eliminate the prototype's fan noise. For a proponent of Zen meditation, the constant hum was both irritating and intrusive. For Wozniak, building a silent machine fell way down the priority list behind the capabilities of its circuit board and microprocessor, while the fan's role in stopping the computer from overheating made it irreplaceable.

Jobs was nevertheless insistent on finding a better solution, and turned to Al Alcorn, his old boss at Atari for advice, who in turn pointed him in the direction of Rod Holt, one of the company's old engineers and widely regarded as one of the best talents in the Silicon Valley area for analogue circuitry. Always determined to work with the best people he could find, Jobs heeded Alcorn's advice, and approached the middle-aged engineer, despite being fully aware that Apple's diminishing cash flow probably meant his fledgling company wouldn't be able to afford him. 'He just conned me into working', Holt once recalled.

This hire beyond Apple's then means would be an early example of Jobs's much vaunted 'reality distortion field,' a self-assured belief that would present itself throughout both his business and private life, where the impossible was possible and where truths were often subjective.

According to Daniel Kottke, the trait had been inspired by Robert Friedland, his charismatic friend from Reed, whose commune out on the All One Farm near Portland had provided both a refuge and inspiration for the young Jobs. '[Friedland] was charismatic and a bit of a con man and could bend situations to his very strong will. He was mercurial, sure of himself, a little dictatorial. Steve admired that, and he became more like that after spending time with Robert,' Kottke told biographer Walter Isaacson. Later in life, Friedland would go on to use his knack of persuasion to become a billionaire mining magnate. During the early 1990s, this would see him face trouble over accusations surrounding environmental damage caused by his company Ivanhoe Mines. The situation would become a major political issue, to the extent that Friedland called up Jobs to see if he could speak with the then president Bill Clinton. Jobs refused to help, later commenting on his relationship with his former mentor: 'It was a strange thing to have one of the spiritual people in your young life turn out to be, symbolically and in reality, a gold miner.'

While Jobs may have been economical with the truth surrounding Apple's ability to pay him, Holt hadn't gone into signing up with Apple with his eyes closed. He suspected Jobs didn't have the cash – but his

apple II
disk II
disk II

# The Seven Leadership Mantras of Steve Jobs

Steve Jobs was an unconventional leader. He rarely took a consultative or consensus-building approach to management. His penchant for delivering stark criticism to staff and tough demands for excellence are well documented.

Nevertheless, his skill at articulating his unique vision, passion for simplicity and ability to learn lessons from previous career setbacks made him unique among his Silicon Valley peers.

## Always keep it simple

When Jobs came back to Apple in 1997, arguably the most important thing he did was simplify its huge product line down to just four items (iMac, Power Macintosh, iBook, Powerbook G3). From here the company built its way back up. Famously he directed designers to lose all buttons on the iPod, resulting in the iconic scroll wheel.

## Secrecy is power

Confidentiality was like a religion at Apple under Jobs. With the company divided into often detached cells, everything was on a need to know basis. Keeping a lid on new products built up interest and anticipation for keynotes and unveilings among techies, and, more crucially, the world's press.

## Don't be afraid to be ruthless

Jobs's ability to know the right time to pull the plug on a project or product line was as much a part of his success as his ability to identify new opportunities. Having directed huge resources towards developing a rival to the Palm Pilot, Jobs canned the project when realising that the era of the smartphone was on its way, rendering such a device obsolete. The decision allowed engineers to work on the then formative iPod project.

## Go for experts

When Apple entered retail, Jobs recruited experience to the board in the form of The Gap's Mickey Drexler. For the NeXT Computers logo he hired one of the world's leading architects, I. M. Pei.

## Sell dreams

Empathy with the customer and understanding their aspirations was a crucial business tenet for Jobs. Throughout its history, Apple's marketing has focused primarily on the emotional benefits of its products and persuasion, with the promise of a better world. During the company's 'Get a Mac' campaign, a 2006 ad famously read 'Why get a new PC and just upgrade your computer, when you can get a Mac and upgrade your entire computer experience?'

## Aim for perfect

Jobs's obsession with the quality of his products, from packaging to the clicking sound made by an iPod jack, is legendary. This regularly cost time and caused frustration to staff, but users of Apple products often reaped the rewards.

## Tell a rehearsed story

Jobs's command of the stage during a keynote was absolute. His often-breathless presentations rarely allowed those watching to get distracted at any point. Key to this was developing a story around a relatable problem people were experiencing with the current product choices, allowing the audience to see Apple as the hero and their new product the great solution to their nuisance or nightmare. While Jobs appeared natural and fluid on stage, the slickness was a result of often gruelling hours of rehearsal beforehand.

intuition told him the Apple II was likely to be something special and he was keen to be part of it. Working day and night on the brand new power supply, Holt's design was every bit as revolutionary as the Apple II's ability to use a colour display. Smaller than a small carton of milk, Holt's power supply took household current and switched it on and off rapidly, producing a steady current that generated much less heat, while also proving to be safe for the device's expensive memory chips. The ingenious idea, which also helped to reduce the size of the computer's case, to this day informs the design of current computer power supplies.

With a provisional design for the Apple II almost complete, Jobs knew for the machine to become a reality they would need a substantial cash injection as well as some added expertise in public relations and advertising, and so the word was put out for potential investors. A Canadian calculator company and Commodore were both at one point potential suitors, however both backed out, the latter deciding to build its own computer after balking at Jobs and Wozniak's valuation of Apple at $100,000.

With news that Nolan Bushnell had just sold Atari to Warner Communications for a tidy $14million, Jobs turned to his former boss for investment. Bushnell declined, instead introducing him to venture capitalist Don Valentine, who had recently founded Sequoia Capital – a company that focused primarily on small, risky tech firms.

Despite the unquestionable promise shown by Jobs and Wozniak, Valentine was put off by the pair's naivety, claiming they 'weren't thinking anywhere near big enough', in turn giving them the name of another potential investor.

A former early employee of Intel, A.C. 'Mike' Markkula was in his early thirties living off his investments. He'd earned himself an early retirement by making millions from the chip firm's first stock sale to the public and was now on the lookout for a new venture. Having turned up at the Jobs's garage, he was instantly impressed with what the pair were working on. 'It was what I had wanted since I left high school,' Markkula said when recalling the duo's demonstration of the Apple II prototype.

For a one-third equity stake in Apple, Markkula offered an investment of $92,000 out of his own pocket along with the promise of a $250,000 line of credit secured with the Bank of America. Wozniak and Jobs would each own 26% of stock, allowing room to attract further investment.

Markkula's business plan for the company dovetailed with Jobs's vision of getting beyond the hobbyist market, while both Jobs and Wozniak felt reassured that their suitor understood their product and their hopes for the company. 'He talked about introducing the computer to regular people in regular homes, doing things like keeping track of your favorite recipes or balancing your checkbook,' Wozniak recalled. Relaxed and unassuming, while seemingly decent and fair, the pair agreed he was a good fit.

For Jobs the decision was simple; for Wozniak it was less clean cut. Still wishing to maintain his role at HP, he felt uncomfortable assuming a position of authority. With Markkula unwilling to agree a deal without Wozniak's full-time commitment, a frantic few days followed with Jobs and Woz's friends and family desperately trying to convince him to agree to the deal before the offer was withdrawn.

Among those who offered to bend Wozniak's ear was his father Jerry. He had previously intervened in his son's role at Apple around the time of Commodore's interest, accusing Jobs of taking advantage of his son. Jerry argued that the pair should not be equal partners in the company given Jobs's limited role in the creation and design of the Apple I and II. Reduced to tears by the confrontation, Jobs told Wozniak that if they weren't to be equal partners, Wozniak could have the whole company. Highlighting the pair's need for each other, Woz resolved the situation by pointing out that none of their early success would have been possible without Jobs. It was, after all, his friend who had turned his ideas into a business by dissuading him to give away his designs for free at the Homebrew Computer Club.

With Markkula ready to walk away, this time around Jerry Wozniak supported Jobs and a host of friends in trying to influence his son. After days of the phone ringing off the hook, Wozniak Jnr eventually felt reassured that saying yes would allow him to earn his fortune as an engineer with the new Apple partnership without having to become a boss and a deal was struck. On 3 January 1977, Wozniak left the security of his job at HP, the contracts were signed, and the new Apple Computer was born.

Chapter Seven

# Inventing tomorrow

7

apple ][
RESET
REPT
BEL
SHIFT

'I don't deny that Woz designed a good machine,' McKenna once said, 'but that machine would be sitting in hobby shops today were it not for Steve Jobs. Woz was fortunate to hook up with an evangelist.'

While securing Markkula's partnership, Jobs had also been piecing together other parts of the new Apple company puzzle by seeking out marketing expertise. Averse to the hype and slickness of the advertising world and with a steadfast belief in pure engineering, Wozniak left his partner to seek out an agency. As with his pursuit of Rod Holt, Jobs was intent on working with the best talent and was again relentless once he'd identified a potential target.

He'd admired a recent groundbreaking advertising campaign by the agency Regis McKenna for Intel which highlighted the strengths of the chip company without being laden with weighty tech detail.

Jobs's initial approaches to the agency, which specialised in startups, were met with cold disinterest. However, following a campaign of persistently calling the company's new business manager, Frank Burge, he eventually made a breakthrough, arranging a meeting with its founder McKenna at the agency's office. The fact that the young entrepreneur managed to convince the experienced McKenna to handle his promising, but undeniably risky company at this point was a measure of Jobs's growing power of persuasion.

'I don't deny that Woz designed a good machine,' McKenna once said, 'but that machine would be sitting in hobby shops today were it not for Steve Jobs. Woz was fortunate to hook up with an evangelist.'+

'The real genius of the product was that Steve Wozniak designed such a flexible product from the technology standpoint. But then Steve Jobs came along and made it all happen. It was the combination that made them so powerful.'

Having taken on the Apple account, McKenna was determined to redesign the fledgling company's over-complicated logo, with the agency's chief art director Rob Janoff explicitly briefed to come up with

The real genius of the product was that Steve Wozniak designed such a flexible product from the technology standpoint. But then Steve Jobs came along and made it all happen. It was the combination that made them so powerful.

Macintosh
hello.

something simple and direct. His initial designs would feature the now familiar multicoloured apple with a bite taken out of the side – supposedly a reflection of Apple's tagline at the time ('Byte into an Apple'); Janoff would say in a later interview that his primary aim was to 'prevent the apple from looking like a cherry tomato'. While Jobs liked the accessible design with the logo's rainbow-like stripes representing the Apple II's colour display, his attention to detail saw him rejig the logo's chromatic order so that green would be at the top where the leaf was.

The final design would get its big unveiling in the spring of 1977 alongside the Apple II at the West Coast Computer Faire, where a huge unmissable version of the logo on backlit Plexiglas welcomed guests to Apple's stand. The first major computer trade show on the west coast, Jobs had had the foresight to sign Apple up early as an exhibitor, managing to secure a prime spot at the entrance of the show floor at the San Francisco Civic Auditorium & Brooks Hall for a cool $5,000. The substantial fee shocked Wozniak, but Jobs felt assured that the show would be an ideal event to launch their new computer.

Alongside the prominent logo, Jobs had taken meticulous care with how the rest of the stand looked, decorating the space with black velvet drapes. On display were the only three working Apple II computers, with empty boxes piled high at the back to kid visitors into thinking they were already rolling off the production line. To get the stand up to Steve's exacting standards, the Apple team worked frantically through the night. The perfectionism extended to the newly arrived cases for the Apple IIs, which much to Jobs's dismay had arrived with tiny blemishes, resulting in him taking some of the team back to the garage to sand and polish them. The presentation effort didn't stop there, with Markkula persuading Jobs and Wozniak to sharpen up and wear tuxedos for the show.

The hard work paid dividends. The stand and the Apple II stood out from the other exhibitors with their poster board signs and ugly metal-clad machines. Over the course of the three-day event, over 300 orders were taken for the Apple II, with a major international agreement also made with a Japanese dealer.

The success of the Apple II soon meant expansion beyond Paul Jobs's garage, with the company moving into rented offices in Cupertino. Alongside the three partners, the team was augmented by engineer Rod Holt, Jobs's and Wozniak's friend Bill Fernandez, plus young programmers Randy Wigginton

# Steve the master showman

## Breaking down Jobs's keynote brilliance

### Lay out a theme and reinforce

During the introduction of the iPhone in 2007, Jobs delivered the memorable line, 'Today Apple reinvents the phone,' with the same words flashed up on a slide in unison. Jobs would slip in the phrase 'reinvent the phone' a further four times throughout the presentation.

### Energy from enthusiasm

Jobs's passion for a product or feature was never restrained during keynotes. During his Macworld 2008 presentation his sincere, repeated use of words like "extraordinary", "amazing" and "cool" when demonstrating the iPhone's updated location feature added a layer of excitement to a relatively mundane reveal.

### Explain the problem

Jobs would rarely take the wraps off something new without explaining the problem with the current products or services it would be competing against. For the original iPhone launch Jobs lambasted rival smartphones as being 'not so smart and they're not so easy to use.' Jobs then picked apart several smartphones from competitors, highlighting their weakness for being unintuitive.

### Get the visuals right

Jobs's credo for simplicity in Apple's design and engineering also extended to his approach to presentations. While many of his contemporaries would go big on data and text-heavy slides, Jobs did the opposite, often showing a single image to get his point across.

### Meaningful magic numbers

Figures rarely make an impact unless they're placed in context. When announcing Apple had sold its 4 millionth iPhone in 2008, he added perspective by saying 'That's 20,000 iPhones every day, on average.' Jobs went on to say, 'What does that mean to the overall market?' before detailing a breakdown of the US smartphone market and Apple's share of it to demonstrate just how impressive the number actually was.

### Sell the benefits

When unveiling a new device, most presenters will promote its features. Jobs would go big on selling its benefits, clearly stating what was in it for the listening audience without making them guess.

and Chris Espinosa. The fast rate of change coincided with Jobs becoming increasingly impatient and demanding of Apple's staff, in particular the two programmers who were both still at college and working hours either side of their studies.

In a bid to bring order to the often chaotic air surrounding the company, as well as keep the intensely passionate Jobs in check, Markkula drafted in a president, a move that a reticent Jobs only reluctantly agreed to: 'I was only twenty-two, and I knew I wasn't ready to run a real company,' Jobs once recalled. 'But Apple was my baby, and I didn't want to give it up.' For the less management-inclined Wozniak, the appointment came as a relief as it now meant there was someone to intervene in Jobs's conflicts.

Markkula's choice for the role was Mike Scott, who he had previously worked with at Fairchild. 'Scotty', who had experience as a director at Fairchild, would focus on manufacturing, Markkula the money and marketing, leaving Wozniak to focus on the engineering and Jobs with a remit of the Apple II and all other office matters.

With an eye for detail and a working knowledge of computers and programming, Scotty had a no-nonsense, sometimes combative management style. As Jobs was previously used to micromanaging Apple's affairs, it was somewhat inevitable that the pair would clash. An early flashpoint came with the awarding of employee numbers, with Jobs incensed that he had been handed the dishonour of being staff member number two, behind Wozniak at one. The perceived slight by Scotty reduced Jobs to tears, leading him to demand he be given number zero on the roster. The new president relented, however with Apple's bank requiring positive numbers for payroll, Jobs's position remained number two.

On another occasion, Scotty took Jobs outside into the office's parking area for what Steve expected to be a regular chat about strategy, only to be taken aback when Scotty confronted him about the touchy subject of body odour. When Jobs defensively insisted he didn't need to shower often because his fruit-based diet meant he didn't sweat as much, Scotty dismissively countered by making it clear that none of his colleagues in the office could stand working near him.

On other occasions, Scott would sometimes concede that it was easier to let the often obsessive Jobs have his way. One such occasion saw the president back down when Jobs insisted that the company needed to have customers on their side, demanding that the Apple II would come with a one-year warranty, unlike much of the competition's guarantee of just ninety days.

By the summer of 1977, Steve was sharing a suburban ranch house with his on–off girlfriend, Chrisann, and Dan Kottke, who had recently moved back to the area following a stint on the east coast. Within a few months of moving in, Chrisann, who had recently taken a job as an assembler at Apple, became pregnant. Having not been involved with any other men at the time, Brennan was sure Jobs was the father. He angrily denied it, and also made it clear he had no interest in getting married. While in favour of Chrisann having an abortion, despite his background he discouraged her from putting the baby up for adoption. As time went on, and with Chrisann deciding to keep the baby, Jobs would disassociate himself from both her and the situation, seemingly viewing the state of affairs as a distraction.

Devastated by Jobs's cold treatment, and by her own admission emotionally unstable, Brennan quit her job and moved to Robert Friedland's All One Farm in Oregon. It was there she would later give birth to their daughter, in May 1978. A few days after his daughter's birth, Jobs would jet out to be with her and Chrisann. Those living on the Friedland's commune were encouraged to give their children a spiritual name, but Jobs was insistent that the baby shouldn't be saddled with an Eastern handle and should have a 'normal' American name that would allow her to fit in. The pair agreed on naming their daughter Lisa Nicole Brennan, without taking Jobs as a surname.

The months that followed, however, would see Steve maintain that he was not Lisa's father, outright refusing to pay child support. Unable to muster up a fight to sue her former lover, Chrisann moved with Lisa to a run-down home in Menlo Park, with the pair becoming reliant upon welfare. A court-ordered paternity test would eventually establish that Jobs was Lisa's father with a 94.4% likelihood, resulting in a court order for him to pay child support of $385 a month.

Chrisann raised their daughter on her own in a small house in Menlo Park, with years passing before Jobs would play a significant role in Lisa's upbringing. He would go on to purchase them a house in Palo Alto and pay for Lisa's education. Steve, who was twenty-three when his daughter was born – the same age his paternal father was when he rejected him – would later express his regret over the abandonment of his child.

'I wish I had handled it differently. I could not see myself as a father then, so I didn't face up to it ... if I could do it over, I would do a better job.'

Chapter Eight

# Just make it great

By the time Jobs had reached his twenty-third birthday he and Markkula had both sold $1million worth of Apple stock, bringing his overall worth to $10million.

Two crucial new developments for the Apple II had helped push its sales into the stratosphere. The Disk II, a floppy disk drive peripheral first unveiled at the Consumer Electronics Show in January 1978, had addressed the computer's biggest weakness – its lack of storage – while also opening up a new way for software by third parties to be sold for the system. Meanwhile, the release of VisiCalc for the Apple II, the world's first spreadsheet and finance program, made the computer a must-have for both business and households alike.

Having been valued at $5,309 when it was formed, by the following year the company was worth around $3 million, with new investment beginning to flood into the burgeoning tech firm. The image of Jobs as Silicon Valley's golden boy that Regis McKenna had begun projecting to the nation's media was becoming self-fulfilling. By the time Jobs had reached his twenty-third birthday he and Markkula had both sold $1million worth of Apple stock, bringing his overall worth to $10million.

Aiming to keep sales of the Apple II buoyant, which by 1979 had helped the company earn $47 million in revenues, a modestly updated version of the computer called the Apple II Plus was released in June of that year, featuring increased RAM and an updated version of Applesoft BASIC.

As sales continued to rise, the company's headcount also grew, with more engineers hired to work on the company's next projects. Among those joining the company was Jef Raskin, a former college professor who had originally been drafted into the company to work on Apple's user manuals. Raskin had been let loose on a side project to devise a consumer-oriented computer with a sub $1,000 price tag. Raskin planned to call his machine the Macintosh after his favourite

ORAGE

Think different.

type of apple. While Jobs was intrigued by the machine's premise, he initially dismissed Raskin's concept as being too slow and ugly.

Somewhat further along the line in development was the Apple III, at this point code-named 'Sara'. Based on feedback from customers and retailers, new features planned for the machine included the ability to display upper- and lower-case letters to a width of eighty characters, not forty as per its predecessor; as well as being able to address more memory, allowing for more sophisticated programs to be made for the platform. Unlike Apples I and II, which were primarily the work of Wozniak, the Apple III would be created via a committee of engineers and requests from marketing. Jobs took on the responsibility of the design of the external case, insisting that it needed to be markedly smaller than its predecessor, a decision that would prove problematic, with the final design being too small to adequately house the computer's internal components.

The Apple III was meant to be Apple's bold entry into the business market but it would ultimately become the company's first commercial failure. The ill-sized case would mean computers were shipped without properly working; the blame for this was placed on the engineers rather than Jobs, who had by this point turned his interest to a more radical third new computer project that would be developed in tandem with the others.

Two engineers from Hewlett-Packard were drafted in to develop the machine which Jobs had already given the eyebrow-raising name of Lisa. With Jobs having not yet fully admitted that his daughter was indeed his, it was a branding that many around the company felt uncomfortable with. Regis McKenna came up with a meaningless acronym – 'local integrated systems architecture' – as an official explanation for the name to press and retailers. Engineers within the four walls of Apple jokingly used their own acronym 'Lisa: invented stupid acronym'.

Unlike Raskin's Macintosh project, the Lisa team's focus was on producing an absolute high-end computer, with the aim of creating a machine that would boast a 16-bit microprocessor – double the power of the 8-bit Apple II, with a hefty mooted $2,000 price tag. Lacking the ingenuity of Wozniak who was still occupied with the Apple II, early work by the engineering team working on the Lisa left Jobs decidedly underwhelmed. Despite its extra power, it didn't appear to be able to do much more than its predecessor.

Much-needed inspiration for the Lisa would come during a visit to one of Apple's recent investors. For some time Raskin had been urging senior management to take notice of some of the groundbreaking work being done by the team at Xerox's Palo Alto Research Center (PARC), the company's innovations lab in Palo Alto where he had spent some time on a sabbatical. PARC would become known for inventing integral pieces of technology that helped fuel the PC revolution, such as Ethernet networking and object-oriented programming.

Raskin's suggestion to arrange a demonstration had previously fallen on deaf ears, particularly from Jobs who was generally dismissive of him. Nevertheless, the former academic remained determined for his superiors to see what Xerox had been developing and called on Bill Atkinson, a young programmer at Apple, to raise the idea of a visit to PARC once again with Jobs. Raskin had drafted in Atkinson to Apple after teaching him during his time at the University of California, San Diego. Unlike Raskin, who Steve saw as a pedantic academic, Atkinson was already respected across the company and by Jobs in particular as being an inspired talent.

Xerox's earlier purchase of $1million in Apple stock had come in exchange for access to the PARC facilities. Making good on the arrangement and heeding the advice of Raskin and Atkinson, a delegation of Apple engineers and executives made two visits to the lab, a ten-minute drive from Cupertino, with Jobs leading the second trip.

On the latter occasion, an engineer named Larry Tesler conducted a demonstration of the Xerox Alto, a personal computer he had been working on, leaving Jobs awestruck.

Instead of typing in commands on the keyboard to direct the computer, Tesler used a block-like input device with three buttons, which the PARC team referred to as a 'mouse'. Using the device he moved a cursor around the Alto's display, clicking to select icons and text on the screen. Opening and closing 'windows', and deftly moving from one task to another on a version of the desktop environment that is today so familiar to computer users was a revelatory moment for Jobs and his team.

Xerox management didn't appear to understand the revolutionary potential of what the PARC engineers and programmers had created. Jobs, in contrast, recognised the goldmine immediately. 'Why hasn't this

# Apple's incredible cash reserve

In July 2011, Apple had more cash to spend than the United States government (US Treasury reserves: $73.7bn; Apple's reserves: $76.4bn). By May 2017, Apple's cash holdings had more than tripled to $256.8bn. That amount of cash could buy you...

982

NEYMARS

Transfer fee from Barcelona to PSG, $261m

257 MILLION

iPhone X

64gb iPhone X $999

4,505

SpaceX Falcon 9

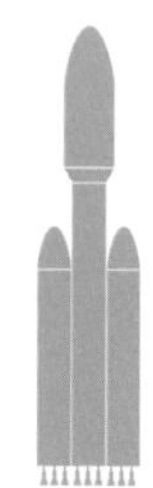

SpaceX Falcon 9 rocket launches, $57 million circa 2012

12,229

Bombardier Learjet

Bombardier Learjet 85 luxury private plane $21million

4,142

## Private islands

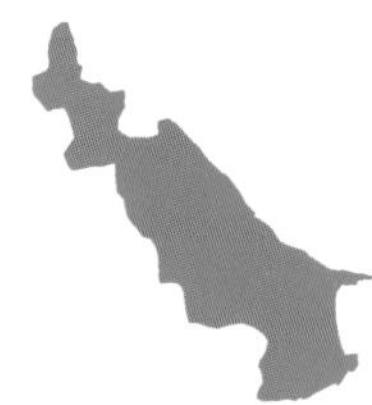

Spectabilis Island, Exuma Cays
$62 million in 2017

3.21 MILLION DOLLARS

## Bonus to all Apple employees in US

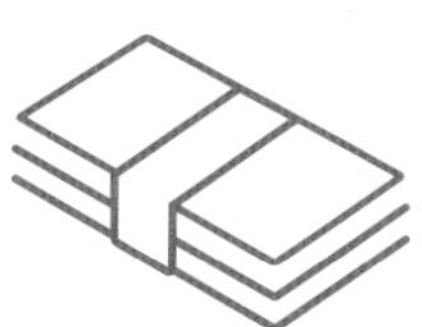

$3.21 million bonus for all 80,000 Apple employees in the US

## All of these companies

SONY

NETFLIX

Twitter $13bn / Snapchat $25bn / AirBnB $31bn / Sony $43bn / Uber $68bn / Netflix $70bn

company brought this to market?' a blown-away Jobs exclaimed during the demo. 'I don't get it!'

His disbelief wasn't lost on PARC's frustrated innovators. Apple 'understood what we had a lot better than Xerox did,' Tesler recalled.

> 'They showed me really three things. But I was so blinded by the first one that I didn't even really see the other two,' Jobs recalled in an interview with PBS. 'One of the things they showed me was object-oriented programming – they showed me that but I didn't even see that. The other one they showed me was a networked computer system... they had over a hundred Alto computers all networked using email etc., etc., I didn't even see that. I was so blinded by the first thing they showed me, which was the graphical user interface. I thought it was the best thing I'd ever seen in my life.
>
> 'Now remember it was very flawed. What we saw was incomplete, they'd done a bunch of things wrong. But we didn't know that at the time... the germ of the idea was there and they'd done it very well. And within – you know – ten minutes it was obvious to me that all computers would work like this someday. It was obvious. You could argue about how many years it would take. You could argue about who the winners and losers might be. You couldn't argue about the inevitability, it was so obvious.'

Jobs raced back to Apple following the demo, demanding that the team working on the company's next generation of personal computers should adapt the Alto's graphical user interface (GUI) and make its concepts the foundation for the Lisa project. Jobs now wanted a mouse, menus and windows. While Xerox appeared happy to have such revolutionary ideas seemingly hidden away in stasis, Jobs knew Apple could take the concepts and bring them to market, fully realising the great potential.

Xerox wouldn't sell a computer featuring the Alto technology until 1981. Aimed at businesses rather than consumers, the Xerox STAR was slow, underpowered and eye-wateringly expensive at $16,000 a unit. While Apple would take the GUI ball and run with it, Xerox would withdraw from personal computers altogether, following underwhelming sales of the STAR.

In later years when accusations were levelled at Jobs that Apple had stolen Xerox's ideas, he didn't discourage the charge: 'Picasso had a saying – "good artists copy, great artists steal" – and we have always been shameless about stealing great ideas... They [Xerox management] were copier-heads who had no clue about what a computer could do... Xerox could have owned the entire computer industry.'

Chapter Nine

# Insanely great

9

## Energised by the mind-blowing Xerox Alto demo, Jobs quickly set about adapting and improving the magic they had witnessed in Palo Alto.

Steve began to muscle in on the day-to-day management of the Lisa project, which was being headed up at that time by John Couch. Often sidelining the former HP engineer, Jobs would go directly with his own ideas to Atkinson and Larry Tesler – a recent poach from Xerox following the flop of the STAR. Jobs would pump up the team by telling them they had a chance to make history as it would be the first consumer machine to feature a graphical user interface and a mouse.

Always focused on the user experience, Jobs wanted Apple's mouse to be smooth in use and be able to travel in any direction, unlike Xerox's cumbersome peripheral which used two wheels and was limited to just four-way movement. This would require using a ball in the design, something the engineer chiefed with the task insisted wasn't possible. Once Jobs got wind of the engineer's defeatist attitude he was sacked on the spot. Jobs's passion for simplicity meant Apple's mouse would feature just one button rather than the Alto's three, with the developers introducing a double-click option to make up for any perceived loss of functionality.

The Lisa project saw Atkinson emerge as one of Apple's key talents, with the young programmer coming up with a host of novel ideas and solutions for the GUI. Arguably his most impressive breakthrough was a graphical effect that allowed windows to overlap – a feature taken for granted today. Atkinson had pushed himself to create the complex code because he thought he had seen this capability during his visit to Xerox PARC. When former PARC programmers saw what he had accomplished they were amazed, pointing out to him that he must have mis-seen or misremembered the demo as the Alto hadn't in fact had such a capability.

While much of the Lisa team found Jobs's enthusiasm infectious and his ideas exciting to work on, his interventions were beginning to cause problems within the ranks, with Couch unsurprisingly feeling undermined on what was supposed to be his project. The agreed company vision for the Lisa had been for the computer to be a purely business-focused machine; Jobs however was intent on creating a computer that was accessible and friendly for an individual. With no unified plan for the computer being acted upon, development inevitably ran into problems. Scott and Markkula were growing increasingly concerned that Apple's flagship new computer was set to be both late and too expensive. With Crouch escalating his grievances to them regarding Jobs's disruptiveness, the pair decided to act. Steve was taken off the Lisa project with Couch made the undisputed manager of the project. Jobs's wings were clipped further, with Markkula and Scott deciding to remove him from his role as vice president for research and development, shifting him to a new position as non-executive chairman of the board.

His new remit would now see him concentrate on promoting the brand, remaining as Apple's public face. Reduced to what was effectively an ambassador role with no operating control, Jobs was incensed and felt abandoned by Markkula in particular. The pain and humiliation of being cut down to size had hit Jobs hard, but it did at least allow him to concentrate on what was to be a landmark moment in Apple's history.

On 12 December 1980, Apple Computer Inc. stock was traded publicly for the first time. The event would go down as the largest IPO since Ford Motor Company sold shares in 1956. Demand for the 4.6 million shares was feverish, with the price shooting up from an initial $22 to $29 within the first day.

With a shareholding of 15% of the company, the 25-year-old Jobs was now one of the country's richest self-made men, worth around $220 million. In just four short years since Steve and Woz had been working out of Jobs's dad's garage, Apple had become a Fortune 500 company valued at a staggering $1.79 billion, with the sale in turn also making at least forty members of staff millionaires.

Years later, Jobs would refer to the day of Apple's IPO as being the most important of his career, as it meant those who had contributed to Apple's early success would make life-changing amounts of money. For some key employees who had been at Apple from the get-go, however, such words would have rung very hollow.

Non-salaried staff who were paid by the hour were not awarded shares. Among those who fell under that category were Bill Fernandez and Daniel Kottke – two of Jobs's oldest friends who had been with Apple since the very start. For Kottke in particular the snub was a very bitter blow. He'd been there during good times and bad, having been Steve's buddy since college, and had travelled alongside Jobs on their adventure to India as well as giving his support when Chrisann became pregnant, but this all seemed to matter little, with his friend denying him what many would have felt a deserved fortune for trivial bureaucratic reasons. When confronted by Kottke over the issue, Jobs would coldly brush him off, pointing him in the direction of his line manager if he needed an explanation. 'Our friendship was all gone. It was so sad,' Kottke would later reflect. Rod Holt, the engineer who had developed the Apple II power supply, tried to encourage Jobs to change his mind and include Kottke in the cash bonanza, suggesting they each give him some of their own shares. 'Whatever you give him, I will match it,' said Holt. 'Okay, I will give him zero,' was Jobs's reply. Whatever their place in Apple's history, they were now no longer key contributors to Apple as far as he was concerned.

It was an attitude far removed from that of Wozniak, who prior to the stock bonanza had sold two thousand of his own shares at a discount to forty mid-ranked staff members. Despite a costly divorce settlement with his wife Alice soon after they married, which saw her receive one-third of his Apple stock, Wozniak would nevertheless later give out shares to Kottke and Fernandez and a number of other employees he felt had been short-changed.

An air of heady excitement took over Apple's offices following the IPO, but the new abundance of wealth across the company soon began to prove a distraction, with luxury houses, high-end cars and even plastic surgery for partners becoming common topics of conversation for staff at the water cooler.

Jobs was determined not to let the money change him and remain grounded, keen to maintain the antimaterialistic stance that had informed his outlook since college. His only real outward concessions to his new wealthy status were a Mercedes coupe, bought as much for his admiration of its superior design, and occasional art purchases (a Maxfield Parrish painting being one of the few concessions to decoration

# Jobs v Gates

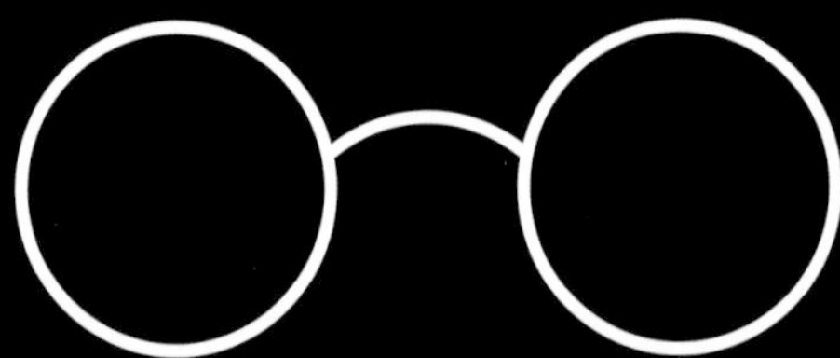

| Born | Founded company | First product |
|---|---|---|
| 24 February 1955 | 1976 (Apple) | Apple I (1976) |
| **Full name** | **Children** | **Age became a millionaire** |
| Steven Paul Jobs | 4 | 25 |
| **Hometown** | **Married** | **Age became a billionaire** |
| San Francisco | March 1991 | 40 |
| **Age at time of first job** | **Religion** | **Retired** |
| 13 (Summer job at HP) | Practicing Zen Buddhist | August 2011 (death) |
| **Education** | **Other associated companies** | **Highest net worth** |
| Reed College Portland (Did not complete degree) | NeXT, Pixar, Disney | $8.3 billion (2011) |

'Design is not just what it looks like and feels like. Design is how it works.'
'Innovation distinguishes between a leader and a follower.'
'We hire people who want to make the best things in the world.'
'Being the richest man in the cemetery doesn't matter to me.'
'I want to put a ding in the universe.'

**Steve Jobs**

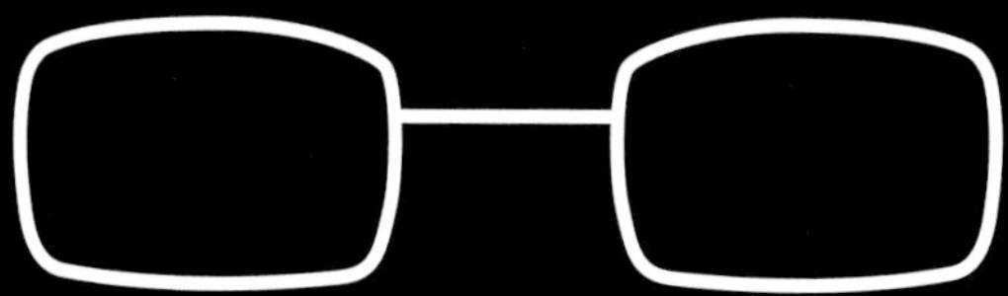

| Born | Founded company | First product |
|---|---|---|
| 28 October 1955 | 1975 (Microsoft) | BASIC (1975) |
| **Full name** | **Children** | **Age became a millionaire** |
| William Henry Gates III | 3 | 26 |
| **Hometown** | **Married** | **Age became a billionaire** |
| Seattle | January 1994 | 31 |
| **Age at time of first job** | **Religion** | **Retired** |
| 16 (Administrator at Bonneville Power) | Agnostic | June 2008 |
| **Education** | **Other associated companies** | **Highest net worth** |
| Harvard University (Did not complete degree) | Corbis | $86 billion (2017) |

'Your most unhappy customers are your greatest source of learning.'
'Success is a lousy teacher. It seduces smart people into thinking they can't lose.'
'It's fine to celebrate success but it is more important to heed the lessons of failure.'
'I never took a day off in my twenties. Not one.'
'I wish I wasn't [the world's richest man]. There's nothing good that comes out of that.'

**Bill Gates**

# Rotten Apples

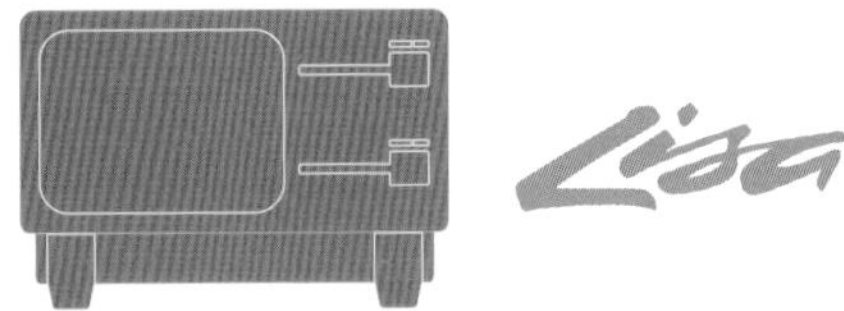

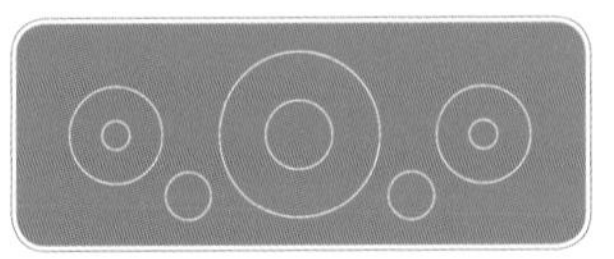

**iPod Hi-Fi**

Power Mac G4 Cube

## Apple Lisa

**Release date:** July 2008
**Discontinued:** June 2012
**Original price:** $9,995

The first mass-market personal computer to be based around a graphical user interface, it also included groundbreaking features such as multitasking and memory protection.

**Why did it fail?** Despite its advancements, it's prohibitive $9,995 price tag and unreliable floppy disk drive meant it was dead on arrival.

## Pippin

**Release date:** September 1996
**Discontinued:** 1997
**Original price:** $599

Apple's inauspicious entry into the already saturated videogame market. Based on PowerPC Macs, it was released shortly before Jobs's return to Apple. Once back in charge, he quickly lost enthusiasm for the loss-making gaming venture and promptly called time on production of the console.

**Why did it fail:** The only company that licensed the platform was Japanese toy maker Bandai. Its key selling point – network-enabled gameplay – was hamstrung by a slow 14.4kbit/s modem, while its dated processor made for sluggish loading times. Along with a limited roster of games and stiff competition in the forms of the significantly cheaper Sega Saturn and Sony PlayStation, only 42,000 of the estimated 100,000 units made were sold.

## iPod Hi-Fi

**Release date:** February 2006
**Discontinued:** September 2007
**Original price:** $349

Bulky white speaker system developed and manufactured in-house by Apple for use with iPods.

**Why did it fail:** While it sounded fine, it was too big for most living spaces. It was also too expensive, especially as it came up against a steadily increasing wave of compatible third-party iPod docks from more recognised audio brands such as Bose.

## Power Mac G4 Cube

**Release date:** July 2000
**Discontinued:** July 2001
**Original price:** $1,799

One of designer Jony Ive's most striking works. An 8x8x8-inch cube suspended in acrylic, it marked a stark contrast to the beige tower PCs of the era. The New York Museum of Modern Art holds a G4 Cube, along with its complementing Harman Kardon transparent speakers, as part of its collection.

**Why did it fail?** The ultimate example of Apple placing form before function and style over power. Its processing capacity didn't quite match its great design, while its hefty $1,799 price tag – a huge sum for the time considering that it didn't include a monitor – ultimately resulted in the Cube selling a third of the units Apple had expected it to.

## MobileMe

**Release date:** July 2008
**Discontinued:** June 2012
**Original price:** Annual subscriptions $99 for 20GB of storage

Following .Mac and iTools - earlier Apple false starts at consumer cloud computing platforms - MobileMe gave users remote access and management of email, contacts, calendar, photos and files.

**Why did it fail:** The platform's reputation never fully recovered from the fallout of an infamously buggy launch that saw users unable to access emails. During a dressing down of the development team responsible for the service shortly after launch, an eyewitness claims Jobs delivered the brutal reprimand: 'You've tarnished Apple's reputation... You should hate each other for having let each other down.'

in his main living area). He took pleasure in seeing his parents pay off their mortgage after he gave them stock worth $750,000, while the IPO also allowed him to finance a charitable organisation concerned with blindness in Nepal and India.

The IPO had confirmed Apple's status as a technology heavyweight, but new challengers in the realm of personal computing were about to enter the fray, the most significant of which would be IBM, the most dominant computer company in the world. For Jobs, Apple's next progressive step needed to be for the company to produce an affordable and accessible computer.

The Macintosh project dovetailed into this vision. Having been exiled from the Lisa division, Jobs began to exert his influence over the direction of what was supposed to be Jef Raskin's project. Steve wanted the Macintosh to now incorporate some of the innovations seen at Xerox, including an Alto-style graphical user interface. As part of this, Jobs wanted the Macintosh to give users the option of multiple fonts that would be beautifully displayed with proportional spacing, which could be resized, italicised and placed in bold.

Up to this point personal computers had only been able to display text in a single typeface which would be designed to be clear to read on TVs and cheap displays – blocky, jagged and just plain ugly. Jobs also wanted the Macintosh to use the same cutting edge Motorola 68000 microprocessor earmarked for the Lisa, which would enable it to produce the sort of graphical tricks that had wowed the Apple delegation on their visit to Xerox PARC. This went against Raskin's plan for the computer to use the cheap and far less capable Motorola 6809. Raskin saw no way of delivering a machine that featured such high-end components and grand feature ideas while maintaining his original goal of creating an affordable computer. Jobs in turn felt Raskin was compromising with costs, turning a potentially beautiful, exciting machine into something horrible, but Raskin remained resistant to Steve's reality distortion field.

The clashes in both philosophy and personality between the two inevitably came to a head. Unable to take the meddling in the project anymore, like John Couch before him, Raskin complained to Mike Scott about Jobs. A showdown with the two warring factions took place later that afternoon in a meeting called by Scotty in his office with Markkula also present. Both men passionately argued their case, with Jobs crying

# Apple Lisa

Release date

19 January 1983

Price

$9,995 (equivalent to $24,768.63 in 2017)

Ports

1 parallel, 2 serial ports, 1 mouse port

Total units sold

100,000

Development time

Four years

GUI

First commercial computer to feature a graphical user interface and a mouse controller

Display

12-inch monochrome monitor, 720 X 364 graphics

Storage

Two 51/4-inch floppy drives, external 5 Meg hard drive

Development cost

$50 million

as he stated his belief in his vision for the Macintosh. Unlike the flashpoint with Couch, this time Scotty and Markkula took Steve's side, with Raskin ordered to take a leave of absence.

Whatever the motivation was for Scotty and Markkula in opting for Jobs, over time the decision would prove to be a sound one. The Jobs-helmed Macintosh (or Mac) would fall some way short of delivering on its original aim of having a sub-$1000 price tag, but under Steve's stewardship the company would create and market a device that would revolutionise personal computing.

With Raskin ousted, Jobs set about augmenting his team further, aiming to fill his squad with 'A-list' players. One such talented individual identified for Steve's dream team was Andy Hertzfeld, a young engineer working on the Apple II.

Sounding Hertzfeld out for a role, Jobs asked: 'Are you any good? We only want really good people working on the Mac, and I'm not sure you're good enough.' Hertzfeld confidently confirmed that he was indeed, pretty good. Later that afternoon, Jobs returned to Hertzfeld's cubicle, offering him a place on the Mac team. The young programmer expressed his delight, but explained he still had a few days' work left on the Apple II to do. Unwilling to wait for him to finish work on a machine Jobs said would 'be dead in two years', he unplugged Hertzfeld's computer, wiping out the code he was working on, before escorting him over to his new home on the Mac team. 'The Macintosh is the future of Apple, and you're going to start on it now!' Jobs would declare, before ushering him to a desk formally occupied by Jef Raskin.

Keen to revive the spirit of the old days in Paul Jobs's garage, as well as harness his untouchable talent, Steve attempted to bring Wozniak onboard the Mac project. The reunion wasn't to be however, as near-tragedy struck.

Attempting a takeoff at Sky Park Airport in Scotts Valley, California, Wozniak crashed his newly purchased turbocharged single-engine, six-seat Beechcraft Bonanza A36TC. Having climbed too abruptly, the plane stalled and careened through two fences into the car park of an ice-skating rink.

Onboard the plane with him was his fiancée, Candi Clark, her brother and her brother's girlfriend. Miraculously, nobody died in the crash, although Wozniak barely survived. After sustaining head injuries, Woz ended up with partial amnesia. It would take several weeks for his memory to fully return, during which time he decided to take an extended break from Apple. A decade after dropping out, Woz would return to Berkeley to finally get his degree, mischievously enrolling under the name of Rocky Raccoon Clark.

The first few months of 1981 saw much upheaval at Apple. The now twenty-strong Mac team moved out of the Apple Campus, setting up a new HQ in a building a short walk away that would become fondly known as Texaco Towers on account of it being next door to a petrol station. Just weeks later, Mike Scott was forced out as Apple's president.

His fate was sealed when, in an uncharacteristically ruthless move, he shocked employees by unceremoniously sacking forty members of staff he deemed not good enough. The unexpected round of layoffs had a profound negative effect on morale across the company, with many members of staff calling into question his judgment.

Concerned at the deterioration of Scotty's relationship with staff, Markkula called together a meeting of Apple management while the president was on leave in Hawaii. The meeting established there was a broad consensus among the likes of Jobs and John Crouch that Scotty's position was now untenable, and a decision was made to let him go. With the conflict-averse Markkula slotting in as interim president, Jobs found he could now lead the Mac division with next to no interference.

The next few years would see Steve drive home his manifesto to the Mac team of producing a machine that was 'insanely great'. HIs charm and exuberance would regularly push team members to produce the seemingly impossible, his cutting criticisms of staff striking fear.

Recalling the Mac's development, software development team manager Bud Tribble said: 'In his presence, reality is malleable... He can convince anyone of practically anything. It wears off when he's not around.'

His meticulous attention to detail saw him obsess over the smallest details during the Mac's development. Insisting on a pinstripe design at the top of window panes, Jobs forced the developers of the GUI to do version after version, insisting on one tiny tweak after another. When the developers protested that they had better things to do he shouted, 'Can you imagine looking at that every day? It's not just a little thing. It's something we have to do right.'

Jobs's reverence for good product design came to the fore during the making of the Macintosh. In order for it to take up less desk space,

Jobs pushed for the main unit to be taller and smaller, while a radical departure from the Apple II saw it feature a detached keyboard. Initial prototypes of the case were too boxy for Jobs's taste. 'It's got to be more curvaceous,' he would feed back.

Even the look of the computer's internals were a major consideration, with Jobs ordering key members of the division to sign their names to the mould of the machine's casing. Though no one but repair technicians would likely ever see the signatures, Steve's reasoning was that all great artists sign their work.

Instead of using the cumbersome 5¼-inch floppy disks that the Apple II helped standardise, the Mac's disk drive neatly situated underneath the display would use 3½-inch mini-floppies. These disks could fit in a shirt pocket and came with a built-in protective cover, making them far less vulnerable to damage than standard floppies.

While the Mac would be a groundbreaking machine on an aesthetic level, not all the design decisions were sound. Jobs pushed through questionable choices despite well-founded reservations from his team, with most relating to his insistence on keeping the machine's footprint as small as possible. Despite the demands on processing to run the Mac's GUI, he agreed to a design with only a meagre 128 kilobytes (or 128,000 bytes) of memory – almost ten times less than what the Lisa would be able to boast. In an effort to encourage use of the mouse for cursor movement, Jobs did away with the keyboard's arrow keys. In a similar act of design over functionality he refused to put a hard drive in the Mac because he didn't want to add a noisy fan to keep it cool, leaving users reliant on floppy disk drives for storage.

Jobs liked to put himself on the other side of the table, adopting the position of a customer when reviewing designs and prototypes. Somewhat ambitiously estimating that five million people would one day be using the machine, he cooked up the notion which he put to developer Larry Kenyon that slashing ten seconds from the startup time would save fifty million seconds every day. 'Over a year, that's probably dozens of lifetimes,' he told Kenyon, before adding, 'if you could make it boot ten seconds faster, you'll save a dozen lives. That's really worth it, don't you think?' As was so often the case, Jobs's knack for motivating by illustrating the bigger picture scored the desired result. Just a few weeks later, Kenyon successfully demoed the machine booting up an impressive twenty-eight seconds faster.

His insistence for staff to do better and better work became all the more pressing when International Business Machines emerged as fierce competitors. The technology giant released the IBM Personal Computer in August of 1981, an event Apple somewhat arrogantly marked with a full-page ad in *The Wall Street Journal* that read, 'Welcome IBM. Seriously. Welcome to the most exciting and important marketplace since the computer revolution began 35 years ago...'.

Many at Apple dismissed IBM's machine as being both dull and inferior, but it would later play out that the young upstart company had perhaps underestimated the clout of its more mature computing rival. IBM's reputation among business buyers, coupled with the might and marketing of its sales force, ensured that sales of its machine would grow at a ominously rapid rate.

Chapter Ten

# The times they are a changin’

10

AMERICAN
ACADEMY OF ACHIEVEMENT
SALUTE
EXCELLENCE
WEEKEND
GUEST OF
HONOR

Jobs's profile remained in its ascendance. Rather than name a person of the year as was the magazine's way, in 1982 *Time* magazine named the personal computer as its Machine of the Year.

Having agreed to an interview with the magazine for the issue, Jobs had suspected he would be awarded the former honour. While that wasn't to be, only one person was nevertheless profiled in the issue, with Jobs offered as the sole face of the new computer revolution. 'It is Steven Jobs, more than anyone, who kicked open the door and let the personal computer move in,' the magazine exclaimed. Arriving quietly on the outside lane, however, was another young pioneer who would soon be talked of in the same glowing terms.

Along with his business partner Paul Allen, Bill Gates had provided versions of the BASIC language for the Altair and the Apple II. His company was now set to go stratospheric, with Gates having clinched a deal to have Microsoft's MS-DOS operating system software come preloaded on every IBM PC that went out the door. Crucially, Gates had managed to work a deal which allowed Microsoft the right to license MS-DOS to other computer makers in the future.

Software programs as well as hardware were now a major selling point for computers, and having an attractive array of programs would become a key to the success of the Macintosh. To that end, in late 1981, Jobs travelled to Seattle in a bid to secure a deal with Microsoft for new software for the Mac which would make use of its revolutionary graphical user interface. Gates, however, wasn't overly impressed with what he saw as a limited platform – or Jobs's attitude.

> 'It was kind of a weird seduction visit where Steve was saying we don't really need you and we're doing this great thing, and it's under the cover. He's in his Steve Jobs sales mode, but kind of the sales mode that also says, "I don't need you, but I might let you be involved",' Gates would later reveal.

# What was on Steve's iPod?

During his keynote address on 1 September 2010, Jobs inadvertently offered a glimpse at his favourite albums while demonstrating Apple's now defunct, music-oriented social network iTunes Ping.

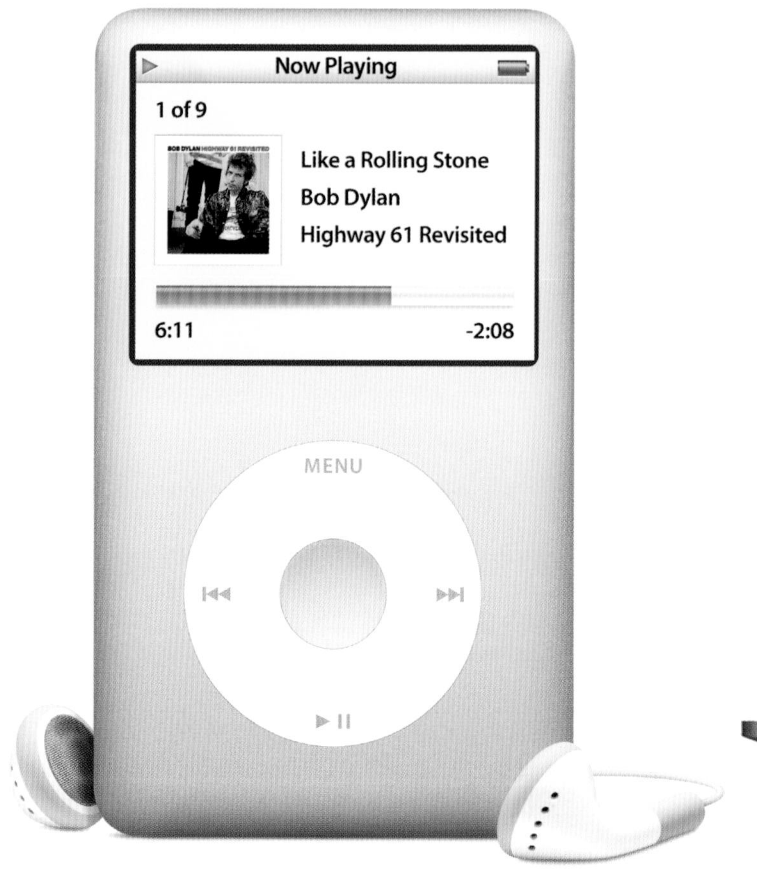

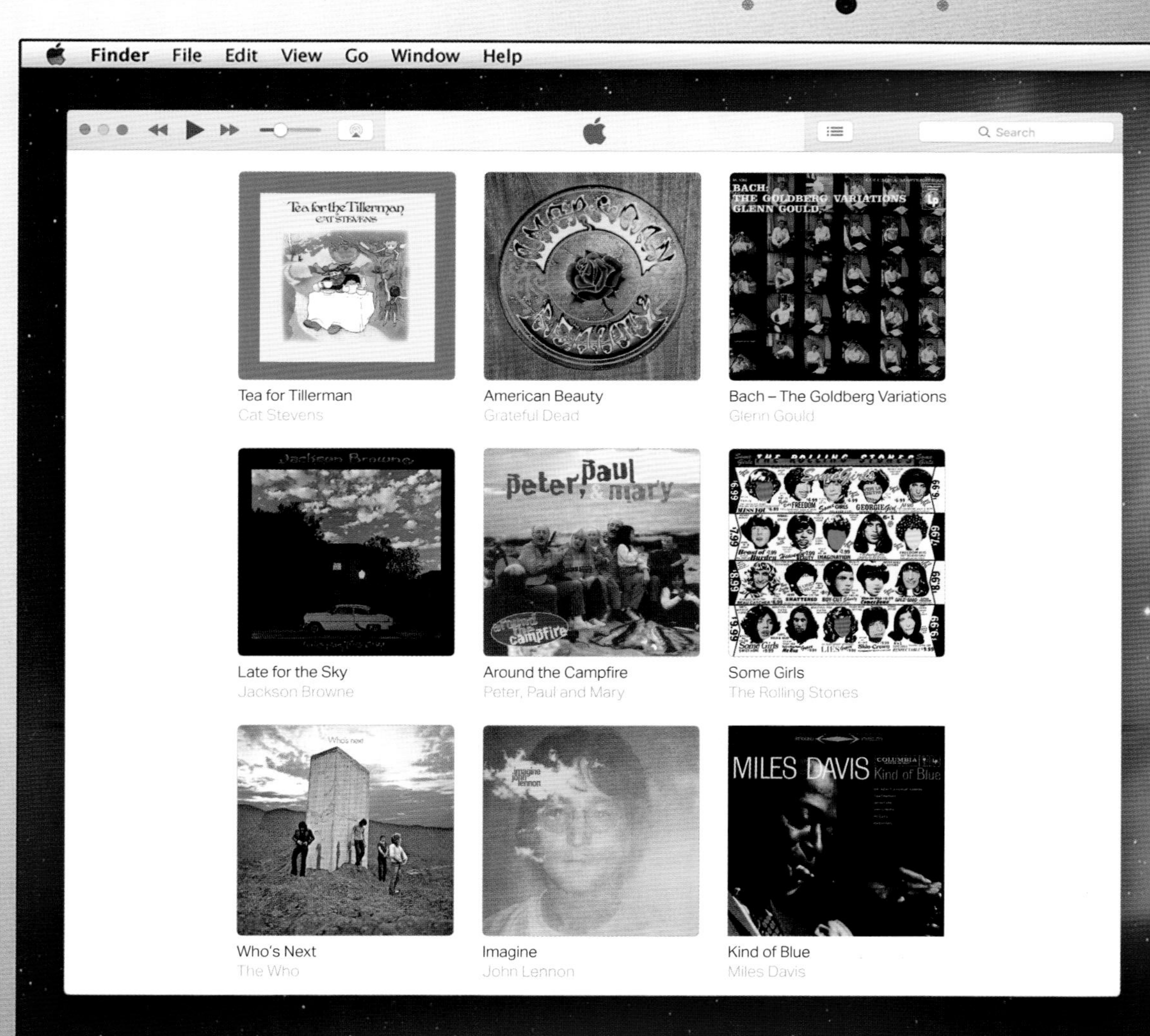
Finder File Edit View Go Window Help
Search
Tea for Tillerman
Cat Stevens
American Beauty
Grateful Dead
Bach – The Goldberg Variations
Glenn Gould
Late for the Sky
Jackson Browne
Around the Campfire
Peter, Paul and Mary
Some Girls
The Rolling Stones
Who's Next
The Who
Imagine
John Lennon
Kind of Blue
Miles Davis
MacBook Air

# Evolution of the Apple logo

Original Apple logo featuring Isaac Newton under the fabled apple tree.

Rainbow Apple logo, used from late 1976 to early 1998.

First incarnation of the glass Apple logo appeared in 1998.

After a two-year gap, the revised glass logo returned in 2001 until around 2007.

This version of the glass stylisation remained for seven years between 2007 and 2014.

Monochrome Apple logo first appeared between 1998 and 2000, making a long-term return in 2014.

Despite reservations on how likely the Mac would deliver on Jobs's many promises, Gates nevertheless agreed to provide graphical versions of a new spreadsheet called Excel, a word-processing program called Word, and a new version of BASIC.

Over the course of three decades, Jobs and Gates would go from being cagey allies to frosty rivals before arriving at a place of respectful admiration that approached genuine friendship. Their route into the computer business had gone via different lanes, one taking a primarily hardware route, the other software. There was also a divergence from the start in terms of what both men saw as the future path for the desktop computer. For Jobs, the computer would prove to be a deeply personal tool, a machine with which users would become emotionally invested, and one that would come to be embraced as much by students and in progressive homes, as it would by middle managers and secretaries. For Gates the outlook was perhaps bigger yet also much simpler – that the primary market for computers was always going to be as a workaday business tool – a machine that would help companies communicate, account and sell. Over the course of the next two decades at least, it would be Gates's forecast that would prove to be the more prescient, with his company eventually leading the way.

Towards the end of 1982, Apple was still riding the wave of success that was the Apple II, having sold a record 700,000 units of its hit computer over the course of the financial year. While its flawed successor would never achieve such highs, the Apple III still managed to notch up a creditable $583 million in sales during the same period, turning into a reality Markkula's confident prediction that Apple would become a Fortune 500 company.

The Apple II couldn't go on forever as the company's cash cow, and with the Apple III clearly not set to make up similar numbers, a huge weight of expectation was placed on the success of Apple's follow-up machine. The Lisa would become the next Apple computer to make it to market, hitting shelves in a blaze of publicity in January 1983, following a gestation period that had cost the company $50 million.

Much to Jobs's disappointment, the Lisa had made it out into the wild before his own pet project, the Macintosh, meaning it could lay claim to being the first personal computer to use a mouse and the first to offer a GUI featuring menus and a file system. It could also boast generous amounts of memory, two floppy drives and seven bundled software programs (LisaWrite, LisaCalc, LisaDraw, LisaGraph, LisaProject, LisaList and LisaTerminal) which could be quickly mastered by users.

As the public face of Apple, Jobs was tasked with introducing the Lisa to the press during its unveiling at the Carlyle Hotel in New York, along with a round of interviews. Unable to contain his passion about his own project, Jobs used the opportunity to refer to the Macintosh, mentioning it would be less expensive and incompatible with the Lisa. Jobs's comments about the Mac made it into much of the coverage that followed the Lisa launch, undermining its big introduction to the world.

The tech press were nevertheless rapturous in its acclaim for the Lisa, with the then influential *Byte* magazine declaring it 'the most important development in computers in the last five years, easily outpacing [the IBM PC]'.

While critics marvelled at its technological advancements, it soon became apparent that the machine had a number of fundamental problems. The graphical interface sapped much of the computer's resources, thus making it impractical for high-end users, while the Lisa's software offering beyond what was bundled with the machine was scant. The biggest barrier to its success, however, was its bloated launch price of $9,995 which put off both business customers and individuals alike. The Lisa had launched a revolution in the way consumers interacted with personal computers, but it would not result in transformative sales for Apple.

One interested onlooker at the Lisa launch event had been John Sculley, President of the Pepsi-Cola division of PepsiCo. Sculley was seen as one of the leading lights of the marketing world, having overseen the Pepsi Challenge campaign, one of the most successful international advertising triumphs of the era. Sculley's presence at the event came amid a series of courtship meetings with Jobs and corporate headhunter Gerry Roche, with Jobs and Markkula having identified the soft drinks marketer as the ideal fit to take over the role of president at Apple.

Markkula had reluctantly assumed the role of CEO following Mike Scott's departure in 1981, but was now ready to step down, fully aware that the company was becoming dysfunctional – a true leader was needed to bring together Apple's new computer divisions which seemed to now be battling each other. While Jobs had coveted the president's

# The iPod era

1st Gen iPod (Classic) 10GB

**2001**

2nd Gen iPod (Classic) 20GB

**2002**

3rd Gen iPod (Classic) 30GB

**2003**

4th Gen iPod (iPod Photo) 40GB

iPod Mini 1st / 2nd Gen / 6GB

**2004**

5th Gen iPod 60GB

1st Gen iPod Nano / 4GB

1st Gen iPod Shuffle / 1GB

**2005**

**The iPod advert boost**
Seven songs that featured in iconic adverts

2004

Black Eyed Peas 'Hey Mama' iPod 3G

2004

Jet 'Are You Gonna Be My Girl?' iPod 3G

2004

U2 'Vertigo' Special-Edition iPod

The times they are a changin'

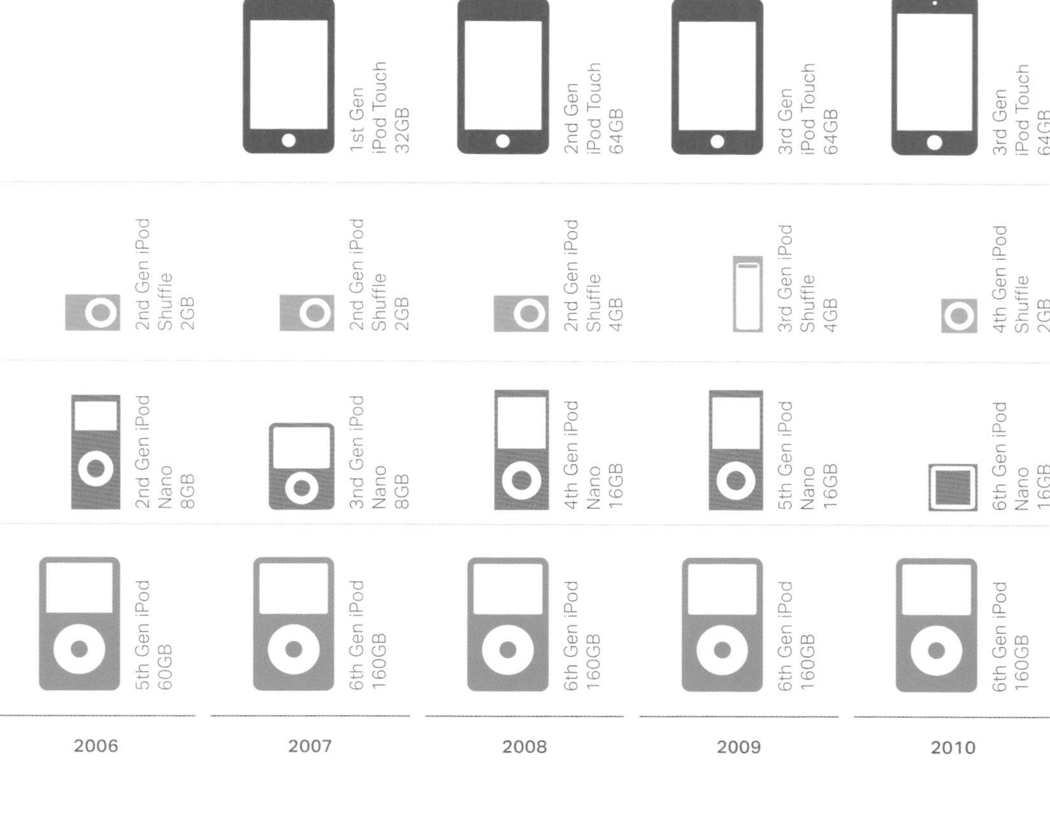


2005

Caesars
'Jerk It Out'
iPod Shuffle

2005

Daft Punk
'Technologic'
iPod

2007

Feist
'1 2 3 4'
iPod Nano

2008

Ting Ting's 'Shut Up
And Let Me Go'
iPod

role himself, deep down he knew he was neither experienced nor mature enough to run the company himself. It was a view that Markkula agreed with so a plan was hatched to bring in someone from the outside.

Their original target for the role had been IBM's Don Estridge, who had masterminded the formation of the company's now widely successful personal computer division, but Apple's $2 million salary and bonus offer was not enough to prise the principled executive away from their rival.

Following the knockback, Jobs and Markkula enlisted Roche to help with their search. It was decided that the hunt should no longer be focused on technology executives; what was needed was experience in consumer marketing – someone with a strong corporate profile who would play well on Wall Street.

The pursuit of Sculley would play out for months, with meetings taking place across both coasts before Jobs's charm offensive finally won out.

Following a visit to New York, Jobs laid down a challenge that sealed the deal: 'do you want to spend the rest of your life selling sugared water or do you want a chance to change the world?'

In the spring of 1983 at the age of forty-four, Sculley uprooted from New York to join Apple in Cupertino, accepting a deal similar to the one rejected by Don Estridge.

Chapter Eleven

# How to think differently

11

apple

In the beginning, Jobs and Sculley got along famously. 'I was smitten by him,' Sculley later admitted. 'Steve was one of the brightest people I'd ever met. I shared with him a passion for ideas.'

When Jobs had agreed to the hire, it was as much about installing a mentor who could give him a better understanding of the business world, as it was an effort to add a disciplined leader to an unfocused company.

The two would regularly go out on long walks together, often making trips to the mountains outside Cupertino for hikes. They were so close that over breakfast one day at Jobs's house, Jobs told Sculley and his wife why he was in such a hurry. 'We all have a short period of time on this earth,' Jobs said. 'We probably only have the opportunity to do a few things really great and do them really well... My feeling is I've got to accomplish a lot of these things while I'm young.'

So entwined were the two, the pair would often finish each other's sentences. During a dinner party ahead of the Macintosh launch, Sculley said, 'Apple has one leader, Steve and me.'

While some employees were initially put off by his corporate-friendly business suit and tie – a rare look in the casual Apple office, usually only reserved for when executives had to impress outsiders – most staff were excited with the plans laid out by Sculley for the company.

With the IBM PC now going great guns and other 'clone' computers now able to use MS-DOS as well, Microsoft's operating system was becoming the de facto standard platform for personal computers, with a huge range of compatible programs available from third-party publishers, leaving Apple marginalised with its own incompatible ecosystem.

Acknowledging how the company would have to change to compete with IBM, Sculley told staff that Apple needed to maintain its entrepreneurial spirit even as the company expanded into new markets. He also planned to diversify Apple, which he rightly felt was far too reliant on the Apple II for its revenues.

A further challenge for the company came towards the end of 1983,

# The Steve Jobs look

1998 1999 2000 2001 2003 2004

2005 2006 2007 2008 2009 2010

just weeks before the Mac would be launched. In a shock move, Microsoft announced it would create a new operating system for IBM- and DOS-compatible machines which would be named Windows. Like the Mac operating system, it would feature a GUI incorporating icons, windows and the use of a mouse.

Gates had previously agreed with Apple to wait a year after the Mac was released before selling such a system, but with the Mac having fallen almost a year behind its scheduled launch date, Microsoft were within their rights to pounce.

As the news emerged, Jobs furiously summoned Gates to Apple's Cupertino headquarters, demanding an explanation. Gates arrived the following day alone to find himself surrounded by ten Apple employees. 'You're ripping us off,' Jobs shouted. Unperturbed, Gates hit back: 'Well, Steve, I think there's more than one way of looking at it. I think it's more like we both had this rich neighbour named Xerox and I broke into his house to steal the TV set and found out that you had already stolen it.'

It would take Microsoft a further two years to launch Windows 1.0, a buggy, ugly first attempt at a graphical user interface that would compare unfavourably to Apple's elegant GUI. It did badly with both critics and consumers, but it provided a starting point for Microsoft from where it would make Windows better and then dominant. Even in his final years, Jobs would remain bitter about how Windows emerged, accusing Gates of shamelessly ripping Apple off. While that may have been an unfair accusation, particularly in light of how Apple had capitalised on Xerox's original ideas, one wonders if Jobs's real issue with Gates was that the Microsoft operating system ended up winning the war, despite Apple's take on a graphical OS being more imaginative and elegant in its execution.

As work progressed on the Macintosh, Jobs tried his best to rally his troops by holding an off-site retreat in Carmel. Kicking off proceedings, he delivered three 'Sayings from Chairman Jobs':

1. Real artists ship.
2. It's better to be a pirate than join the navy.
3. Mac in a book by 1986.

While the third slogan was a means of encouraging the team to think innovatively about future products ('Mac in a book' refers to the team's early concepts about making a laptop device – it would take six years before Apple would ship the fifteen-pound Mac Portable), the first two were very much about the current task ahead for the division.

Slogan number one, 'Real artists ship', would serve as a friendly warning that it was crunch time and deadlines needed to be hit to get their product out. The second implied that his rebellious group's technology was much better than what everyone else was offering, including the internal rivals working on the Lisa. From that point the building which housed the band of pirates flew a skull and crossbones.

While Sculley's appointment had initially brought Jobs much optimism and excitement, as time went on the decision to bring him in would prove to be one of the biggest mistakes of his career. Sculley's marketing skills were proven and strong, but his experience and understanding of computers was limited. Upon arriving in Cupertino he hired a technical assistant to tutor him on digital technology as well as give him a crash course on the Apple II in his office. Jobs soon began to resent Sculley for not appearing to share his passion for great products, and started to question how much the new president actually offered to the company. For his part, Sculley didn't like the way that Jobs treated other staff members.

Their first real flashpoint came during a meeting to decide the pricing of the Macintosh. In the same way that pioneers such as Henry Ford and Edwin Land, founder of Polaroid, had taken hugely expensive products and managed to make them affordable via more efficient manufacturing, Jobs wanted the Macintosh to be a computer for the masses, not one for corporate tech departments.

To make that vision a reality, Jobs felt it was fundamental that the Mac was sold at $2,000. With the project already way over budget, and Jobs wanting a huge war chest for advertising, Sculley put his foot down; if he wanted to spend so much on marketing, it would have to be absorbed into the computer's price. Jobs was furious, but ultimately opted for the marketing budget. This resulted in the Macintosh being given a price tag of $2,495, a figure Jobs thought was too high for the machine to realise its mass market goal.

The bumper marketing allocation allowed Jobs to hand advertising agency Chiat\Day a $900,000 budget for a TV advert.

Directed by Ridley Scott, who was fresh from filming the visually stunning science fiction epic *Blade Runner*, the result was the classic

# Four key ingredients to the Steve Jobs look

Levi's 501s – $69.50. Usually opting for light blue stonewashed denim, Jobs famously unveiled the iPod Nano for the first time by taking it from the small 'watch pocket' of the jeans he was wearing during its launch in 2005.

Issey Miyake black turtleneck – $270. Arguably Jobs's most iconic clothing item, Jobs adopted the austere knitwear after being impressed by the Japanese designer's uniforms for Sony staff following a visit to the Far East in the 1980s.

Lunor glasses, by Robert Marc – $495. Originally custom-built for Jobs in 1998, the frameless Gandhi-style round lens glasses were eventually released to the public following Jobs's death in tribute.

Jobs wore variants of the grey 991 series of running shoes by American footwear manufacturer New Balance – with the 991s being his most regularly worn shoe at keynotes and launches.

'1984' ad, based on George Orwell's novel of the same name, casting IBM as the villain and the Macintosh as the hero.

The commercial begins in monochrome with an army of downtrodden, zombie-like skinheads marching into an assembly as a Big Brother figure fiercely lectures them from a huge screen on the virtues of censorship: 'Today we celebrate the first glorious anniversary of the Information Purification Directives...'

The scene is interspersed with shots of a sprinting blond heroine in a white vest and bright red shorts, carrying a mallet, pursued by stormtrooper-like security guards. She bursts into the assembly and swings the mallet at the screen, unleashing an explosion and a blast of fresh air, as a voice-over reads the text of a product launch scheduled for two days hence: 'On January 24th, Apple Computer will introduce Macintosh. And you'll see why 1984 won't be like "1984".'

Jobs was suitably thrilled by Scott's finished edit, but Sculley, for whom advertising was an area of expertise, along with the rest of the board of directors hated it. Despite the board's opposition, Apple's marketing executives made the final decision to run with the advert.

The advert ran in its full sixty-second length only once on national television – during the third quarter of Super Bowl XVIII on 22 January 1984. (It was shown a month earlier on a TV station in Twin Falls, Idaho, to preserve its eligibility for advertising awards, and subsequently with previews in some movie theatres.)

Response to the ad was so emphatic that Apple bought months of ad time on ScreenVision, a company that sold ad time in movie theatres. Because they were so enamoured with the commercial, some owners re-aired the ad for months after Apple's contract ran out.

Now commonly regarded as one of the most important adverts of all time, before Super Bowl XVIII, nobody watched the game 'just for the commercials'. But '1984' would go on to define the Super Bowl advert as a cultural phenomenon, creating the annual commercial frenzy that now often overshadows the actual sporting event.

Along with the '1984' spot, Apple bought spreads in major newspapers and magazines, including a huge twenty-page advertising supplement in *Newsweek*. In an initiative devised by Sculley, potential customers with a credit card could try out the product with the 'Test Drive a Macintosh' promotion, letting them take home a Macintosh for twenty-

# The 1984 commercial

Amount of extras hired for the ad, many of them real-life London skinheads

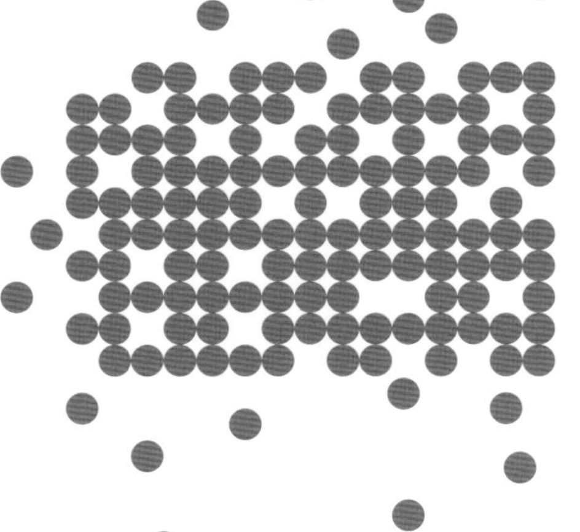

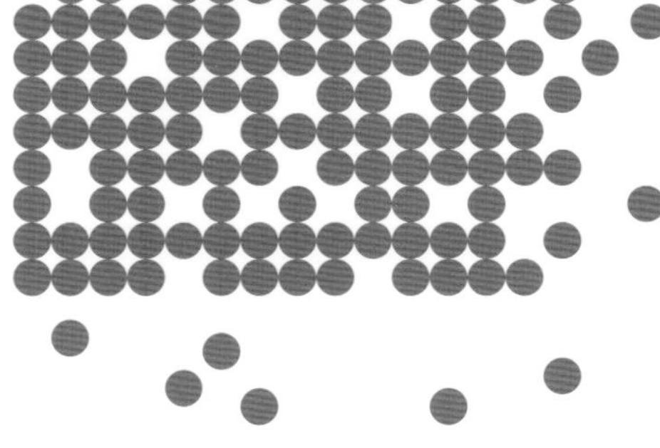

Running length of advert

Number of days spent shooting the advert at Shepperton Studios in Surrey, England

Day rate for actors appearing in the advert

Average score for an advert using market research firm ASI's test for effectiveness

Number of times advert was shown nationally (its only airing was on 22 January 1984, during a break in the third quarter of the telecast of Super Bowl XVIII by CBS)

Position in *Advertising Age's* list of 50 greatest commercials of all time

four hours and return it to a dealer afterwards. In an effort to differentiate its offering from the 'square' IBM, Apple also gifted Macs to major celebrities, including Michael Jackson, Andy Warhol and Mick Jagger.

Two days after the Super Bowl advert, Jobs officially unveiled the Mac at the Apple annual stockholders meeting. Emotively using Vangelis's stirring theme from *Chariots of Fire* during a showreel of its capabilities, the demo ended with the Mac 'talking' to the audience, delivering a segment of the presentation via its speech synthesis feature. Funny, slick and purposeful in the way he pitted Apple against the growing threat of IBM, Jobs gave a masterclass in the sort of clear presentation that would punctuate the near legendary keynote speeches he would give in the future. The dazzling show at the Flint Center on the De Anza College campus near the company's headquarters in Cupertino, earned him a wild five-minute standing ovation.

Hands-on reviews of the machine were equally as rapturous. *Consumer Reports* raved about the Mac. 'The Macintosh ... is charting a simpler and more accessible path to computing – a path that almost allows you to abandon the notion that you are using a computer rather than accomplishing a task with a tool.' Confidently claiming that the Macintosh would change PCs forever, Byte's Gregg Williams said the machine brought the world 'one step closer to the ideal of computer as appliance.'

It wasn't without its faults – once you installed the operating system, the Mac's 128KB of memory left it with just enough space for 8.5 pages of typed text. It didn't have colour graphics, not much in the way of third-party software, and was, of course, incompatible with MS-DOS.

Nevertheless Jobs's band of pirates had delivered on their promise of creating something 'insanely great', with many regarding it as a vision of the future, including Bill Gates. 'The next generation of interesting software', he told *Businessweek*, 'will be done on Macintosh, not the IBM PC.'

Initial sales of the Macintosh were nothing short of extraordinary, with Apple selling around 70,000 within the first hundred days, far more than the IBM PC had managed following its launch.

The euphoria, however, wasn't about to last.

# Complex vs simple

## Comparing use of plain English by Steve Jobs and Bill Gates

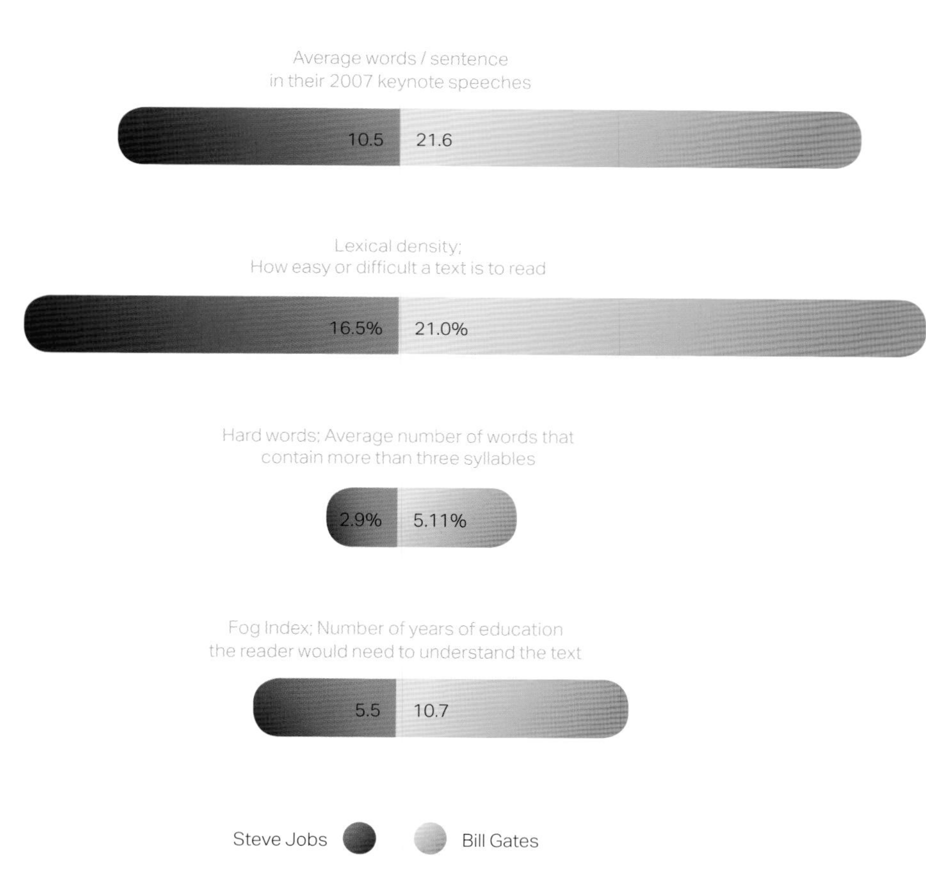

# Three is the magic number

From the French revolution motto of 'liberty, equality and fraternity' to the 'Snap, Crackle, Pop' zinger from Kellogg's copywriters in the 1930s, the power of breaking things down into three points has long been established in communications.

The principle works on the well-established idea that we are limited to holding only a small amount of information in short-term, or 'active,' memory. Steve Jobs was a strict adherent of the rule throughout his career, with some of his most impactful slogans and persuasive phrases deployed during his keynotes serving as great examples of the principle.

2007 – iPhone launch

Primes audience by repeatedly saying how he was about to unveil a trio of revolutionary products – a new iPod, a phone and an Internet communications device, before finally revealing a revolutionary single device able to handle all three tasks.

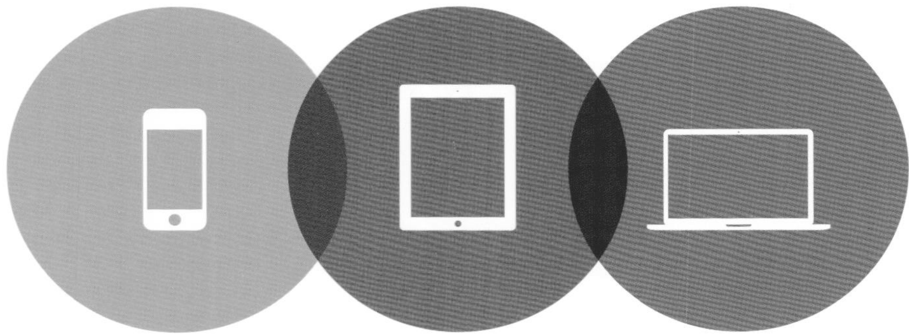

2010 – iPad launch

Using a slide, Jobs emphasised how the new device should be perceived as a 'third device' between a smartphone and a laptop.

2011 – iPad 2 launch

Highlighting the key improvements over its predecessor, Jobs introduces the iPad 2 as being 'thinner, lighter and faster' than the original. The use of the three adjectives is used verbatim in almost all blog and newspaper coverage of the launch.

# Five iconic keynote moments

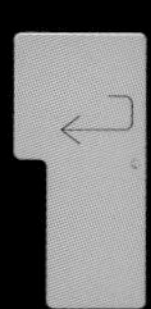

### The return of the founder, WWDC, 1997

After being fired by the Apple board in 1985, Jobs's return from exile was a huge moment for the company. Introduced by Vice President of Developer Relations David Krathwohl, Jobs received a sustained standing ovation as he took to the stage, before setting out his vision for the future in a Q&A with developers.

### The new power of Wi-Fi, MacWorld, New York, 1999

Signalling the start of the wireless era, few Apple demos have managed to capture the imagination of the attending audience in the same way as when Jobs showed off the new Wi-Fi feature on the iBook laptop. Like a magic show, Jobs used a hula hoop to show that the laptop was untethered, yet still able to browse a website.

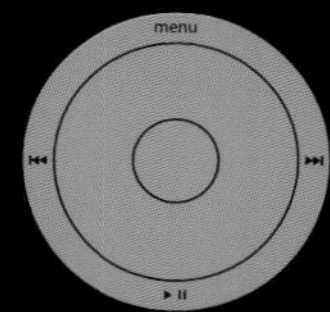


### iPod unveiled, Apple Town Hall, Cupertino, October 2001

When Jobs initially began detailing the features of its new product line, the audience appeared to be somewhat muted. However, once he pulled the device out of his pocket and showed the world its size and iconic white design, the crowd erupted as the penny dropped that this new device could revolutionise the music industry.

### The iPhone tease, Macworld, San Francisco, 2007

When Jobs announced the first iPhone, he initially made it sound like he was priming the audience for three new devices: 'An iPod... a phone... and an internet communicator.' He then showcased the iPhone, which he pitched as all three gadgets rolled up into one device before prank-calling a local Starbucks on stage and ordering 4,000 lattes for the crowd.

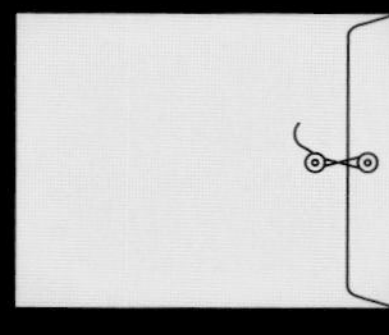

### The perfect prop, Macworld, San Francisco, 2008

Arguably the high point of Apple's industrial design during the second Jobs era, his reveal of the Macbook Air perfectly illustrated its key feature. Holding a humdrum A4 manila envelope, Jobs proceeded to pull from inside what he declared the 'world's thinnest laptop', ushering in a new age of high-powered, yet low-weight laptops.

Chapter Twelve

# Why one home run is much better than two doubles

12

3.4
4.0
FQ1
FQ2

## After an encouraging early flurry following its launch, sales of the Macintosh soon started to tail off. Jobs had forecast that Apple would sell two million Macs by 1985, but only 250,000 were shifted.

Jobs would primarily blame the computer's $2,500 price tag as its Achilles' heel, but its problems went much deeper. While the machine's advanced graphical capabilities wowed, its meagre memory would get eaten up by its visual demands, making it a woefully slow computer when carrying out general tasks. Meanwhile, Jobs's purely aesthetic choice to omit a fan meant the Macintosh would regularly overheat and fail, earning the computer the unwanted nickname of 'the beige toaster'.

The company's marketing arm also appeared to be dropping the baton. Another costly attempt at a blockbuster Super Bowl commercial backfired in 1985. With its depiction of corporate PC users as 'lemmings', following one another off a cliff, the bleak TV spot came across as both arrogant and tone deaf to the emerging dominant computer buyer. Apple's stock was tanking. Having reached a peak of $63.50 a share around the time of the Lisa launch, it then slipped so far that the value of Jobs's personal holding dropped from $450 million to $200 million. 'It's hardly the most insightful or valuable thing that's happened to me in the past ten years,' he would joke when quizzed on the heavy loss.

There was further disappointment for Jobs at the start of 1985 with news that his old friend and 'likemind' Steve Wozniak had decided to leave the company to concentrate on his new startup, CL 9, which would create the world's first universal remote control. Woz had returned to the fold at Apple two years earlier after completing his degree at Berkeley, and had rejoined the Apple II team. But the company founder had become unsettled by how big the company had become and disenfranchised by the way it was placing all its attention and resources on its new machines, therefore ignoring the Apple II, the computer that was still providing the company with the bulk of its revenue. He would remain on the payroll on a modest retainer, working as a consultant and brand ambassador.

48 billion

Estimated average number of iPhone sessions per day

85 million

Number of iPhone users in the US

$0.36

Estimated amount an iPhone will cost you in energy per year

395

Average number of iPhones sold every minute

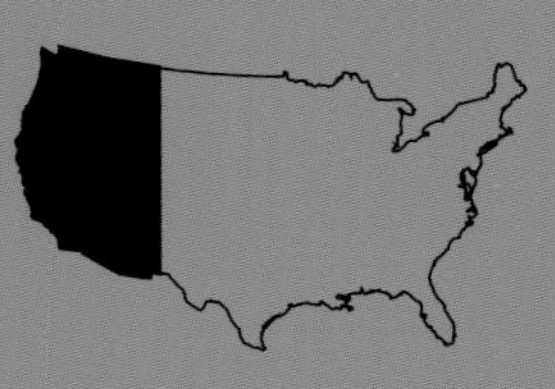

79%

Apple's share of global smartphone profits in 2016

94%

Percentage of smartphone industry profits that go to Apple

Within the walls of Apple's HQ, tension was beginning to mount. The company published the first quarterly loss in its history and was preparing to release a fifth of its staff. With both sides blaming the other for the failing Macintosh, the fighting between Sculley and Jobs became so intense that the board felt compelled to step in, urging the president to take the reins of the company rather than share them with his younger dissenter.

Sculley would eventually act upon the board's advice in March 1985, almost two years after arriving at the company. He took Jobs aside in his office and told him that he was taking him off the Macintosh team. His new planned role would see him represent the company externally as Apple's chairman without influencing the core business.

Talking in 2012, Sculley gave his recollections of the incident:

> 'When the Macintosh Office [Apple's ambitious hardware and software solution for businesses which included networked Macintosh computers, file server, and a laser printer] was introduced in 1985 and failed Steve went into a very deep funk. He was depressed, and he and I had a major disagreement where he wanted to cut the price of the Macintosh and I wanted to focus on the Apple II because we were a public company.
>
> 'We had to have the profits of the Apple II and we couldn't afford to cut the price of the Macintosh because we needed the profits from the Apple II to show our earnings – not just to cover the Mac's problems.'

Unable to accept the demotion, Jobs was determined not to go down without a fight. In May of that year, with Sculley travelling to Beijing to sign an agreement to allow Apple to sell its computers in China, Jobs seized the opportunity to try and take back control of the company.

Desperate and somewhat naive, he confided in some senior members of his own team, detailing his plans. Among those he tried to charm was Jean-Louis Gassée, Apple's Director of European Operations, but revealing his plan for a coup to him proved to be a huge mistake. Gassée's loyalties lay with Sculley, and he was only over in Cupertino because the president was lining him up to take over Jobs's role. 'I made my choice,' Gassée recalled years later. 'At that point I'd rather work with Sculley than work with Steve, who was absolutely out of control.' Gassée warned Sculley of the plan, telling him, 'If you go to China, you're dead.'

The following morning, Jobs was shocked to find Sculley present at the weekly executive staff meeting. Sculley then proceeded to confront Steve over his disloyalty in front of the whole board, asking if the rumours of his plotting were true. Jobs said they were, and Sculley once again asked the board to choose between the two of them – him or Jobs. One by one, around the table, everyone explained they would back Sculley – the support Steve had been expecting just wasn't there.

The following Friday, Jobs received a final humiliation when he was handed a further demotion after being reduced to the role of a non-executive chairman and given an office in another building away from Sculley.

Less than eighteen months after the launch of the Macintosh brought Jobs international acclaim, he was being edged out of the company he'd founded. Jobs was left devastated by his ousting – Apple had been just about the only focus of his adult life – and his subsequent behaviour left some of his closest friends fearing he may have even been contemplating suicide. 'I hired the wrong guy, and he destroyed everything I'd spent ten years working for,' he would bitterly reflect in a 1995 interview.

One of his final acts for Apple was to suggest to the board that they consider buying the Graphics Group from *Star Wars* director George Lucas's company Lucasfilm. Made up of cutting-edge computer graphics technicians, Jobs had been blown away by a demo of the group's groundbreaking work on 3D animation during a visit to the company's California base. 'These guys were way ahead of us on graphics, way ahead,' Jobs would explain. 'They were way, way ahead of anybody. I just knew in my bones that this was going to be very important.' With Steve's influence among staff at rock bottom, his advice fell on deaf ears, Apple passed up the opportunity to buy the company which would eventually become Pixar.

Jobs would spend the rest of the summer travelling across Europe and Russia as an Apple ambassador, where he was still thought of as a 'revolutionary business figure'. On his trips back and forth he tried to forge an idea of what he would do next. He contemplated running for office, despite never voting, and even applied to fly on the Space Shuttle as a civilian. His trips abroad as Apple's emissary would see him meet with heads of state, university presidents, artists and, crucially, scientists.

Towards the end of the summer he met Nobel Prize-winning biochemist Paul Berg, who confided that current computers were

# Roots of the iPhone

In December 1999, rumours began to mount that Apple was planning to enter the cellular market, after the company registered the domain iPhone.org. It would be almost seven years before the device would eventually become a reality.

### September 2002

During an interview with the *International Herald Tribune*, Jobs fails to rule out that the company is working on a cellular device.

### October 2002

The UK, Singapore and Australia become the latest regions where Apple has filed a trademark for 'iPhone ™'.

### September 2005

Motorola releases the ROKR – its iTunes-enabled phone – amid much anticipation. A storage limit of just 100 songs, coupled with its inability to download songs wirelessly sees it come under criticism from tech press and gains lukewarm reaction from consumers.

### October 2005

In a *Fortune* magazine interview, Jobs says the ROKR will not be Apple's last foray into cell phone business.

### November 2006

Apple is granted a patent for the iPhone.

### December 2006

A complication for Apple, as Cisco – who have owned the iPhone name since 2000, launch a VOIP device using the title.

**January 2007**
Steve Jobs officially unveils the iPhone during his Macworld keynote speech.

**February 2007**
Apple and Cisco settle trademark dispute – opting to share the name.

**May 2007**
Inaccurate rumours of a delay to the iPhone published online cause Apple stock to drop by almost $4 billion.

**June 2007**
The iPhone is released as planned in the US on 29 June 2007.

**November 2007**
The iPhone becomes available in the UK via O2.

**December 2007**
The iPhone is lauded as the invention of the year by *Time* magazine.

falling short in speeding up scientific research, with both Macs and PCs underpowered for the kind of computational modelling he and his peers were looking to carry out. The conversation was hugely inspiring for Jobs, leading him to concoct a vision of a new, radically high-end computer 'workstation' that would primarily be targeted at universities and the broader education market that could fulfil the sort of demanding tasks that Berg had spoken about.

It began to occur to Jobs that he still loved what he did, he had the nucleus for another great product, and he could pursue his vision and his passion now without the interference of a board and CEO he felt had held him back. So, he decided to start a new company.

Jobs would fund his new venture by raising $135 million from the divestment of his Apple stock over the preceding months, selling 1,499,099 shares of his stock – only keeping one single share to ensure he would continue to get his annual report.

Apple were initially supportive of Jobs's plans to start a new company, even offering investment. All that changed when it emerged he was set to take five members of Apple staff with him, including key engineers, resulting in an incensed Sculley threatening to sue Jobs and his new company because of its use of his company's staff and intellectual property. Apple would go on to agree to settle on the basis that Jobs agreed not to release any competing products before 1985. His new company would also need to show all of its products before they were announced to the press, allowing Apple to file suits before the products got to consumers.

Following Jobs's departure, Apple would experience something of a turnaround, with the Macintosh eventually finding its feet in the market. This was in no small part thanks to the popularity of its laser printer peripheral which had been released just before Steve's exit. The combination of the printer and the Mac's unique handling of fonts made it a compelling choice for anyone looking to create professional-looking documents and presentations. Under Sculley's stewardship, Apple's sales grew to $8 billion by 1993; however the company's fortunes would change markedly as the decade progressed, as Microsoft's and Windows' dominance of the market became near total.

Alongside his new computing venture, Jobs also paid Lucasfilm $5 million for the computer graphics company that Apple had rejected. Steve would invest a further $5 million into the business and would change its name from the Graphics Group to Pixar.

As well as providing early CGI effects and animation for the movie industry, the company had been developing its own computer software and hardware. Its flagship product was the Pixar Image Computer, a $30,000 commercial image-processing machine targeted at the medical and graphics industry. Jobs had originally envisioned producing a cheaper version of the highly advanced computer for the mass market. Disney was a major purchaser of the machine but there were not enough high-volume sales to sustain the division. The poor uptake forced Jobs to eventually sell off the hardware side of the business to Vicom Systems for $2 million in 1990, allowing Pixar to concentrate on becoming primarily a graphics production company.

By early 1986, things began to move at pace for Jobs's new computer company, which was tentatively titled Next. Untethered by the cautious arm of a CEO like Sculley, Jobs was free to indulge his passion for exceptional design, bestowing his new venture with a visual identity by the renowned graphic designer Paul Rand for a then unheard of fee of $100,000.

Rand, who had previously designed logos for UPS, ABC and IBM, among others, delivered a cube-shaped design to reflect the planned shape for Jobs's new machines, coupled with colourful type, including a lowercase 'e', which he told Jobs could mean 'education, excellence, expertise, exceptional, excitement, $e = mc^2$.' Jobs was delighted with the design, and particularly enthused by the concept of using a lower case letter. From this point on the company would be known as NeXT, with the unconventional use of capitalisation informing the naming conventions of Jobs's projects throughout the rest of his life.

$31,600,000,000. The value of 11% stake
in Apple at the time of Jobs's death.

# How cashing in cost Jobs a fortune

Jobs famously sold 1,499,999 shares of his stock in Apple after being ousted from the company. He only kept one share so he could continue to get his annual report. Had he held onto them, the holding would have placed him within the top five richest people in the world at the time of his death.

$130,000,000. The then value of the 11 per cent stake in Apple which Jobs sold in 1984.

Chapter Thirteen

# Stay hungry

# 13

NeXT

By early 1986, Jobs's small but talented NeXT team had set up camp in offices in Redwood City, California, and had begun the process of creating Steve's dream machine.

As was ever the case with Jobs, his design sensibilities at times took precedence over more practical concerns, in this case insisting on a cube design for the computer, despite the shape creating issues in housing the machine's motherboard. He wanted a machine with enough power to run fully-fledged laboratory simulations yet still cheap enough for college students to use in their dormitory rooms. Engineers and programmers were charged with a delivery date of summer 1987 and a target shelf price of $3,000 – much like Jobs's past projects at Apple, both of these goals would prove to be overly ambitious.

One of the key innovations of the final product would be the inclusion of built-in Ethernet capabilities, with Jobs correctly predicting that networked computing would eventually change the world. Showing impressive foresight, he would declare at the time that 'the most exciting thing of the early nineties is going to be to link these islands of personal computers together into interpersonal computing'.

Underpinning the hardware would be NeXTSTEP, the computer's elegant operating system. Much like the Macintosh, it used an intuitive graphic user interface controlled with a mouse, but it took the concept much further. It boasted full multitasking which allowed several programs to be run at once, while its software technology made it much easier to create sophisticated, feature-rich programs.

After seeing the November 1986 PBS documentary *The Entrepreneurs*, which featured Steve Jobs and NeXT as a new startup, Texas billionaire Ross Perot immediately invested $20 million for a 16% share in the company, with further funding coming from Stanford and Carnegie Mellon universities.

While NeXT was starting to take shape, things were less positive on the family front for Jobs. His adoptive mother, Clara, had been diagnosed with lung cancer, and Steve spent every spare moment he could at her bedside.

# The NeXT Computer

Launched at a gala event in 1988, the NeXT Computer, Jobs's first product since leaving Apple, combined powerful hardware and software in ways that had never been achieved before.

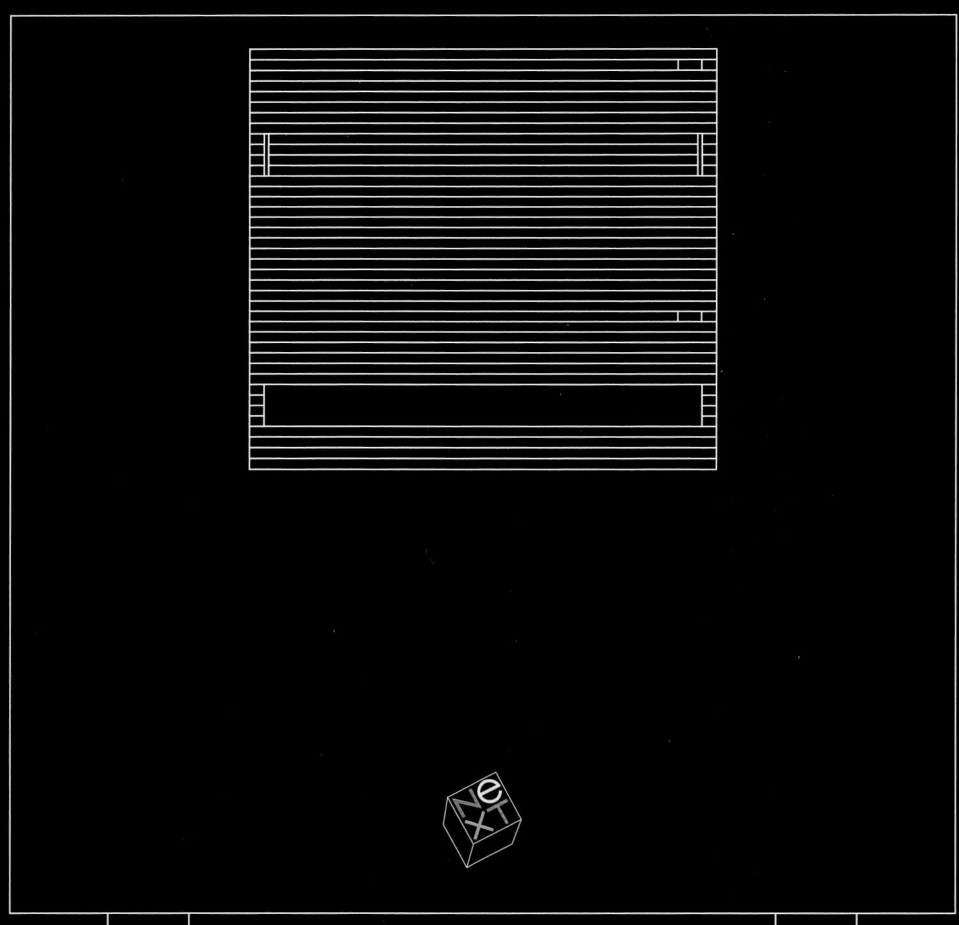

### $6,500 introductory price

Additional cassette tape interface allowed the user to save program data – a precursor to a floppy disk drive.

### No floppy or hard drives

The original NeXt Computer used a 256MB Canon magneto-optical drive for primary data storage along with a removable data cartridge.

### NeXTSTEP

Groundbreaking, Unix-based operating system, featuring proprietary GUI using a Display PostScript-based back end

### 17-inch monochrome monitor

Greyscale display with 1120 x 832 resolution, later versions would offer colour screens

### 8MB of onboard RAM

Expandable to 64MB

### Built-in DSP chip

Delivering CD-quality, stereo sound

### CP

Motorola 68030 running at 25 MHz

Jobs had always wanted to know more about his birth parents and had enlisted a private detective to trace his birth mother, Joanne Schieble. Shortly before Clara's death, Jobs was contacted by the detectives to let him know they had indeed found her. Not wishing to upset his father further, Steve waited until after Clara's death to ask him for his blessing in contacting Joanne, which he duly gave.

And so, after thirty-one years separated, mother and son met face to face for an unsurprisingly emotional reunion. During the meeting at her house in Los Angeles, Joanne would apologise repeatedly for her decision to give him up, saying she had always missed him. Jobs would discover that his father was Abdulfattah 'John' Jandali, a Syrian who had become a political science professor, and that Abdulfattah and Joanne did in fact get married after he was adopted. The marriage didn't last long, but before they parted, the couple had another child, a girl they named Mona. After the split, Joanne had remarried.

Mona, who had also been unaware of her sibling, was a writer. She was currently working at the literary journal *Paris Review* and writing the hit novel called *Anywhere But Here*, based on her experiences with an absentee father. Steve and Mona agreed to meet in New York where she lived. The pair hit it off immediately, discovering they shared similar tastes and character traits – both enjoyed long walks and design, while Mona was also intense in her attitude to work, and very strong-willed.

While Jobs had never really been close to his adoptive sister Patty, his relationship with Mona quickly blossomed into one of the most important in his life.

Having tracked him down in Sacramento, Mona arranged to meet their biological father and asked Steve if he would join her. Explaining his decision to decline his sister's invite, Jobs later said: 'When I was looking for my biological mother, obviously, you know, I was looking for my biological father at the same time, and I learned a little bit about him and I didn't like what I learned. I asked her to not tell him that we ever met... not tell him anything about me.'

Mona managed to keep to her word not to mention Steve, even when Jandali told her that he and Joanne had given her older brother up for adoption. 'We'll never see that baby again,' he told her. The meeting went well, but as she was leaving, Jandali, who at this point was managing a coffee shop, said something amazing: 'I wish you could have seen me when I was running a bigger restaurant...', before explaining that he used to run a popular Mediterranean eatery in Silicon Valley. 'Everybody used to come there. Even Steve Jobs used to eat there. Yeah, he was a great tipper.'

Amazed by the revelation, Jobs began to recall the encounter. 'He was Syrian. Balding. We shook hands.' Jobs didn't want to meet his father, but it appeared he already had. Despite this unbeknown encounter, Jobs would never reach out to his biological dad, with Jandali only discovering from news stories that Steve was his son. He blamed Syrian pride on stopping him from getting in contact with Jobs, although following his son's death, he admitted he had sent him short email birthday wishes over the years.

1987 came and went and with it the NeXT Computer's proposed release. This was partly due to the new features that were added during development and partly due to Steve's perfectionist attitude, which saw him spend months deliberating over the computer's patented monitor stand, his fastidiousness even extending to having the NeXT factory completely repainted when he didn't like the shade of grey used.

The high-end desktop computer would eventually get its unveiling at Davies Symphony Hall in San Francisco in October 1988. The venue had been booked because of its good acoustics, to show off the computer's then groundbreaking full stereo sound.

Meticulously planned, Jobs's presentation, which saw him talk in almost nothing but hyperbole, was another early showcase for his unique marketing style. Unlike many other CEOs, Jobs wrote his presentations himself, toiling over every slide and demo. The preparation showed, and the debut was a success, with the machine's multimedia abilities showcased to stunning effect.

'To many of us gathered in the hall,' William J. Hawkins wrote in a *Popular Science* story on the launch, 'Steve Jobs' revolutionary new computer represents American entrepreneurship at its best – he's an incurable romantic nobody wants to see fail.' *Byte* magazine meanwhile listed the NeXT Computer among the 'Excellence' winners of its annual awards, stating that it showed 'what can be done when a personal computer is designed as a system, and not a collection of hardware elements'. *Newsweek* used the cover line 'Mr. Chips' and showed Jobs leaning on the sleek black NeXT, which it proclaimed to be 'the most exciting machine in years'.

While the keynote wowed, it also delivered news of a $6,500 price tag, an eye-watering figure that was far higher than the sub $3,000 price his academic advisors had pushed for and which Jobs had promised. The outlay for many wouldn't end there, with a hefty $2,000 price being given to the

# The NeXT legacy

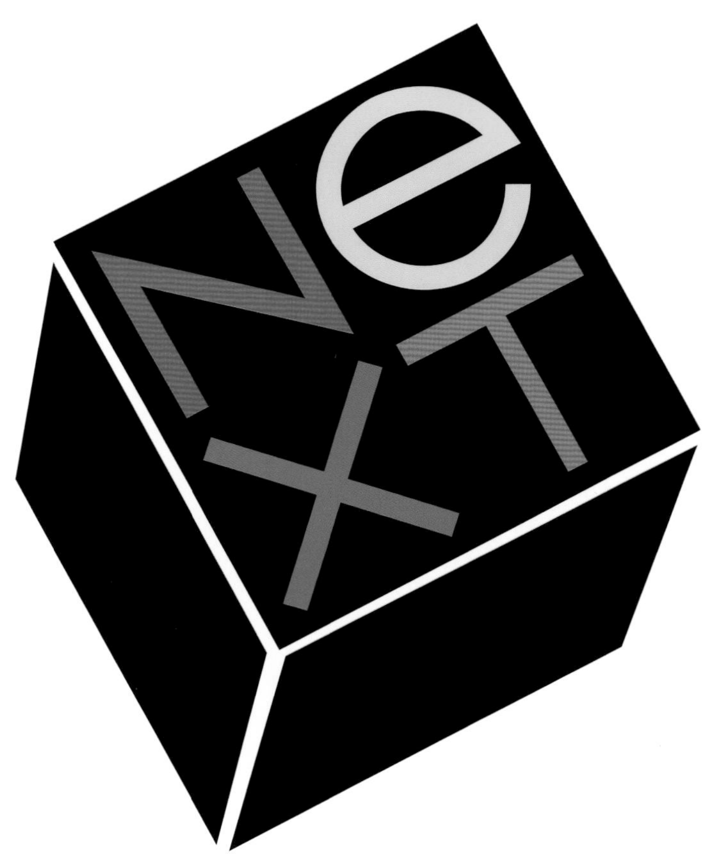

## The dock

One of the breakthrough UI features of NeXTSTEP was its dock – a bar of icons situated on the left hand side of the screen, providing easy access to regularly used apps. While positioned on the bottom of the screen by default rather than on the side, the version of the dock that features in MacOS has the same functionality and is an integral piece of UI Apple's current operating system.

## The Pinwheel / Beachball of Death

One of computing's most unwelcome icons and animations, the spinning sphere warning that a Mac is performing a task and cannot accept any further input, started life, albeit in monochrome form, on NeXTSTEP.

## Grab

Like MacOS, NeXTSTEP had Grab – an application used to take screenshots. The original camera flash animated icon for the utility was still in use as recently as 2007's OS X 10.5 (Leopard).

## Chess

Save for the recent addition of online play via Apple's Game Center, the version of Chess that was built-in to NeXTSTEP is incredibly similar to the version that's bundled in with MacOS.

## System sounds

Basso, Frog, Funk, Ping, Pop and Tink – the large majority of alert sounds that have become a familiar part of working on a Mac since the turn of the century were ported over from NeXTSTEP.

optional printer. Meanwhile, the computer's much-heralded optical disk for storage was frustratingly slow in use, meaning the additional purchase of a $2,500 external hard drive was almost essential.

NeXT Computer's state-of-the-art robot-led factory had been readied to roll off 10,000 units a month, but when the machine finally went on sale in the summer of 1989, the plant was mainly idle, with sales trickling in at a hugely underwhelming 400 a month. The venture was beginning to lose money at a worryingly rapid rate.

While Jobs's business affairs were causing concern, his private life was about to take a turn for the better.

Since leaving Chrisann Brennan, Jobs had had a series of girlfriends, including the folk singer Joan Baez and the Pulitzer Prize-winning novelist Jennifer Egan. His first real long-term relationship would take place with Tina Redse, a graphic designer. The pair shared a turbulent two-year relationship. She would prove a catalyst in Jobs improving his relationship with his daughter Lisa, pushing him to visit his child more frequently. Jobs would eventually propose, but Redse was ultimately unable to put up with how cold and uncaring Jobs could be at times and how hurtful he could be to her and others, forcing her to decline and eventually leave. 'I would have sucked at it on many levels. In our personal interactions, I couldn't abide his unkindness. I didn't want to hurt him, yet I didn't want to stand by and watch him hurt other people either. It was painful and exhausting.'

In October 1989, Jobs agreed to give a lecture at Stanford Business School. While waiting to be called on stage, he began chatting with Laurene Powell, who, unable to find a seat in the packed auditorium, had unwittingly taken a reserved spot next to him.

Jobs raced through the lecture, hoping to spend more time with the pretty, young graduate student. After his talk, he cut short a chat with the school's dean upon noticing that Laurene was leaving. They chatted for a few minutes more before Jobs headed to his car to travel on to a NeXT meeting, before changing his mind.

'I was in the parking lot with the key in the car, and I thought to myself, "If this is my last night on earth, would I rather spend it at a business meeting or with this woman?" I ran across the parking lot [and] asked her if she'd have dinner with me.'

Jobs would gush to his colleagues at NeXT over the following days about Powell. Vegetarian, smart and beautiful, Powell had worked at Goldman Sachs before she entered Stanford, where she presciently told her roommate that she wanted to marry 'a Silicon Valley millionaire like Steve Jobs'.

The two would start seeing each other regularly, creating an unintended spectacle at both NeXT and Stanford. When Powell stayed overnight at Jobs's Jackling House mansion, she would drive to classes in his BMW with 'NEXT' vanity plates, while Jobs would be regularly spotted having lunch at the campus café. After completing her course at Stanford, Powell moved in with Jobs. On the morning of New Year's Day 1990, Jobs welcomed in the decade by proposing to Laurene.

In line with Jobs's antimaterialistic outlook, their wedding would not be an extravagant affair to appease the press, with the pair arranging to be wed in a modest ceremony at Yosemite National Park by Jobs's old Zen master, Kobun Chino.

Six months after the man who had regularly been referred to in the business press as the world's most eligible bachelor relinquished his title, Jobs settled into a new guise as a family man. Laurene gave birth to Jobs's first son in September 1991, and following months of Jobs's characteristic deliberating he was named Reed Paul Jobs after Steve's alma mater and his father. Jobs abandoned the Jackling House and relocated his family to a large home in old Palo Alto, with Chrisann allowing Lisa to move in with them.

His new settled personal life would prove a welcome refuge from the dire state of both of his business concerns. With sales of only 500 systems per month, NeXT released new updated versions of its systems and options, including a faster CPU, 16-bit colour graphics instead of greyscale, and internal hard drives.

The improvements made for a much more compelling machine, but sales were nevertheless slow, forcing a decision to be made. In February of 1993, with around just 50,000 systems sold and the company burning through hundreds of millions of dollars from investors, including vast sums from Japanese multinational Canon, the company abandoned the production of computers. In order to save money it would now focus on porting the NeXTSTEP operating system to Intel's 486 computer chip, allowing it to run on the now-dominant Microsoft Windows-based computers.

While NeXT sold relatively few machines, their influence was nevertheless wide reaching. Tim Berners-Lee famously used a NeXTCube workstation to lay down the foundation of the first web server and web browser software. Using the same computer, John Carmack wrote *Wolfenstein 3D* and *Doom* – two video games commonly regarded as being among the most influential of all time.

Chapter Fourteen

# Life's change agent

14

DISNEY · PIXAR
TOY STORY

Shortly before Jobs purchased Pixar in 1986, the company gained some clout in the movie industry. A short called *Luxo Jr,* by young animator John Lasseter, became the first CGI film to be nominated for an Oscar.

Lasseter had been drafted in by Pixar founders Ed Catmull and Alvy Ray Smith to add animation expertise to the company after working for Disney on a number of never-released computer graphic-led animation projects.

Essentially a demo to show off the capabilities of the Pixar Image Computer, the company's graphic designing machine, *Luxo Jr* focused on the attempts of an anamorphic desk lamp to play with its parent. Full of character and genuine humour, while it would miss out on the award for Best Short Animated Film, the short would go on to inspire a new logo design for the struggling company and serve as its mascot.

Despite *Luxo Jr*'s success, by 1991 the company was in financial dire straits, having lost over $8 million over the course of the previous year. With the company's hardware arm now sold off, Jobs had been hoping Pixar's RenderMan 3D animation software, which had been recently used in James Cameron's sci-fi epics *The Abyss* and *Terminator 2*, could be adapted into a consumer offering, empowering untrained people to create animations on their home computers. The Pixar team would, however, struggle to create a program intuitive enough for amateurs to use, with the fate of the project later sealed when it was decided that there just wasn't enough demand for such a tool from ordinary consumers. Like the hardware arm before it, the call was made to shutter the consumer part of Pixar's software division, leaving just the professional software arm and its creative animation division as ongoing concerns.

In a bid to turn profit, Pixar began producing commercials for brands such as Life Savers Candy and Listerine, but these small commissions would do little to prop up the failing company.

Until this point NeXT had been Jobs's key focus when it came to his two precarious companies. But as Pixar's financial situation worsened, he became more hands-on. Intent on stopping the company failing, Jobs invested

# The Pixar years

**1979** The Graphics Group, a part of the computer division of Lucasfilm, is formed. The group primarily works on computer hardware.

**1982** Team begins working on film sequences with Lucasfilm's Industrial Light and Magic special effects division.

**1986** Jobs pays George Lucas $5 million for The Graphics Group's technology rights and invests a further $5 million as capital into the company. Pixar is established as as an independent company.

The company releases groundbreaking computer animated short film, *Luxo Jr.*, directed by founder John Lasseter.

**1988** Pixar's *Tin Toy* becomes the first computer-animated film to receive an Academy Award (Best Animated Short).

**1989** Pixar releases its first version of Renderman - a computer graphics animation program that has since gone on to become an industry standard

**1991** Pixar agrees £26 million deal with Disney to produce three computer-animated feature films.

**1994** Jobs examines selling Pixar, with Microsoft a potential suitor.

**1995** *Toy Story*, the first feature-length animated film, is released to critical and commercial success. Pixar holds initial public offering, with stock priced at $22 per share.

**1997** Pixar enters into new agreement with Disney to produce a further five films together over ten years.

**2000** Pixar builds new dedicated studio in Emeryville, California.

**2004** Jobs and Disney chief executive Michael Eisner fail to negotiate a new partnership.

**2006** New Disney CEO Bob Iger reaches agreement to buy Pixar in an all stock deal. As part of the agreement Jobs becomes The Walt Disney Company's largest single shareholder with approximately 7% of the company's stock.

# Box Office vs Budget

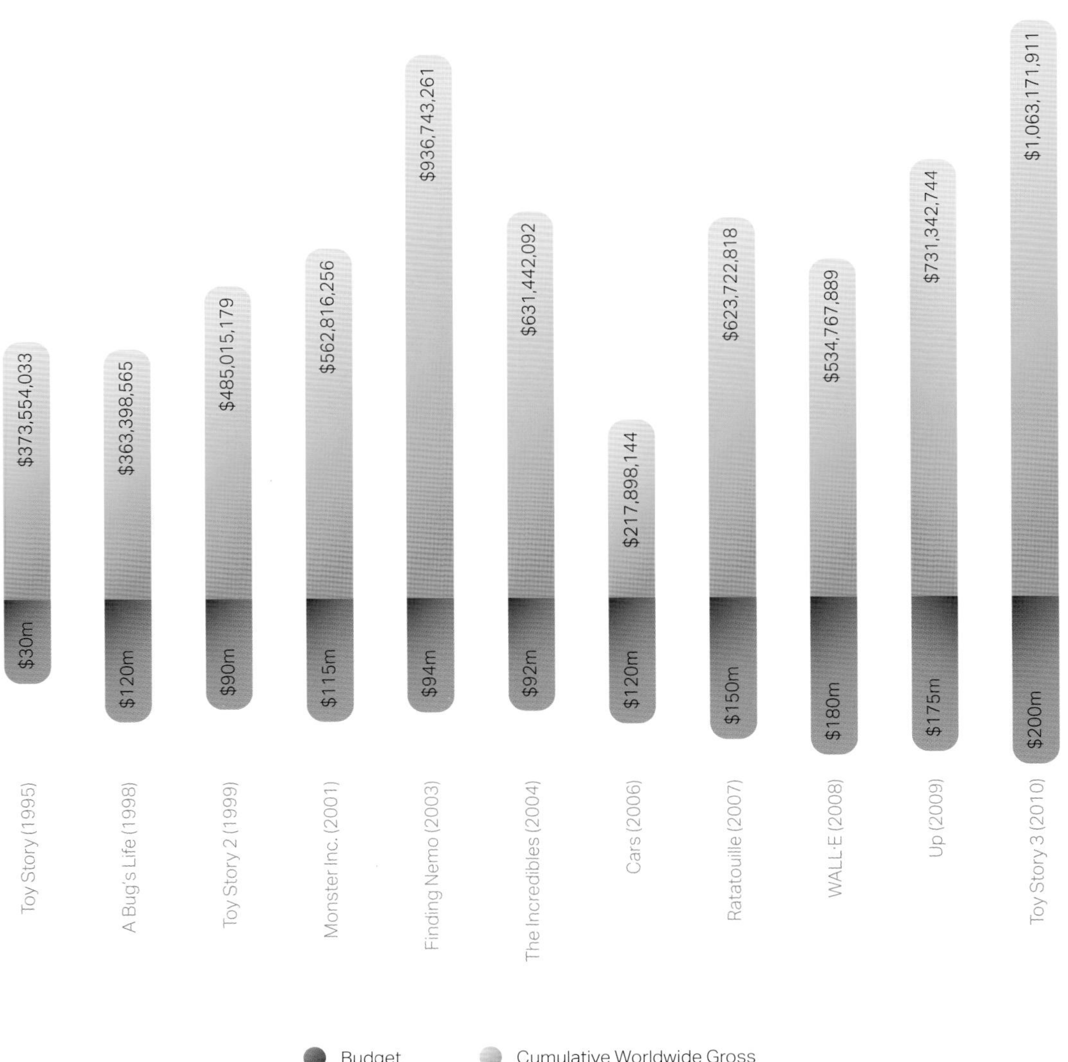

more money in exchange for an increased stake, reducing the proportion of management and employee ownership until eventually his total investment of $50 million gave him control of the entire company.

With a third of its staff having been laid off and the cash drain so severe, Jobs began to contemplate selling the remaining parts of the business. But a lifeline then presented itself.

Enamoured with Lasseter's work on *Luxo Jr's* follow-up, *Tin Toy* – an even more advanced five-minute short that had won Best Animated Short Film at the 1988 Academy Awards – a resurgent Disney expressed an interest in funding a full-length Pixar movie.

Steve Jobs flew to Anaheim to join Smith and Catmull during negotiations with Jeffrey Katzenberg, Head of Disney Studios, to finalise a deal centred on Lasseter's idea for a film about toys that yearned for kids to play with them.

Like Jobs, Katzenberg was used to getting his own way. The pair had already had a heated argument during a sales call months before, when Jobs tried to sell Disney a lab of NeXT Computers, leading Smith and Catmull to become concerned that Steve's abrasive negotiating could scupper Pixar's last chance as a company.

While Jobs did push back on some of Katzenberg's demands (he refused to hand over rights to all Pixar's 3D computing technology), he nevertheless managed to get a deal over the line. Under the agreement Pixar would not get ownership of the films or their characters nor a cut of the video revenues. Disney would fund the production of Lasseter's film and have the option to fund two more movies as well. Pixar would get 12.5% of the box office and a chance at survival.

Work on *Toy Story* was ponderous and at times fraught. Alvy Ray Smith quit Pixar following a disagreement with Jobs over the use of a whiteboard. It was an unwritten rule that no one other than Jobs was allowed to use it, a rule Smith decided to break in front of everyone after Jobs went 'total street bully' on him, resulting in the pair screaming into each other's face 'in full bull rage'.

Yet Disney executives were blown away by an initial thirty-second trailer for the film. Despite his inexperience as a writer, Lasseter's outline script centring around a toy cowboy, Woody, and his conflict with a new space action figure was green lit. Impressed with the trailer, Tom Hanks and Tim Allen signed on to the project for little more than union voice fees.

Production ran into trouble on 19 November 1993, however, on what would become known within Pixar as Black Friday, after a rough version of the

# US smartphone market share

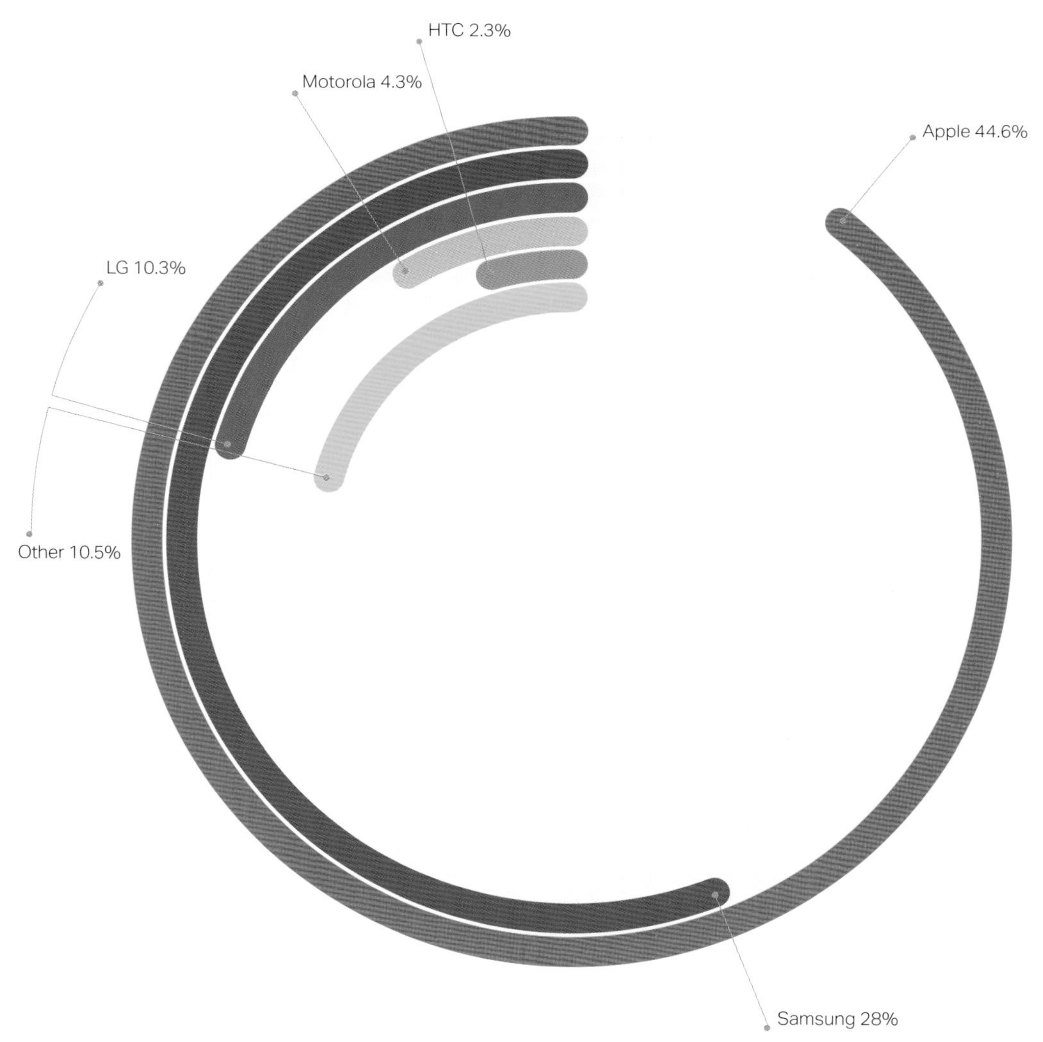

# Breaking down Steve's estate

7% stake in Disney
$7,400,000,000

Estimated value at the time of his death: $7.4 billion. Jobs acquired 138 million shares when Disney bought Pixar Animation Studios in 2006, becoming the company's largest shareholder.

0.5% stake in Apple
$2,100,000,000

Estimated value at the time of his death: $2.1 billion (5.5 million shares).

Venus superyacht
$130,000,000

260ft-long vessel designed by Steve Jobs with Philippe Starck, completed shortly after his death. Estimated value at the time of his death: $130 million.

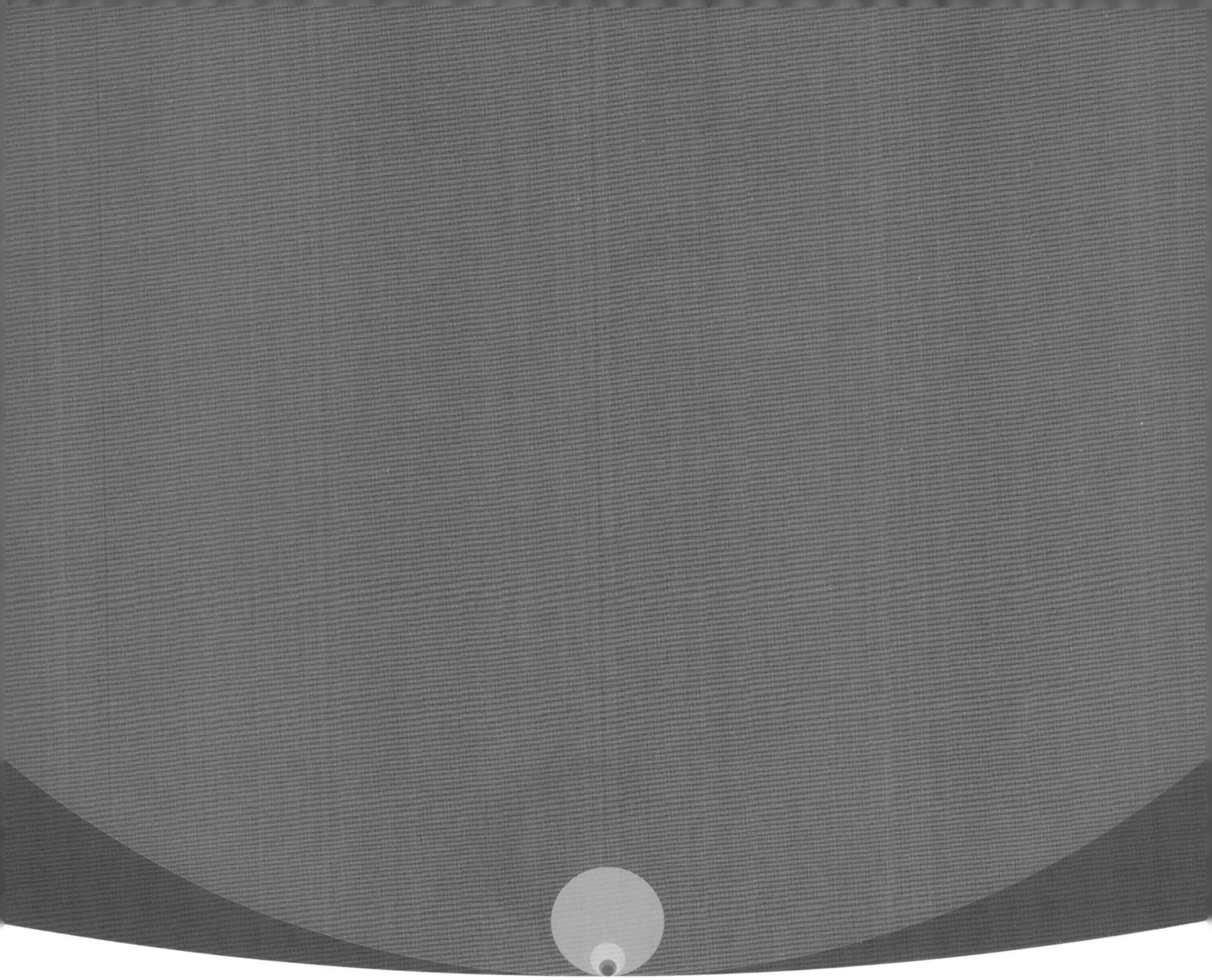

Gulfstream V Jet
$40,000,000

Offered to him by the Apple board when he officially became the company's CEO. Estimated value at the time of his death: $40 million.

Palo Alto Home
$8,000,000

Estimated value at the time of his death: $8 million.

Jackling House
$2,000,000

Purchased in 1984, redevelopment plans were only completed after his death following local objections. Value circa 1984: $2 million.

film caused panic among Disney executives. Selfish, sarcastic and outright mean, the film's main character, Woody, was distinctly unlikeable. Ordering a rewrite from Lasseter, Katzenberg halted production on the film with the entire deal left in doubt.

The blow came at a particularly difficult time for Jobs. Once feted as the golden boy of technology, his reputation as a businessman was being openly called into question by the media. A stinging profile piece in the *The Wall Street Journal* in mid-1993 read: 'His NeXT workstation seems destined to become a high-tech museum relic. He himself is fighting to show he still matters in the computer industry.' A further quote in the same article given by the respected industry analyst Richard Shaffer was even more damning: 'People have stopped paying attention to him ... It's sad.'

To compound matters, his adoptive father had recently passed away at the age of seventy. Paul Jobs had been immensely proud of his son and his accomplishments, and had been a supportive presence at his launches and keynotes up until the end.

While Lasseter and his team battled to whip *Toy Story* into shape, Jobs began privately inviting offers for Pixar, with Microsoft cofounder Paul Allen and Oracle CEO Larry Ellison both sounded out. As a sale beckoned, confidence in *Toy Story* began to return. Lasseter's reworked script added scenes to the film before Buzz Lightyear arrived, showing Woody as a more endearing leader of the toys. Delighted with the changes, Disney gave the go-ahead for production to restart, with Katzenberg handing the film a coveted Thanksgiving release date.

Buoyed by Disney's faith in the film and the growing buzz surrounding the movie, Jobs decided to hang on. Upping his commitment, he decided that Pixar shares would be put on sale to the public shortly after the movie's opening, and hired a chief financial officer to sell the idea to Wall Street. In light of the company's modest revenue and continual losses, it was a bold move, but one that would prove a business masterstroke. Amid the growing excitement with Pixar and *Toy Story*, Jobs became a father once again, with Laurene giving birth to a baby girl named Erin Siena.

On a storming opening weekend, *Toy Story* earned $39.1 million, enough to easily recoup its production costs. An eventual worldwide box office haul of $373 million saw it rank third behind *Aladdin* and *The Lion King* in terms of the most successful animated movie blockbusters up until that point.

# Apple the media master

By 2010 the iTunes Store had delivered on Steve Jobs's vision of positioning Apple as a leading media distribution company, with Apple now a major player in publishing, TV and movies as well as music.

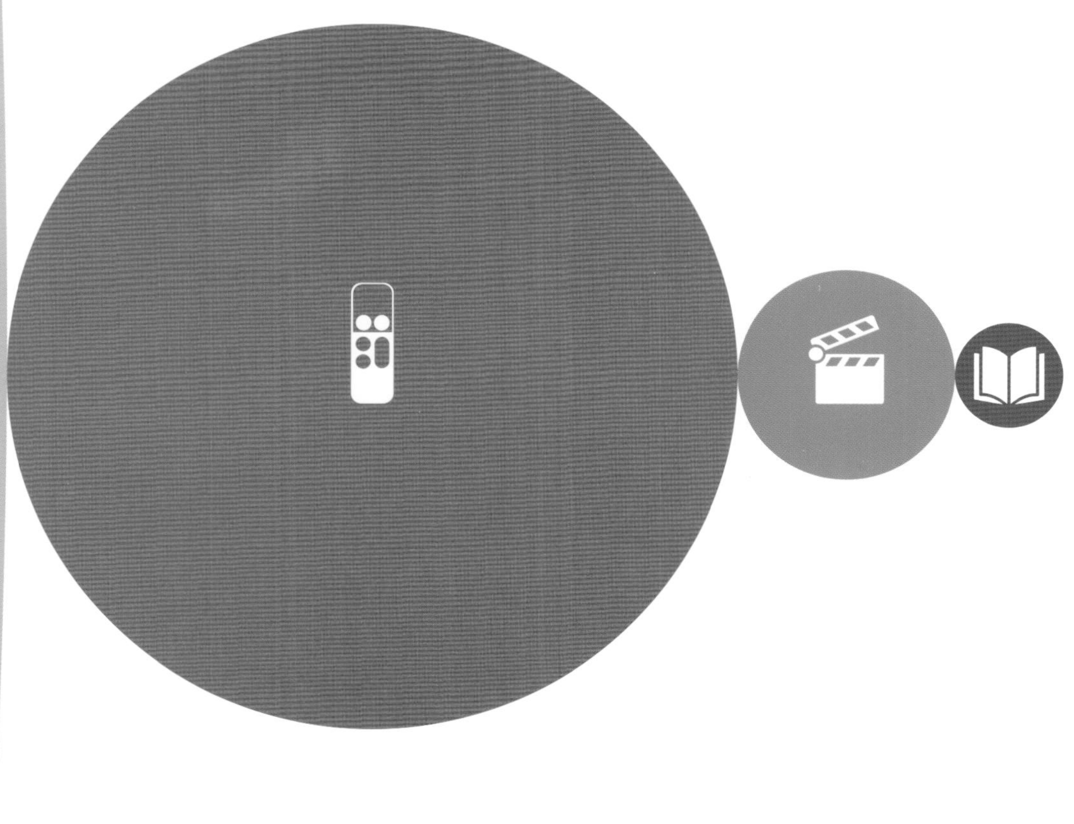

11.7 billion songs | 450 million TV episodes | 100 million movies | 35 million books

Just ten days after *Toy Story's* release, Pixar floated 6.9 million shares on the stock market. Priced at $22 per share, PIXR, as it would appear on the NASDAQ, would hit a high of $49.50 on the day of the IPO, closing at $39.

The sale had made Jobs, who owned upward of 80% of the company, a billionaire for the first time. As the stock hit the market, he called his friend Larry Ellison, founder of Oracle, and already a member of the billionaire club. All Jobs said was, 'Larry, I made it.'

Jobs had always hated the Disney deal. The wild success of *Toy Story* now meant Pixar was no longer dependent on the company to finance its movies. Taking full advantage of the leverage handed to him, Jobs audaciously arranged a meeting with Disney's CEO, Michael Eisner, where he demanded half of future profits from Pixar's next few films along with equal branding. With Disney's paranoia at its height surrounding the recent founding of rival studio DreamWorks by its former executive Jeffrey Katzenberg, music mogul David Geffen and Hollywood director Steven Spielberg – an obvious new home if Jobs and Pixar walked – Eisner eventually agreed. A new five-movie deal was agreed, with Jobs's demands met, although Disney retained the rights to the characters.

The Pixar experience had revealed a new business maturity in Jobs. For the first time he hadn't acted as a hands-on micromanager. He had made a success of the company by expertly negotiating deals for the studio, yet had taken a passive creative role, sitting back and letting a group of incredibly gifted people achieve their potential.

Steve's art of persuasion was being keenly missed at Apple. The intervening years following Jobs's departure had seen a dispiriting decline in fortunes.

Sculley's reign during the post-Jobs era had initially been a success with the introduction of the System 7 operating system, which brought colour to the Mac for the first time. Having launched an early attempt at a laptop with the huge and heavy yet powerful Macintosh Portable in 1989, Apple would go on to make a real dent in the nascent laptop market with the introduction of the PowerBook, a lighter and cheaper machine that broke new ground by placing the device's trackball in front of the keyboard.

Amid those successes, Apple began to lose its way. The Newton MessagePad, an ahead-of-its-time yet deeply flawed Personal Digital Assistant (PDA), proved a massive flop, the notoriously unreliable autocorrect function of its handwriting recognition feature becoming a tech industry punchline. Indeed Apple's software engineers were so haunted by a gag in *The Simpsons* poking fun at the feature, that years later the team working on the iPhone's keyboard were given extra development time to ensure the mistakes of the past would not be repeated.

Sculley's biggest miscalculation, however, would be a gamble on a new kind of processor called PowerPC for its desktop machines. Migrating Apple's existing designs over to the new standard came at a huge cost, ensuring Mac prices stayed high while the price of rival Intel x86-based processors became cheaper as PCs grew ever more popular. After an earnings miss that was chiefly blamed on the PowerPC transition, Sculley was fired by the board of directors.

Sculley was superseded by long-time Apple employee Michael Spindler, who had joined the company in 1980. As a way of expanding its meagre market share, Spindler broke with company tradition by introducing licensing of the Mac's operating system to other computer manufacturers, allowing them to make their own Apple-compatible machines. Spindler's hope was that the licensees that came on board, which included Motorola, Power Computing and UMAX, would make lower-end machines. The plan backfired massively, however, with the licensee's targeting high-end users, offering faster yet cheaper machines than Apple. The 'clones', as they became known, would go on to cannibalise sales of Apple's premium machines. Spindler would only last three years at the helm before being ousted by the board following the collapse of buyout talks with Sun Microsystems, Philips and IBM.

Spindler was replaced by board member Gil Amelio in 1996. With the company operating at a loss and Microsoft's Windows 95 now flying off the shelves, the former CEO of National Semiconductor set about averting Apple's apparent death spiral with a dramatic cost-cutting drive, reducing Apple's workforce by a third.

Amelio also cancelled the company's meandering in-house attempt at developing its next desktop operating system, codenamed Copland. Apple's Chief Technology Officer Ellen Hancock, who had been placed in charge of getting development back on track, made the call to try to find a suitable third-party system instead to replace it.

Amelio initially started negotiations to buy BeOS from Be Inc., a company headed by Jean-Louis Gassée, the man who had replaced Jobs at Apple. Negotiations stalled when Gassée overplayed his hand by demanding $275 million, with Apple unwilling to offer more than $200 million. Gassée had believed that Be Inc. was the only game in town. However, there was another player waiting in the wings, led by a man with an even deeper history with Apple.

Chapter Fifteen

# The lightness of being a beginner again

# 15

Steve Jobs had never given up on the idea of a homecoming. Indeed, the groundwork for his eventual return to Apple was laid over a year earlier.

Jobs remained vocal on how he could turn around the company's fortunes, telling *Fortune* magazine in a September 1995 interview: 'You know, I've got a plan that could rescue Apple. I can't say any more than that it's the perfect product and the perfect strategy for Apple. But nobody there will listen to me.'

With a deal for BeOS with Gassée dead in the water, the options open to Apple's new Chief Technical Officer Ellen Hancock in finding a provider for its next operating system were limited. But following an opportunist call from a NeXT sales rep suggesting Apple should consider their platform, Hancock began to view NeXTSTEP as a serious alternative. It was, after all, a finished product, and since NeXT had ceased making its own hardware, it was no longer a proprietary operating system and was easily adapted to other platforms, including the PowerPC. NeXTSTEP also had the key feature of its object-oriented programming environment, which made it simpler for developers to reuse snippets of code in different programs, and therefore far quicker to create software.

Jumping at the opportunity, on 2 December 1996, Jobs returned to Apple's Cupertino campus for the first time in over a decade, meeting with the now CEO Gil Amelio and Hancock to demo NeXTSTEP. Over the course of several sessions, Jobs delivered a masterclass of charm and spellbinding sales skills pinpointing how NeXT's software could make the company's computers nimbler for the approaching internet age and revitalise Apple as a whole. Amelio was sold by Jobs's vision.

Just seven days later, NeXT engineers began workshops with their Apple counterparts on how a Mac OS–NeXTSTEP transition would work and how to preserve Mac OS compatibility.

Having been open to the sale of NeXT in its entirety for some time, Jobs agreed a friendly buyout from Apple for $429 million. At the time the

You know, I've got a plan that could rescue Apple. I can't say any more than that it's the perfect product and the perfect strategy for Apple.

figure seemed a huge price to pay for the failing NeXT, but the acquisition brought more than software to Apple – it brought back Jobs, albeit in an advisory capacity.

While Amelio and Hancock appeared to bring much-needed competence and stability to Apple, it was hoped the returning presence of its founder would bring some greatly sought-after charisma and a valuable public relations boost. As part of the deal, Jobs received $130 million in cash and 1.5 million shares of Apple stock, worth at that time about $22.5 million.

As the news emerged, many industry commentators wondered if by bringing back the company's talismanic founder and giving him a toehold, Amelio had effectively signed his own death note as Apple's CEO. Such assessments inevitably proved prescient.

The writing was on the wall as early as Jobs's official reintroduction during Amelio's keynote address at the Macworld Expo on 7 January 1997. What should have been a triumphant presentation by Amelio was an unqualified mess. Opting to wing it instead of using a script, Amelio's allotted hour-long keynote descended into a rambling, three-hour marathon, covering the company's devastating $120 million loss in the previous quarter followed by an incoherent outlining of his plans for the company's future.

A welcome break from the monotony came around the two-hour mark, with Jobs's appearance from exile drawing a wild reaction from the 2,000-strong crowd of consumers and developers. Rehearsed, direct and engaging, Jobs slickly outlined how Apple would merge elements of Copland with NeXTSTEP to produce a new operating system named Rhapsody.

Jobs understood the importance of luring developers to the new operating system in order for it to succeed, so he spoke directly to them throughout, using the word developer twenty-five times. Moreover, during his concise thirteen-minute segment, Jobs clearly stated a new vision for the company: 'What we want to try to do is provide relevant, compelling solutions that customers can only get from Apple.' At a time when Apple appeared to be fighting to stay relevant, such words felt like a battle cry.

Amelio ended the keynote with a fumbled unveiling of Apple's new Twentieth Anniversary Macintosh – a premium all-in-one computer and the first major project headed up by the company's up-and-coming British industrial designer Jony Ive. The grand finale didn't go as Amelio had hoped. Calling Apple's other founder Steve Wozniak to the stage and announcing he too would be returning to Apple in an advisory capacity, Jobs walked off, preventing the opportunity of Amelio's planned photo op. Following the keynote, Jobs was at pains to point out that he was only a part-time consultant for Apple and said of his new role, 'I'll advise Gil as much as I can, until I think they don't want my help or I decide they're not listening.'

Frustrated with Amelio's lack of urgency in tackling the company's mounting problems, Jobs sold the 1.5 million shares he'd acquired following the NeXT sale. 'I pretty much had given up hope that the Apple board was going to do anything. I didn't think the stock was going up,' he would later explain.

By the beginning of July 1997, Jobs had convinced Apple's increasingly concerned board to oust Amelio and give him control. And so it played out, with Amelio handing in his letter of resignation following heavy pressure from the directors. As Steve Wozniak later put it: 'Steve Jobs meets Gil Amelio. Game over.'

Minutes after Amelio addressed staff in a conference room, informing them of his departure, Jobs walked in. Wearing shorts and sneakers, he posed a question to those gathered: 'What's wrong with this place?'

After a few muted responses, Jobs shouted: 'It's the products! So what's wrong with the products?' Following some more timid replies, Jobs yelled: 'The products suck! There's no sex in them anymore!' Apple's products neither evoked passion among staff, nor were they desirable for consumers.

Fred Anderson, the Chief Financial Officer Amelio had hired at the beginning of his reign at Apple, was initially given day-to-day control of the company, with Jobs heading up a committee to find a new CEO. After interviewing a number of candidates, Steve was eventually given the title Interim CEO (iCEO – a nod to future Apple product lines), beating off competition from Oracle founder Larry Ellison. Taking an infamous, symbolic annual salary of $1, Steve, now aged forty-two, was back and at the helm of Apple. Arguably the single greatest third-act comeback in business history was about to play out.

Having moved into a very small office next to the boardroom with a NeXTstation computer installed (Jobs refused to use a Mac as his personal machine for a number of years until Mac OS X was eventually released as a public beta in 2000), Steve quickly set about reorganising the company. He continued the cost-cutting drive that had been started by Amelio, auditing every project at Apple. As well as lacking direction, Jobs knew Apple was

# The iMac G3

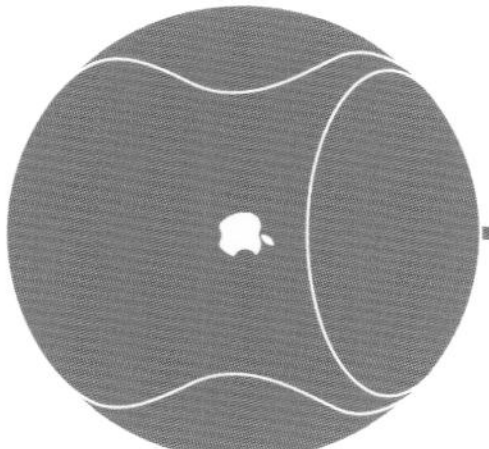

## Unveiling
6 May 1998 at the Flint Center Theater Cupertino, California – the same venue where Jobs had unveiled the original Macintosh back in 1984.

## No floppy drive
Arguing that the format was redundant in the age of the internet and USB storage, the iMac did away with having a $3^1/_2$-inch floppy disk drive. A standard feature on PCs of the time – it was a decision some tech commentators had suggested would cause the iMac to flop. It didn't.

## PowerPC 750 G3 processor
Running at 233 MHz – later revisions would run at 266 MHz and 333 MHz.

## Memory
32 MB, expandable to 512 MB of PC100 SDRAM.

## Display
Built-in 15-inch shadow-mask CRT screen (up to 1024 x 768 pixel resolution).

## Casing
The iMac's unique Bondi Blue translucent housing forced Jony Ive and his team to consider the new computer's exposed components.

## Speakers
2x built-in Harman Kardon speakers for SRS stereo sound.

## Dual headphone jacks
Feature aimed at education-market hopes: allowing a teacher and a student – or two students – to both listen to multimedia audio.

## Infrared port
Port used the IrDA protocol, which could transfer data at up to 4Mbps.

## USB connectivity
The iMac boasted dual USB ports – the first computer to exclusively offer the ports as standard.

## Internal modem
After its unveiling, Apple was forced by consumer pressure to adopt the faster new standard 56 kbit/s speed for its internal modem rather than the 33.6 kbit/s capable component it had originally announced at the machine's unveiling.

## Mouse
While the machine was a huge success, the round, 'hockey puck' design of the supplied Apple USB mouse was derided by consumers and tech critics alike for being uncomfortable, particularly for users with larger hands.

## CD-Rom Drive
Tray-loading drive. Later revisions of the iMac included a slot-loading DVD Rom drive.

## Price
$1299

Here's to the crazy ones.

The misfits. The rebels. The troublemakers.

The round pegs in the square holes.

The ones who see things differently.

They're not fond of rules.

And they have no respect for the status quo.

You can quote them, disagree with them,
glorify or vilify them.

About the only thing you can't do
is ignore them.

Because they change things.

They push the human race forward.

And while some may see them as the crazy ones,
we see genius.

Because the people who are crazy enough to think
they can change the world, are the ones who do.

The spoken monologue from the Think Different advert

Amelia Earhart

Pablo Picasso

Mahatma Gandhi

Miles Davis

Albert Einstein

Yoko Ono and John Lennon

James Watson

Cesar Chavez

Jane Goodall

working on too many products. Project leaders were summoned one by one and asked to justify the existence of the products they were developing. By the end of the process Jobs had reduced the number of active R&D projects from 350 to fewer than 15.

Amid the wiping of the slate, Jobs came up with a lean and coherent new strategy for Apple's business – a back to basics approach focusing on just four great products instead of dozens of mediocre ones. The plan was defined by a basic four-square grid to represent the future of the Mac: two 'for consumer' desktops and portables, and two 'for pro' desktops and portables. Anything that didn't fit in the grid would either be axed or not developed further.

During the company review it emerged that over $1 billion had been spent on the development of the Apple Newton over the course of ten years – had the ill-fated product line been cancelled one year after being initiated, Apple would have had enough money to remain healthily profitable throughout the 1990s.

The wide-scale culling would also see the end of countless ancillary items that were making little if any profit, including Apple's line of printers and digital cameras. He would also kill off the Mac clone market that had cannibalised sales of Apple's own machines by ceasing to license its operating system to third-party computer makers. Elsewhere, the Pippin, Apple's brief and ultimately ill-advised tiptoe into the video gaming console market, was also put out of its misery.

The sometimes brutal cuts would see over 3,000 employees laid off during Jobs's first year as iCEO, but the painful measures at last allowed Apple to focus on creating a range of products that would set them apart significantly from the competition. The new era would also see new talent brought into the fold, including key development staff from NeXT, while a crucial new hire during Jobs's first year would be a new senior vice president for worldwide operations brought in from Compaq Computers. Tim Cook would develop into a vital partner for Jobs in the day-to-day running of Apple. Intense and disciplined, the tall, bookish Alabaman would soon develop a reputation as one of the toughest executives at Apple after being briefed to make Apple's supply chain leaner and more agile, with limited overstock of inventory.

Another decisive, and ultimately pivotal early call made by Jobs came when he moved to set aside the company's long-standing rivalry with Microsoft and enter into a partnership.

# The App Store explosion

By 2010 the App Store had become established as a critical revenue stream for the company.

July 2008

The App Store opens with 500 available apps

July 2009

50,000 apps available

July 2011

425,000 apps available

In August 1997, Jobs took the stage at the Macworld Expo in Boston to announce that Apple had taken a $150 million investment in non-voting shares from its long-time adversary. As part of the deal, Microsoft would continue to develop Office products for the Mac – something that had been in doubt – while Apple would make Microsoft's Internet Explorer the default browser on its computers.

After revealing the tie-up, Jobs introduced Bill Gates via video link-up, with the Microsoft chief appearing on an oversized video screen in scenes unintentionally reminiscent of Apple's '1984' Big Brother advert. The appearance of Gates drew boos and hisses from the audience of Apple faithful. Placating the crowd, Jobs stressed the need for Apple to take a pragmatic approach in order to survive: 'We have to let go of this notion that for Apple to win, Microsoft has to lose,' Jobs said. 'We have to embrace a notion that for Apple to win, Apple has to do a really good job. And if others are going to help us, that's great because we need all the help we can get. And if we screw it and we don't do a good job, it's not somebody's else's fault. It's our fault.'

Around this time Apple dropped a lawsuit related to Microsoft's use of patented code from Apple's Quicktime video software. The dispute had further soured the relationship between the two companies following an earlier legal battle over Microsoft's alleged plagiarism of the look and feel of Mac OS for Windows – a long-running claim which was ultimately rejected by the courts.

Jobs would also become hands on with the company's marketing operations. He fired John Sculley's ad agency, BBDO, and rehired Chiat\Day – the firm that had created the famous '1984' Super Bowl advert. Inspired by the way Nike celebrated athletics and athletes without ever mentioning its shoes, Jobs refused to delegate the project and instead personally laid out a brief for a campaign that reaffirmed Apple's old core values: creativity and the power of the individual.

Presenting the agency's initial ideas for the brief, Lee Clow, now the creative director for Chiat\Day, offered up a new slogan and aesthetic. Featuring the tagline 'Think Different' – a veiled reference to IBM's famous THINK tagline – the treatment featured montages of artists and creative professionals using the Mac. Jobs became enamoured with the underlying concept, but rather than use footage of DreamWorks filmmakers at work, he hit upon the idea of using celebrities and thinkers instead.

Enthused by an idea which fulfilled his aim of celebrating creativity, Jobs handed Clow's team a demanding seventeen-day deadline after approval to complete the vast campaign, which would include a television commercial, a series of international print adverts as well as billboards for major markets such as Los Angeles and New York.

The final TV spot would feature more than a dozen iconic twentieth-century figures including artist Pablo Picasso, aviator Amelia Earhart, inventor Thomas Edison, singers Bob Dylan and John Lennon, and the Reverend Martin Luther King, Jr. The archive footage was soundtracked with a monologue read by *Jaws* actor and avowed Apple fan, Richard Dreyfuss. As well as providing a new manifesto for the company, its sentiments could also adequately sum up the key characteristics of the company's iCEO.

The TV spot debuted on 29 September 1997 and immediately proved hugely popular. With its equally strong complementing print adverts, the campaign would become one of the most successful of the era, running for five years, with the advert winning numerous awards including the first Emmy for a commercial. Its success marked a major turning point for the company.

Jobs himself recorded a version of the 'Here's to the crazy ones' ad narration, but didn't allow it to air, fearing that people would consider it arrogant. The alternative version resurfaced online some years later following Jobs's death.

While the campaign reaffirmed Apple's counterculture credentials in the public's consciousness, notable by their absence in the first run of adverts were any actual Apple products. This had been partly down to Clow and the rest of the creative team being concerned with appearing to exploit the artists whose images they had used, but there was also the small matter that Apple simply didn't have any new products to showcase.

That next piece of the Apple comeback puzzle would be addressed with a radical research project that had survived Jobs's aggressive R&D cuts. Originally titled the Mac NC (for Networked Computer), the design team working on the project would be headed up by Jony Ive.

Chapter Sixteen

# Something's transmitted

16

Prior to Jobs's return Jony Ive had been thinking about quitting, until a company-wide presentation by the returning leader convinced him to stay.

Now thirty years of age, Jony Ive had been at Apple for a few years by this point, having already worked on the Newton MessagePad and the Twentieth Anniversary Macintosh, and prior to Jobs's return had been thinking about quitting, until a company-wide presentation by the returning leader convinced him to stay. For his part, Jobs had been looking to outside star designers ahead of Ive to take on the role of Apple's head of design, but thanks to sharing key elements of their design philosophies, the pair would hit it off.

Entrusted with the iMac project, the new computer would prove to be the purest expression of Ive's creativity yet. The project would also mark the beginnings of one of Jobs's closest professional and personal relationships, with Steve later referring to Ive as his 'spiritual partner'.

Working in total secrecy – a Jobs directive that would become an almost cult-like feature of Apple's workplace culture – Ive's small team was briefed with developing a simple to set up consumer desktop computer that could be sold with a sub-$1,500 price tag. In many ways a throwback to the creation of the original Mac, Jobs wanted a finished product that was radically different from the rest of the market – a machine that would fully encapsulate the company's new 'Think Different' mantra – a machine that would eventually be named 'iMac'.

Ive's team's final designs for the machine's all-in-one, teardrop-shaped housing and its distinctive translucent Bondi blue coloured case, radically redefined the notion of what a desktop computer could look like, signalling a divergence for Apple from the beige boxes that had come to define the accepted look of a PC.

Its internal features were no less radical. Jobs and Jon Rubinstein, Apple's new Senior Vice President of Hardware Engineering who had joined the company as part of the NeXT buyout, decided the new computer would not include a $3^1/_2$-inch floppy disk drive – a standard feature on machines of the time. Many believed Apple had made a huge error and was insane for leaving a floppy disk drive off the iMac. Justifying the move, Jobs quoted the hockey star Wayne Gretzky's famous line: 'Skate where the puck's going, not where it's been.' Within a couple of years most PC manufacturers would be following suit. From CD and DVD drives to VGA display ports, under Jobs Apple would develop a reputation as always being the first computer firm to drop a legacy technology, sometimes even before the rest of the industry would be ready. The iMac would also introduce Universal Serial Bus (USB) connectivity to the masses, with the iMac boasting two of the ports on its rear. The self-contained unit required minimal setup and even had a handle that made it easy to pull out of the box.

While considering the computer's name, as would be his preference, Jobs purposely worked in a small, tight-knit group. Throughout his career, Steve was an avowed sceptic on the benefits of focus groups, preferring to limit the amount of opinions on the table. Under his stewardship Apple rarely carried out any market research or testing.

Ken Segall, Apple's former Creative Director, once recounted Jobs saying to the group working on the machine, 'We already have a name we like a lot, but I want you guys to see if you can beat it. The name is MacMan. After comparing the name to both the classic arcade game *PacMan* and Sony's Walkman, Segall suggested the name that finally stuck: iMac. 'It referenced the Mac, and the "i" meant internet,' according to Segall. 'But it also meant individual, imaginative and all the other things it came to stand for.'

With development of the machine going to the wire, preparations for its launch event were almost derailed when Jobs discovered that the final machine would feature a tray-loading CD-ROM drive, rather than a slot-loading drive akin to those seen on high-end cars of the time that he had personally requested. Furious with the late design change, Jobs threatened to delay the computer before compromise was made with the manufacturing team that the more elegant drive type would feature on future versions.

So successful was Jobs and the team at keeping tight-lipped on the project that when the iMac was eventually unveiled on 6 May 1998 during a press event at the Flint Center Theater, most Apple employees had never even heard of the new computer.

Coming across as much as a pep talk for a recovering company as a product launch, Jobs repeatedly emphasised that Apple was back on track. As ever, he had fastidiously prepared for his presentation, helping to create the slideshow and approving every word in his speech. The iMac's unveiling drew gasps and cheers, as Jobs declared: 'It looks like it's from another planet, a good planet – a planet with better designers.'

While critics bemoaned the lack of a floppy drive and its cutesy and ultimately uncomfortable hockey puck mouse, it was hard to deny Apple had delivered on its promise of creating an insanely great new computer.

Following strong preorders, the machine's first six weeks of availability in North America, Japan and Europe saw Apple sell a then-unprecedented total of 278,000 iMacs, making it the fastest-selling Macintosh model ever.

Announcing its annual financial results on 14 October 1998, Jobs revealed a $106 million profit on revenues of $1.56 billion for the company's fiscal fourth quarter, marking the company's fourth straight profitable quarter and Apple's first profitable year since Spindler had almost crashed the company in 1995.

No one had ever questioned Jobs's status as a tech visionary, nor his skills for negotiating, but the triumph of the iMac and the steadying of the ship of a seemingly doomed Apple, coupled with the ongoing success of Pixar, meant those who had doubted Jobs's aptitude for management and leadership in the past now needed to reassess.

While the good times were now very much rolling, juggling both business concerns for Jobs was nevertheless beginning to prove difficult. Now very much hands-on at Apple, while often regularly making the sixty-mile round trip to keep on top of matters at Pixar, Jobs's increased workload appeared to be beginning to have a major impact on his personal life and his health. 'It was rough, really rough, the worst time in my life,' he would tell biographer Walter Isaacson.

'I had a young family. I had Pixar. I would go to work at 7 a.m. and I'd get back at 9 at night, and the kids would be in bed. And I couldn't speak. I literally couldn't, I was so exhausted.'

Amid this hectic lifestyle, Steve began to develop extremely painful kidney stones. Given these are often caused by a diet high in animal protein, and with Jobs a vegan, many would later speculate that the issue could have been an early sign of the disease that would cruelly later claim his life.

# Rich list

## How Steve Jobs's wealth stacked up to his tech peers in the rich list

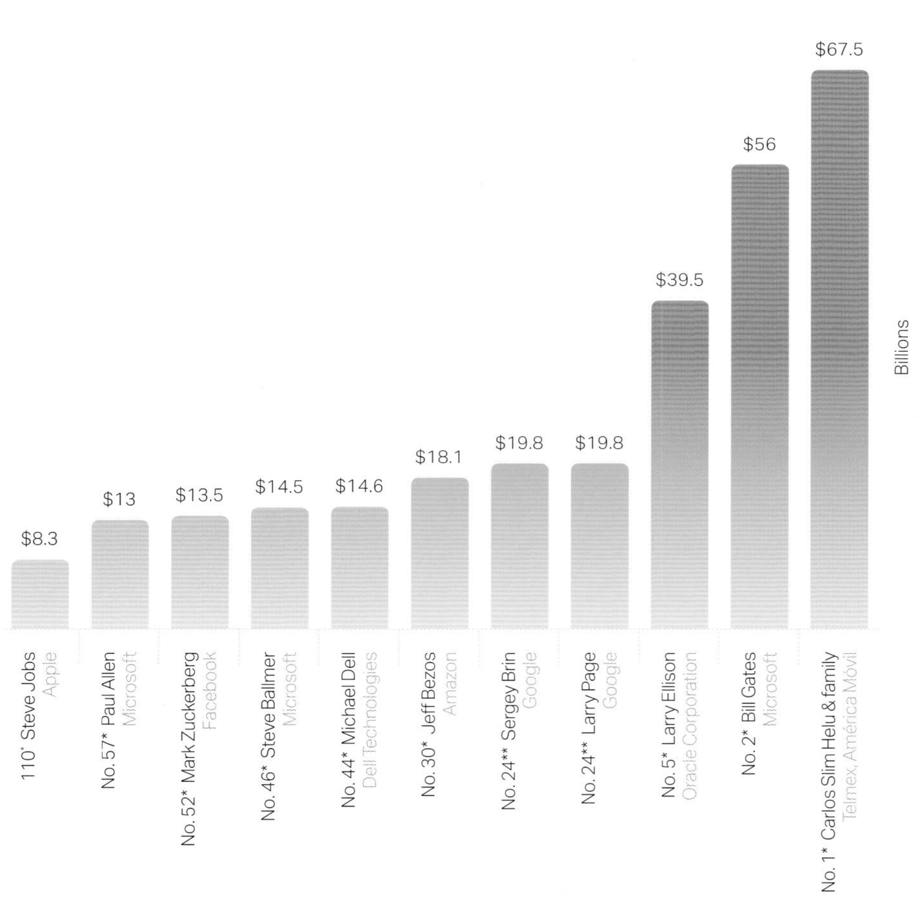


* Position on the Forbes Rich List 2011

** Joint Position

# Jobs's net worth

Forbes Rich List
2007 - 2011

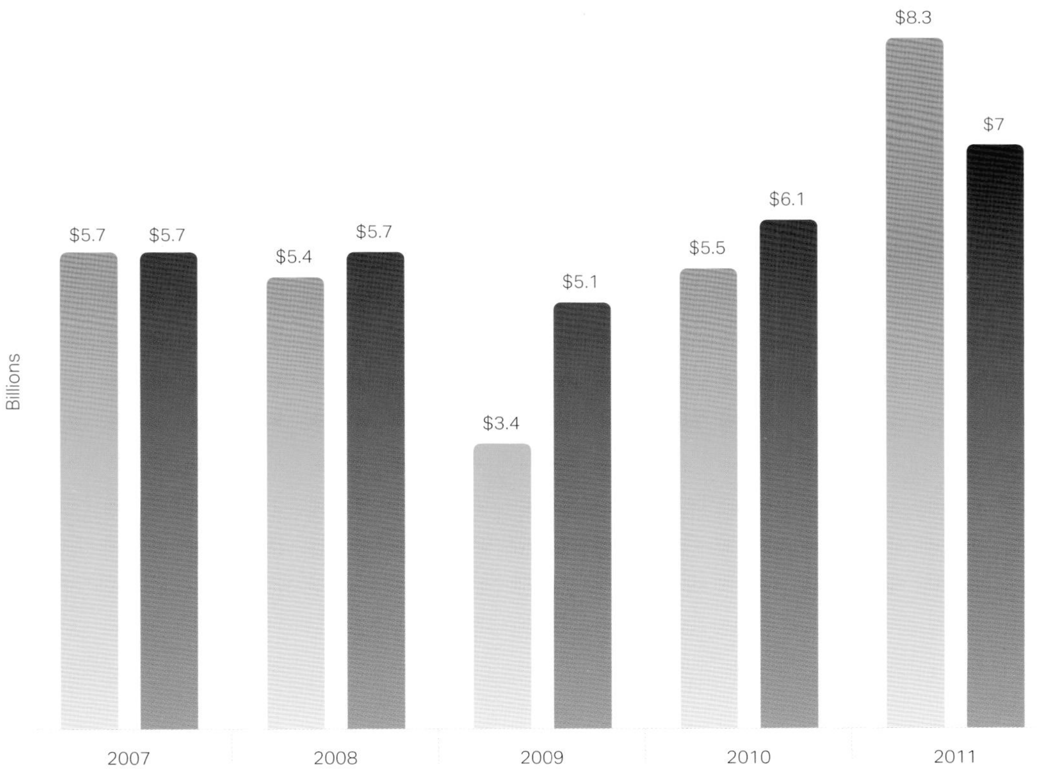


March October

The next few years would nevertheless continue to be a buzz of constant activity for Steve, Pixar and Apple, and in May of 1998, Laurene gave birth to another daughter who they named Eve. Around this time Jobs signed off on a new updated Apple logo, its rainbow colours discarded for a sleek monochrome look that better reflected the company's adherence to sophisticated design.

Complementing the now massively successful iMac, in mid-1999 Apple rolled out a similarly multi-coloured, entry-level laptop called the iBook which boasted a new technology called Wi-Fi, allowing users to connect to the internet without a cable. Demonstrating the then seemingly magical new technology to *Newsweek* reporter Stephen Levy, Jobs couldn't hide his amazement: 'Isn't this why we got into this business in the first place?' Jobs asked.

Pixar, meanwhile, had followed *A Bug's Life* – 1998's best-selling animated movie – with *Toy Story 2*, the blockbuster of the 1999 holiday season, with the two films grossing more than $800 million in ticket sales worldwide.

At the 2000 Macworld Expo, Jobs officially dropped the 'interim' modifier from his title at Apple and became permanent CEO. It came after almost two years of constant encouragement from the board to commit himself to the role, with many left mystified by his insistence on maintaining his $1 salary without stock options (since his return the company's stock had risen phoenix-like from $14 to $102). Jobs would justify his stance by saying, 'I don't want the people I work with at Apple to think I am coming back to get rich.' With Apple stabilised and ready to push into exciting, unchartered territory, Jobs eventually relented, accepting an initial ten million shares in the company along with a Gulfstream V private jet.

The first significant mis-step under Jobs's leadership would come with the Power Mac G4 Cube, introduced on 19 July at the Macworld Expo in New York City. Another experiment in form for the humble computer by Jony Ive, the small desktop machine had a look that was perhaps too radical for consumers. Somewhat reminiscent of the NeXTcube, its internals were housed in an eight-inch (20cm) cube suspended in a beautiful clear perspex casing. Although praised for its innovative industrial design (The New York Museum of Modern Art holds a G4 Cube, along with its distinctive Harman Kardon transparent speakers, as part of its collection), unlike the recent iMac, the Cube didn't prove popular with Apple's crucial market of creative professionals who found it too expensive (after dropping $1,599, you would still need to fork out for a not included monitor), not powerful enough and hard to upgrade. By July 2001, only a third of the 800,000 units predicted had been sold, with Apple forced to put the Cube on ice.

The following year, Mac OS X was finally released. Where Mac OS 8 and 9 had kept things ticking over, OS X was a drastic reimaging of Apple's operating system, based largely on the Unix and Berkeley Software Distribution (BSD) technology that had been at the core of Jobs's NeXT Computers. Its flexibility would also allow a smooth transition for when the company would eventually move to a new CPU architecture for its next wave of Macs. Midway through the decade, the company would shift from expensive and underpowered PowerPC processors supplied by Motorola and IBM, to processors designed and manufactured by Intel, the main supplier for most of Apple's competitors which was now leading the way in terms of speed and power. It also meant that for the first time you could install Windows on a Mac, allowing users to switch between the two competing operating systems.

Adapting OS X for the new processor type was a huge project – what could have been a slow and painful transition was both smooth and delivered on time by the agile, new-look Apple, which rolled out the change by confidently introducing the first MacBook Pro alongside a new iMac, both featuring Intel processors. It was an achievement that drew admiring glances from no less than Bill Gates: 'If you'd said, "Okay, we're going to change our microprocessor chip, and we're not going to lose a beat", that sounds impossible – they basically did that.'

While Apple's competitors were openly talking about the PC revolution being over, Jobs had a far more progressive vision that would define what computing meant in the next decade. No longer simply being a tool for words and numbers, Jobs saw the computer as a 'digital hub' for the consumer's complete 'digital lifestyle', with the computer handling everything from home movies and videos to family photos, books and magazines. One particular medium would be the driving force of the strategy.

For a company so intertwined with the creation of music – its computers had been the de facto choice for recording studios running Pro Tools and Cubase audio workstation software for some time – it was behind the curve in a big way in terms of how music was consumed as the rise of the MP3 file format altered people's listening habits. The rip, mix, burn era would become a fully fledged boom with the emergence of the peer-to-peer file-sharing program Napster.

While music fans were creating playlists and burning their own CDs on PCs, Macs had barely begun to feature drives capable of writing to disks, with Apple instead focusing on DVD playback drives. 'I felt like a dope,' Jobs admitted to *Fortune*. 'I thought we had missed it. We had to work hard to catch up.'

Apple would go some way to rectifying the situation with the purchase of SoundJam MP – a Mac-compatible MP3 player introduced in mid-1998 that had been created by two former Apple developers. Reconfigured, simplified and rebranded as iTunes, Jobs unveiled the rejigged software at Macworld San Francisco in January 2001 with a concession and a promise: 'We're late to this party and we're about to do a leapfrog.'

iTunes mixed Napster's user-friendliness with features that were equally agreeable to the major record labels. While file sharing from the original program was gone, users were nevertheless able to copy compact discs into their iTunes libraries as well as easily search and organise their digital music collections.

There was a longer game at stake, of course. Jobs had far bigger plans than just a Mac-based music player. He envisioned a self-contained ecosystem with iTunes at its heart. Users could purchase high-quality downloads directly from Apple's own music service and play them on a proprietary portable player that integrated with their other products, in turn encouraging them to buy a Mac. The next step was to create that device.

While Apple would rightly gain a well-earned reputation for its innovation during Jobs's reign as CEO, it was also an effective fast follower, refining existing ideas and making a far better product by focusing on improving the customer experience. There would be no better example of that than the iPod.

Jobs loved music. He was also an early owner and had been hugely inspired by the original gadget that had set music free – Sony's Walkman. Jobs, however, hated the then current crop of MP3 players and saw an opening for Apple. Large capacity units like Creative's Nomad Jukebox were too big and unwieldy, while more portable devices had small memory chips that meant you could barely fit a full album on them. As most rival players used USB 1.1 for connecting to computers, transfer speed for tracks to the device were painfully slow, while battery life was invariably poor. Jobs's biggest issue, however, was with the cumbersome and complicated navigation that made sifting through the sometimes thousands of tracks stored on the devices a slow, joyless experience. 'The products stank,' Greg Joswiak, Apple's vice president of iPod product marketing, succinctly summed up during an interview with *Newsweek*.

Apple's head of hardware engineering, Jon Rubinstein, who had held the same position at NeXT, headed up the team entrusted to build the iPod, with Jobs decreeing that the player would need to be in shops by the fall of the following year, in time for the holiday season.

With much of Apple's development teams working on new Macs, Rubinstein brought in outside help in the form of a programmer and an engineer called Tony Fadell. Fadell had plenty of experience devising and creating portable electronic devices, having developed a handheld PC for Philips and a PDA for General Magic. A part-time DJ, Fadell had been working on the concept of a device that would no longer require him to transport his bulky collection of CDs and vinyl to and from gigs. He came to Apple's attention after pitching a concept of a hard-drive-based player that was linked with a content delivery system, where users could legally obtain and download music. Once onboard the project, Fadell shopped around for an existing player to use as the basis of the Apple player. After briefly looking at Rio and Creative, the team found PortalPlayer, a new company that had not yet released, but had been assisting other companies develop MP3 players, including Apple's rival IBM. PortalPlayer's early work showed promise and would give a platform for the team to work from, but their early prototypes would need a great deal of work from Apple's software and industrial design teams to make them a desirable product.

Having identified an LCD (liquid crystal display) screen and a rechargeable lithium battery that would work for the iPod, Rubinstein hit an early stumbling block in trying to find a small, yet capacious hard drive that would live up to the high expectations of the device laid down by Jobs. A decisive moment for the project would come towards the end of 2000 when Rubinstein visited electronic component manufacturer Toshiba while on a trip to Japan. Toshiba had been a maker of hard drives

# The iPhone sales explosion

## 2007 – iPhone

700,000

Apple's revolutionary iPhone goes on sale on Friday, June 29 and almost immediately becomes one of the fastest selling consumer electronics devices of all time. All 164 Apple retail stores in the US stay open until midnight, with customers able to purchase up to two iPhones on a first come, first served basis.

## 2008 – iPhone 3G

1,000,000

Apple sells one million iPhone 3Gs in its first weekend. The new model combines all the revolutionary features of the iPhone plus 3G networking that is twice as fast as the EDGE technology connectivity on its predecessor.

## 2010 – iPhone 4

1,700,000

The new iPhone 4 features Apple's new Retina display. It also features a 5 megapixel camera with LED flash, HD 720p video recording, Apple's A4 processor, a 3-axis gyro and up to 40% longer talk time – in a beautiful all-new design of glass and stainless steel that is the thinnest smartphone in the world.

## 2011 – iPhone 4s

4,000,000

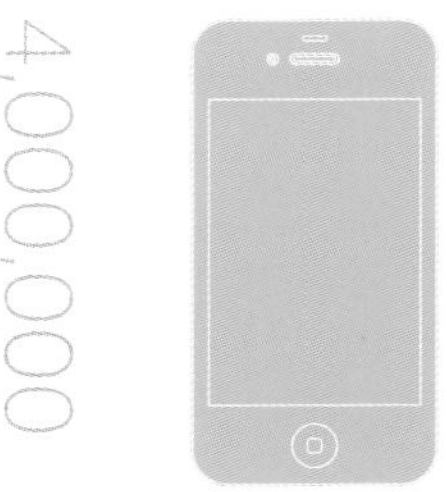

Alongside an improved processor, camera and battery, the 4S introduces Siri - Apple's voice-controlled personal assistant.

## 2012 – iPhone 5

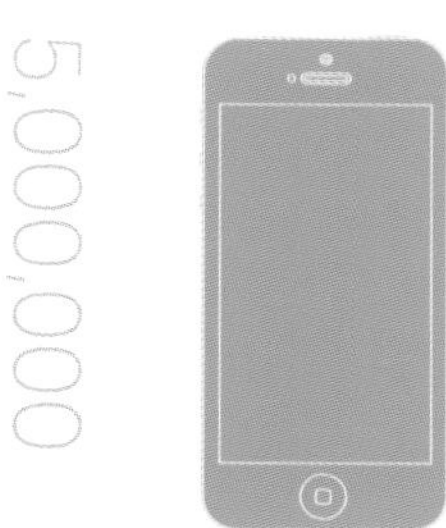


Boasting a much thinner design, the iPhone 5 also featured a longer, more cinematic 16:9 display, Apple's own custom-made A6 processor and Lightning, a new compact dock connector which replaced the 30-pin design used by previous iPhones.

## 2013 – iPhone 5s/5c

Apple announces it has sold a record-breaking nine million new iPhone 5s and iPhone 5c models, just three days after launch on 20 September. In addition, more than 200 million iOS devices are now running the completely redesigned iOS 7, making it the fastest software upgrade in history.

## 2014 – iPhone 6/6 Plus

In response to the rise in populatrity of large screened Android "phablets" the next generation of iPhones came in two size options - both of which were bigger than previous iterations of the device. The 6 had a 4.7-inch display, while the iPhone 6 Plus boasted a 5.5-inch display.

## 2015 – iPhone 6s/6s Plus

Apple sells more than 13 million new iPhone 6s and iPhone 6s Plus models, a new record, just three days after launch. The new iPhones will be available in over 130 countries by the end of 2015.

for personal computers for some time and, during the visit, Rubinstein was shown the company's latest breakthrough in the field – a prototype miniature drive for laptops that could hold five gigabytes of data yet measured less than two inches in diameter. 'They said they didn't know what to do with it. Maybe put it in a small notebook,' Rubinstein recalled.

Small enough to fit into a cigarette pack its comparatively large capacity meant it could hold thousands of audio files. Blown away by the demo and the possibilities of the prototype's small form factor, Rubenstein rushed to visit Jobs who was in Japan for the Tokyo Macworld conference. There he would ask Jobs for a $10 million cheque to buy up all of Toshiba's inventory of the drive, a component that would give the iPod a huge advantage over its competitors. 'I went back to Steve and I said, "I know how to do this. I've got all the parts." He said, "Go for it."'

The team's solution to the transfer speed problem that beset existing MP3 players would be to use Firewire connectivity – a technology originally developed by Apple to transfer video from professional digital movie cameras. Able to shift data thirty times faster than USB 1.1, it would make moving tracks to the device a far less frustrating experience than what the competition offered.

Jobs's enthusiasm for the project ensured he was more hands on than he had been on any other product since his return. Intent on making sure the iPod would not go the way of his predecessor's doomed attempts at releasing a consumer electronics device like the Newton and the Pippin, he dismissed several early prototypes that didn't meet his exacting standards. When the design team presented him with one such early incarnation of the iPod, he examined it for a while in his hand before declaring: 'It's too big.' The engineers countered, saying they had pulled off a miracle of miniaturisation. Incensed, Jobs walked over to the fish tank in the corner of his office and dropped the underwhelming prototype into the water. He then pointed to the bubbles that floated from it to the surface and said: 'That means there's still some space in it. It's too big.'

The big issue for those working on the user interface would be a way of easily navigating its library on a device that could potentially hold thousands of songs. The team's initial ideas did little to improve upon the clunky arrow key buttons found on the unintuitive MP3 players already out there that Jobs despised, before a moment of inspiration came from Apple's affable marketing senior vice president, Phil Schiller. Using the example of Bang & Olufsen's BeoCom phones that had a dial-like interface for navigating lists of phone contacts and calls, Schiller suggested that the iPod's menus should be navigated with a wheel that would scroll faster the longer it was turned. It proved a eureka moment that immediately helped distinguish the iPod from the clunkiness of competing players.

Vinnie Chieco, a copywriter from San Francisco who had been recruited by Apple to be part of a small team tasked with developing the device's initial marketing campaign, claims to have come up with the device's name. During the group's meetings Jobs had settled on the player's memorable tagline – '1,000 songs in your pocket.' This meant the product's name no longer needed to be descriptive nor reference music. Upon seeing the iPod, Chieco's thoughts turned to science fiction: 'As soon as I saw the white iPod, I thought 2001,' said Chieco. 'Open the pod bay door, Hal!' All that was left was to add the 'i' prefix which had by now been used for iTunes, iMac, iBook and iMovie. A year earlier on 24 July 2000, Apple registered the iPod name for 'a public internet kiosk enclosure containing computer equipment', a fact Chieco claims to be either a coincidence or a means of throwing competitors off the scent of what Apple were about to unleash upon the world.

After six months of intense activity, the iPod team met its deadline. 'Hint: It's not a Mac', Apple teased in a special October 2001 invite to Apple's Cupertino HQ for its debut.

'This is a major, major breakthrough,' Jobs told the assembled reporters. Pulling out the pure white and stainless steel, card deck sized device from his jeans pocket, during the launch event, Jobs declared: 'With iPod, listening to music will never be the same again.' It was a bold statement, but one that would in the end prove far more prescient than even Jobs could ever have anticipated.

The finished iPod would hold a thousand songs, could be recharged within an hour and would cost $399. 'Do you remember what it was like when you got your first Walkman?' asked the singer Seal, who alongside other musicians appeared behind Jobs on a giant video screen at the event. The initial reception from the tech press and even some Apple fan sites was less than enthusiastic, with many

# Apple Park

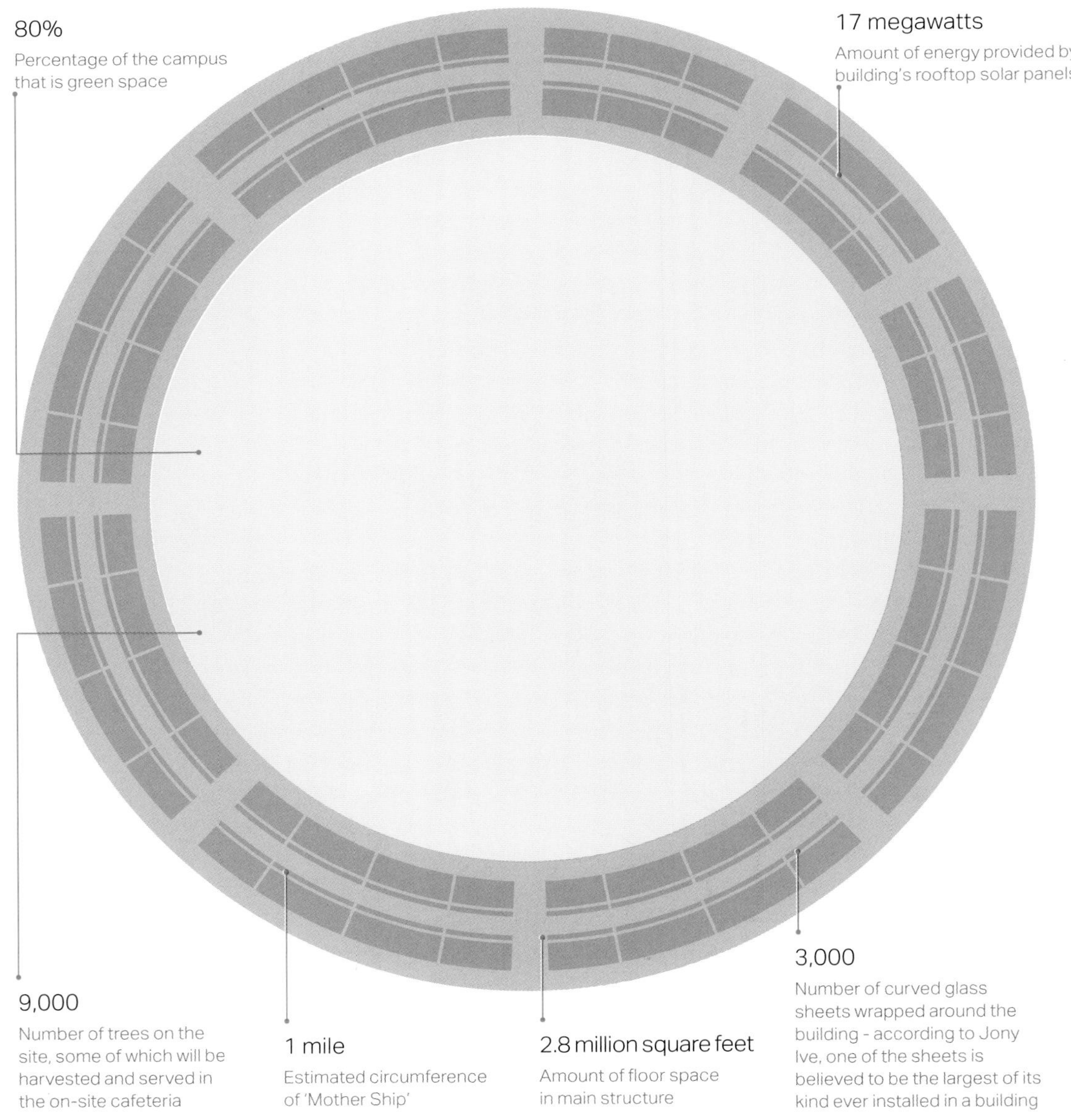
80%
Percentage of the campus that is green space
17 megawatts
Amount of energy provided by building's rooftop solar panels
9,000
Number of trees on the site, some of which will be harvested and served in the on-site cafeteria
1 mile
Estimated circumference of 'Mother Ship'
2.8 million square feet
Amount of floor space in main structure
3,000
Number of curved glass sheets wrapped around the building - according to Jony Ive, one of the sheets is believed to be the largest of its kind ever installed in a building

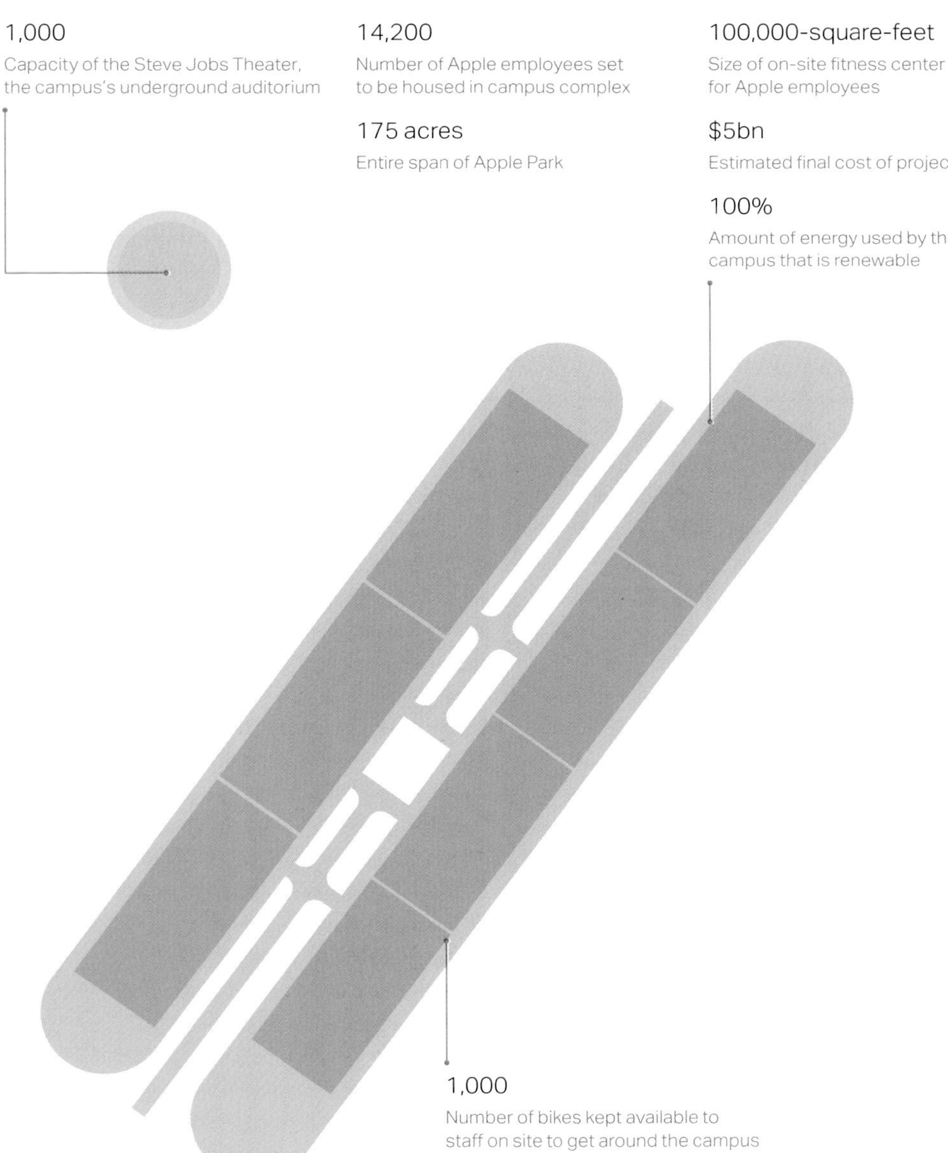
1,000
Capacity of the Steve Jobs Theater, the campus's underground auditorium
14,200
Number of Apple employees set to be housed in campus complex
175 acres
Entire span of Apple Park
100,000-square-feet
Size of on-site fitness center for Apple employees
$5bn
Estimated final cost of project
100%
Amount of energy used by the campus that is renewable
1,000
Number of bikes kept available to staff on site to get around the campus

criticising its lack of support for syncing with Windows machines, its comparatively expensive price tag and its odd name.

The iPod would meet a far more favourable response when it was released in Europe a month later. After a slow start in which 125,000 iPods were sold in its first month and around a million shifted in its first year, sales would begin to gather pace with an entire ecosystem starting to form around the device as new accessories and software products were released. An updated, larger 20GB capacity version of the iPod would arrive in July 2002 that would be compatible for syncing with Windows PCs via third-party software by Musicmatch. Apple also began to offer engraved iPods in time for Christmas 2002, with several acts such as Madonna and Beck, and companies licensing their logos to Apple.

Not everyone was happy with the growing success Apple was having with its digital hub strategy. Testifying before the US Senate Commerce Committee, Disney CEO Michael Eisner accused Apple's 'Rip, Mix, Burn' ads of fostering piracy, arguing that its adverts implied 'that [you] can create a theft if you buy this computer.' Jobs would hit back, defending Apple's position in *The Wall Street Journal*: 'If you legally acquire music, you need to have the right to manage it on all other devices that you own.' Indeed, Jobs's stance that Apple was a force for good for the industry would be bolstered by his next move which would provide a mechanism for the labels to battle back against the ominous threat of web piracy to its bottom line.

While the iPod was beginning to surpass sales expectations, the music industry was in total disarray, with the major labels unable to come to a consensus between them on a standard platform for copy-protecting digital music. Multiple music industry copyright lawsuits had resulted in the demise of Napster, but copycat sites and services like Kazaa and Limewire had become even bigger and more sophisticated, ensuring that free, and largely illegal, file-sharing continued to grow in popularity around the world. The CD had killed vinyl, but the advent of MP3s looked set to decimate a once $40 billion-per-year industry.

Amid the turmoil, executives from Warner Music and Sony Music arranged for a meeting in Cupertino with Jobs in January 2002 with the mission of getting Apple to sign up as a partner in a consortium that would develop a standard file platform for music devices.

Turning to Jobs and the now ascendant Apple was a no-brainer for the labels, as the then Warner Executive Vice President Paul Vidich explained:

> 'Steve made digital music fashionable. The iPod white silhouette campaign was a perfect representation of that. He turned music into a fashion statement, a wearable fashion statement. He made it sexy.'

A few short minutes into the pitch, Jobs dismissively interrupted: 'You guys have your heads up your asses.'

'Everyone else in the room was silent,' recalled Vidich. 'I replied in a hoarse voice, "You're right, Steve. That's why we're here. We need your help."' While Jobs would agree for Apple to join the consortium, no product or standard would get off the ground.

With the growing success of the iPod, Jobs had the ammunition he needed to make a persuasive pitch for his own vision of how music should be sold online. Two months after the meeting, with a beta version of the iTunes Store ready to demo, Steve reached out to Warner Music Group and was called in to give a two-hour walkthrough of the product to Vidich along with a smattering of Warner Music executives. They were blown away.

'It was going to be their storefront, the first thing that consumers saw,' Vidich reminisced to *Rolling Stone* in 2013. 'I remember thinking, "This is so simple. It works. It's great."'

Apple and Warner began to work up a business plan during which the infrastructure for the store was fleshed out ahead of being pitched to the other majors. It would be the Warner executives, not Jobs as is often suggested, who would present the idea that tracks should be sold for 99¢, a major decision considering some labels had wanted to price tracks at $3.49 each.

The straightforward pricing appealed to Jobs's sensibilities for keeping products and consumer choices uncomplicated. 'When we told Steve, he looked at us like we just gave him a gift,' Vidich recalled. 'We knew we needed to alter consumer behaviour in a big way. Below $1 was an emotional threshold for people. It became an acceptable impulse purchase.'

With a Warner deal secured, and the store to all intents ready to roll, Apple began coercing the other big labels, including EMI, Universal, BMG and Sony to get onboard.

# Cash reserve and capitalisation

Apple's huge cash hoard and market capitalisation in comparison to other tech giants in 2011.

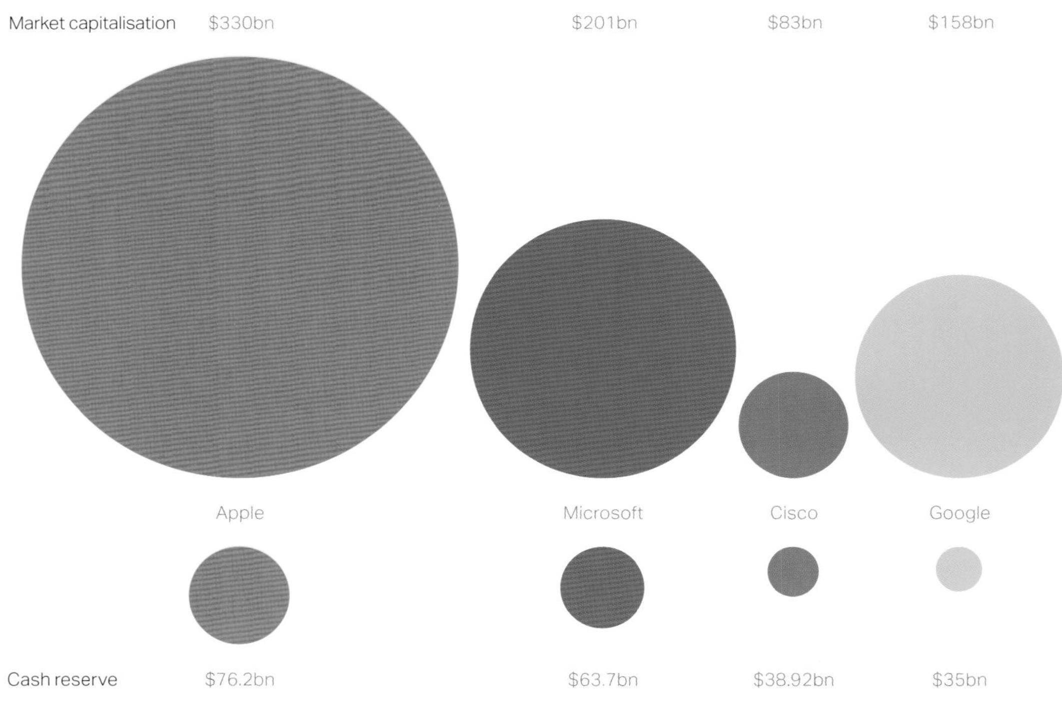

$125bn $85bn $188bn $92bn $102bn $81bn

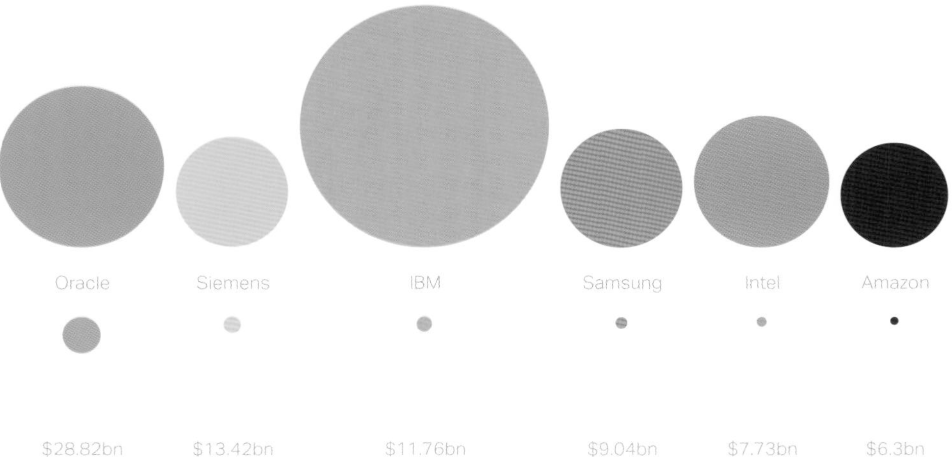

The other labels, however, would prove a harder sell than Warner, with Apple executives encountering resistance on pricing and Jobs's plan of making each track from an album available as an individual purchase. 'Apple certainly had very good people, but they couldn't get the deals done,' recalled Jay Samit, the then president of digital distribution at EMI. 'To the labels, Apple was this small company with 2% market share in PCs. iTunes would have been stillborn if Steve hadn't gotten personally involved.'

Once again Jobs's charm and enthusiasm as a salesman would earn its intended results, with each major eventually falling into place. 'He was a great salesman,' Doug Morris, who was head of Universal Music at the time, recalled. 'He had a clear, complete thought that went from the iPod to iTunes. It made absolute sense to me.'

After a year and a half of negotiations with the labels, in April 2003, the iTunes Music Store was launched with 200,000 songs in its library. Within just a week it had reached the milestone of 1 million tracks sold.

To coincide with the launch, Apple also released a Windows-compatible version of iTunes, dispensing with the need for the third-party Musicmatch software to sync. With all of the pieces in place, the iPod boom began to really take hold. Apple's marketing department went into overdrive. The iconic iPod commercial featuring dancing silhouettes and music, often hand-picked by Jobs, by hip or up-and-coming bands such as The Black Eyed Peas' 'Hey Mama' and Jet's 'Are You Gonna Be My Girl' became ubiquitous, while the company's distinctive white earbuds became as common a sight on the street as a Starbucks paper cup. While riding along Madison Avenue in New York around this time, Jobs noticed on every block there was someone wearing the distinctive white earbuds. He remarked later, 'I thought, "Oh my God, it's starting to happen!"'

Within months, the iTunes Music Store would quickly take over 70% of the legitimate download music business. A year after its launch it had sold an incredible 85 million songs and was named *Fortune*'s product of the year for 2003. iPod sales responded in kind. By the time they peaked at nearly 55 million in 2008, the iTunes Store had taken over Best Buy as the number one music retailer in the US; by February of 2010, iTunes became the number one music retailer on the planet.

The success of the iPod and the store would somewhat inevitably resurrect a legal dispute with one of Jobs's most cherished influences.

In March 2006, Apple Corps, the company that holds the rights to The Beatles' catalogue, sued Apple for violating a trademark agreement. Apple Computer had agreed with its namesake in 1991 to stay out of the music business, but with 10 million songs sold on iTunes at that point, it was becoming unambiguously involved. When the case came before the High Court in London, the judge considered disqualifying himself owing to the fact that he owned an iPod. Apple's lawyers argued that not even 'a moron in a hurry' would mistake the two companies. The case was eventually settled in 2007 in favour of Jobs's company. Much to his relief, the relationship would eventually be patched up between the two parties in 2010 when the entire Beatles back catalogue was finally made available on the iTunes Music Store. Later that year, the flagship Apple Store opened in Midtown Manhattan, its unique glass-cube structure making it a modern New York City landmark.

Amid the triumph of the iPod and iTunes, Jobs had often been complaining of severe pain around his abdomen. A diminished appetite would also see him regularly skip meals, ailments he would dismiss and self-diagnose as being caused by another case of kidney stones. After a chance meeting in October 2003 with the urologist who had treated him previously, he discussed the problems. While not worried about the symptoms, she convinced Jobs to go in for a routine check of his kidneys and ureter, with it having been five years since his last CAT scan.

Unexpectedly, the results were bad with a devastating initial prognosis. A shadow was picked up on his pancreas indicating a tumour. One of the consultants went as far as suggesting he should think about putting his affairs in order.

The scan was followed with a biopsy later that same day that provided a much brighter picture. The shadow was identified as a rare pancreatic neuroendocrine tumour – a slow-growing variant that made it more likely to be treated successfully. Having had his cancer detected early, the tumour could be removed before definitely spreading. To the dismay of family and friends, Jobs decided not to go ahead with any procedure. 'I really didn't want them to open up my body, so I tried to see if a few other things would work,' he explained to biographer Walter Isaacson. Those 'other things' would include a strict vegan diet, acupuncture, herbal remedies and even consulting a psychic.

# Jobs's cancer battle

## 2003 – Diagnosis

Diagnosed with rare form of pancreatic cancer called an islet cell neuroendocrine tumour.

## 2004 – Announcement

August
In an email to staff, Jobs discloses that he has undergone surgery for cancer. Tim Cook takes over Jobs's duties during his recovery.

October
Makes first public appearance since undergoing surgery at unveiling of new Apple Store in Palo Alto, California.

## 2005 – 'I'm fine now'

June
During speech to Stanford University students, Jobs reveals that his initial diagnosis was that he had as little as three months to live, before a biopsy the next day revealed it was curable. He states 'I'm fine now.'

## 2008 – Weight loss

July
With Jobs looking noticeably thinner during recent appearances, Chief Financial Officer Peter Oppenheimer addresses mounting rumours that Apple's CEO is ill again, stating that Jobs has no plans to leave the company and that his 'health is a private matter.'

## 2009 – Medical leave

January
Apple and Jobs issue statement saying that his recent severe weight loss is due to a hormone imbalance issue and that he will continue to run the company. Eleven days later he backtracks and announces he will take medical leave until June. Cook once again deputises.

June
A doctor at the Methodist University Hospital Transplant Institute in Tennessee confirms Jobs received a liver transplant and has an 'excellent prognosis'. He returns to work that same month.

September
Jobs presides over an Apple launch event for the first time in six months. Reveals that liver donor was a young adult who had died in a car crash.

## 2011 – Resignation

January
In a memo to staff, Jobs announces new leave of absence, this time with no set return date and with Cook once again taking over day to day matters.

August
Jobs resigns as Apple CEO, stating that he can no longer meet his duties, but makes no reference to his medical condition.

October
Jobs dies at the age of 56.

# Pancreatic cancer

## Risk factors

Gender

Diabetes

Genetic

Physical inactivity

Tobacco use

Age

## Figures

Position in the leading cause of cancer deaths in the US

3%

Percentage of those diagnosed that survive for five years and beyond (lowest survival rate of all cancers)

12

Position in list of most common causes of cancer deaths

50/50

Affects men & women equally

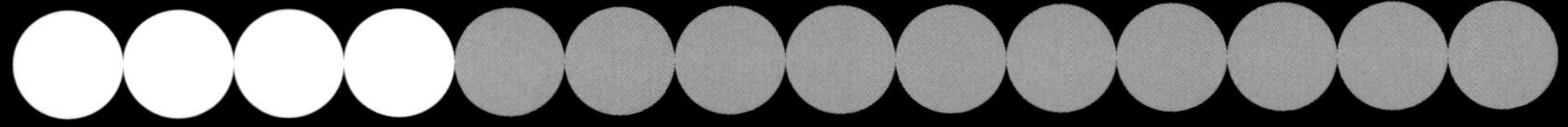

20%–30%

Amount of pancreatic cancer cases thought to be caused by smoking

1 in 65

Average estimated lifetime risk of developing pancreatic cancer

## Treatment

Surgical removal of parts of the pancreas affected by the tumour can extend a patient's life by a few years

Chemotherapy and radiotherapy where surgery is not an option

After nine months it became clear even to Steve that his diets and herbal remedies were not working, when a CAT scan in June 2004 revealed that the tumour had grown and potentially spread. Accepting that there was no other alternative for ridding him of the disease, on 31 July 2004, Jobs underwent surgery at Stanford University Medical Center. While it went well, the procedure wouldn't provide a cure: during the operation, the surgeons had discovered that Jobs's cancer had spread to three spots on his liver. Jobs would admit his regret over his decision not to have the operation when the cancer was first discovered.

Jobs would keep the severity of his situation to himself, telling staff and even fellow members of the management team that the operation had been a success, and that he would return to work by September, telling everyone he had been 'cured'.

Despite his skill as an orator, Jobs rarely gave speeches. 'If you look closely at how he spent his time, you'll see that he hardly ever travelled and he did none of the conferences and get-togethers that so many CEOs attended,' Tim Cook once commented. 'He wanted to be home for dinner.'

He would break with that stance when he accepted an invitation from Stanford to give its June 2005 commencement address to graduates.

The speech's significance could be summed up by how the supremely confident fifty-year-old CEO of one of the world's biggest companies was left paralysed by nerves ahead of the address. 'He woke up with butterflies in his stomach,' Laurene recalled. 'I'd almost never seen him more nervous.'

In a reflective phase of his life following his health issues, the now famous speech would offer a rare moment of Jobs being forthcoming about his cancer to the public, if not entirely frank. 'I had the surgery and I'm fine now,' he would state.

Written with assistance from Aaron Sorkin (the TV and film scriptwriter, famous for his work on *The West Wing* and *A Few Good Men*, who would go on to write the screenplay for a 2015 biographical film on Jobs directed by Danny Boyle), the speech was broken into three stories. The first covered his dropping out of Reed College, the second his devastating ousting from Apple. The final, and most poignant, would focus on his cancer diagnosis and the awareness his recent brush with mortality had brought him.

At times sombre in its tone, Jobs urged the graduates to remember that everyone's future is uncertain and there was no time to waste on an unfulfilling career.

His parting words would be a repeat of the farewell message from the final issue of *The Whole Earth Catalog*, the counterculture magazine that had inspired him during his college years:

Stay Hungry. Stay Foolish.

Chapter Seventeen

# One more thing

17

Following his cancer surgery, Steve had forced himself back to fitness and was intent on getting back to the office as quickly as possible, with colleagues commenting that he appeared even more focused and determined when he eventually returned.

While Apple was a company transformed, he knew that some of his most important work was to come. There was no room for complacency – Apple needed to push on and create even greater products, not least because there was an emerging threat to its current cash cow.

Like Jobs, Apple's team of executives were raising concerns about the iPod's future. The company had notched up sales of two million music players in 2003, ten million in 2004, and would go on to register forty million in 2005, an almost unheard of number for a consumer electronics device. By 2005, there was the iPod, the iPod Mini, the iPod Nano, and the iPod Shuffle, in descending size order. That same year also saw the introduction of the first iPod with video, alongside the ability to buy movies and videos on iTunes. While the iPod was still riding high, it was becoming patently clear that mobile phones were set to cannibalise its market. Compact handsets like Samsung's SPH M100 flip phone were already offering rudimentary MP3 playback, albeit with limited capacity for songs. Elsewhere, bulky but multi-featured business-focused phones based around PDA functionality like Sony Ericsson's P900 and the HTC Himalaya were starting to resemble what would now be categorised as smartphones, offering internet connectivity and email, basic touchscreen functionality via a stylus, and built-in cameras.

While lots of consumers were carrying around both an iPod and their phone, the convenience of only taking one device to work or college would eventually prove too enticing. Sooner rather than later, a competitor would provide a compelling handset combining the two devices.

Apple's initial response to the problem was an attempt at neutralising the threat. This would take the form of a collaboration with Motorola on an 'iTunes phone' that would be exclusive in the US to the Cingular network. Named the Rokr E1, the candy bar-shaped handset would be the first that could play music purchased from the iTunes Music Store. Apple would

# Apple's stock

How much its value changed during
Jobs and Cook era

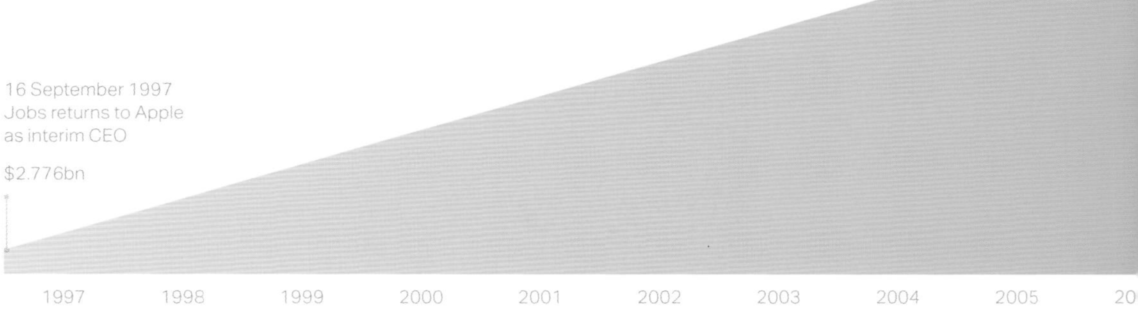

12 September 2017
Cook unveils iPhone X
$830.88bn
25 November 2011
Cook's first product
speech as CEO
$337.91bn
24 August 2011
Jobs steps down as CEO
$348.75bn
07
2008
2009
2010
2011
2012
2013
2014
2015
2016

provide the iTunes software, while Motorola would take care of the design and manufacturing of the hardware. Despite a high-profile advertising campaign featuring Madonna, Iggy Pop and the rapper Common, as well as the handset's unique selling point, the lacklustre phone was doomed from its very inception. To a certain degree, Apple had wilfully hobbled the device by limiting its iTunes functionality to what was offered by the minimal, entry-level iPod Shuffle, with the aim of giving the user a taste of their service so that they would eventually want to upgrade to a premium iPod.

The handset inevitably sold poorly and Apple and Motorola parted ways, but the project had allowed Apple to dip its toes into the mobile market and had also opened up lines of negotiation for the possibility of a further partnership with Cingular, only this time with a product that would be all of Apple's making.

Like the iPod and the iTunes Store, such a move would see Apple moving into a new market it had little experience within, but Jobs was adamant the company needed to go in, all guns blazing. 'Everybody hates their phone and that's not a good thing,' Jobs said. 'There's an opportunity there.' Much like they had done with the MP3 player, Apple's new mission was to fix, transform, then dominate the mobile phone and its market.

The genesis of what would eventually become the iPhone can be traced back to a brainstorming meeting amongst Jony Ive's industrial design team in 2003. The meeting would see designer Duncan Kerr provide a show and tell of the research work he had been collaborating on with Apple's input engineering division who were looking into new methods of input for the Mac. Kerr would give a walkthrough of screens featuring a new multi-touch technology which would leave Ive and his team both astounded and excited by the possibilities it could open up. Kerr's demonstration would show how you could now use two or three fingers instead of one to manipulate on-screen elements in new ways, including zooming and rotating.

The team began to brainstorm ideas around what kinds of hardware they could create around the technology, with a tactile, touchscreen Mac being the obvious conclusion. Ive would later be shown a huge experimental system featuring the technology running an adapted version of OS X that the input engineering team had already set about creating. It featured a huge multi-touch display placed on a table tennis table with a projector positioned above. 'This is going to change everything,' Ive would relay back to his team afterwards. He wanted Jobs to see the system in action, but resisted, opting to wait until the input engineering team had polished up the still very raw concept. 'Because Steve is so quick to give an opinion, I didn't show him stuff in front of other people,' Ive would explain.

When Ive finally showed off the team's work, Jobs was blown away. 'This is the future,' would be the CEO's emphatic response. Steve green-lit the project for further development, with the aim of shrinking the giant capacitive screen into a working, finger-controlled tablet running a modified version of OS X. Within a week, Ive's team had worked up a prototype with a twelve-inch MacBook screen that could recognise pinch to zoom gestures, with an adapted version of Google Maps used to demo its capabilities. The proof-of-concept earned the team further encouragement from Jobs to develop more tablet prototypes with a view to the team working the concept up to an actual product. To further bolster the project, in 2005 Apple secretly acquired Fingerworks, a small Delaware company that had already developed a number of multi-touch interfaces including a gesture-based touchpad for PCs. While it would be five years before the tablet idea would become an actual product, its underpinning technology would first get redirected into Apple's mobile phone project.

Hedging its bets, Apple would have two phones in development at the same time. Project number one was led by Ive and would feature a screen using the multi-touch technology, while project number two was headed up by Tony Fadell, the now vice president of iPod engineering, whose team had begun working up a phone concept based around the recently released iPod Mini and its click wheel interface. As well as acting like a rotary phone dialler, and a rolodex-style interface for flicking through contacts, Fadell's team's concept would also use the click wheel in conjunction with a predictive text feature for composing SMS messages. Apple would file a number of patents related to the text system, with Jobs named as one of the inventors, but Steve would eventually kill off the iPod-influenced phone project. It wouldn't be able to surf the web nor run apps, while its interface was too slow in use and was generally felt too limited.

Apple would instead push ahead with the more promising touchscreen phone concept. Now codenamed Project Purple, Ive was placed in charge of its industrial design, with Fadell overseeing engineering, while Scott Forstall, previously in charge of OS X development, was given the job of adapting the operating system into a version for the new mobile phone. Key staff were moved from Mac and iPod projects onto the secret iPhone division,

# Jobs's final quarter sales

By the time of Steve Jobs's passing, the iPad had become established as Apple's second most important product line

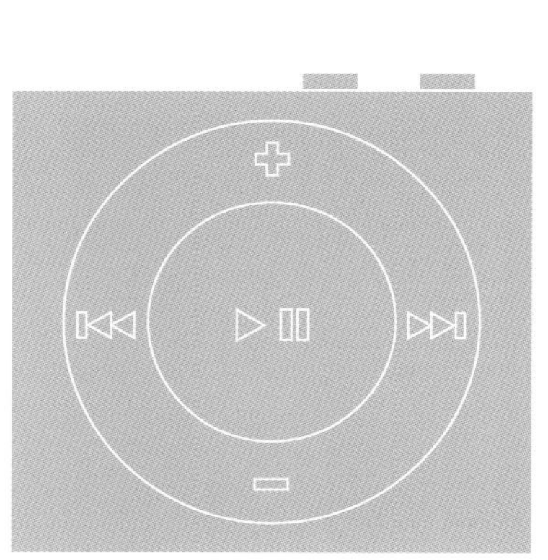

iPods
7.54 million

iPads
9.25 million

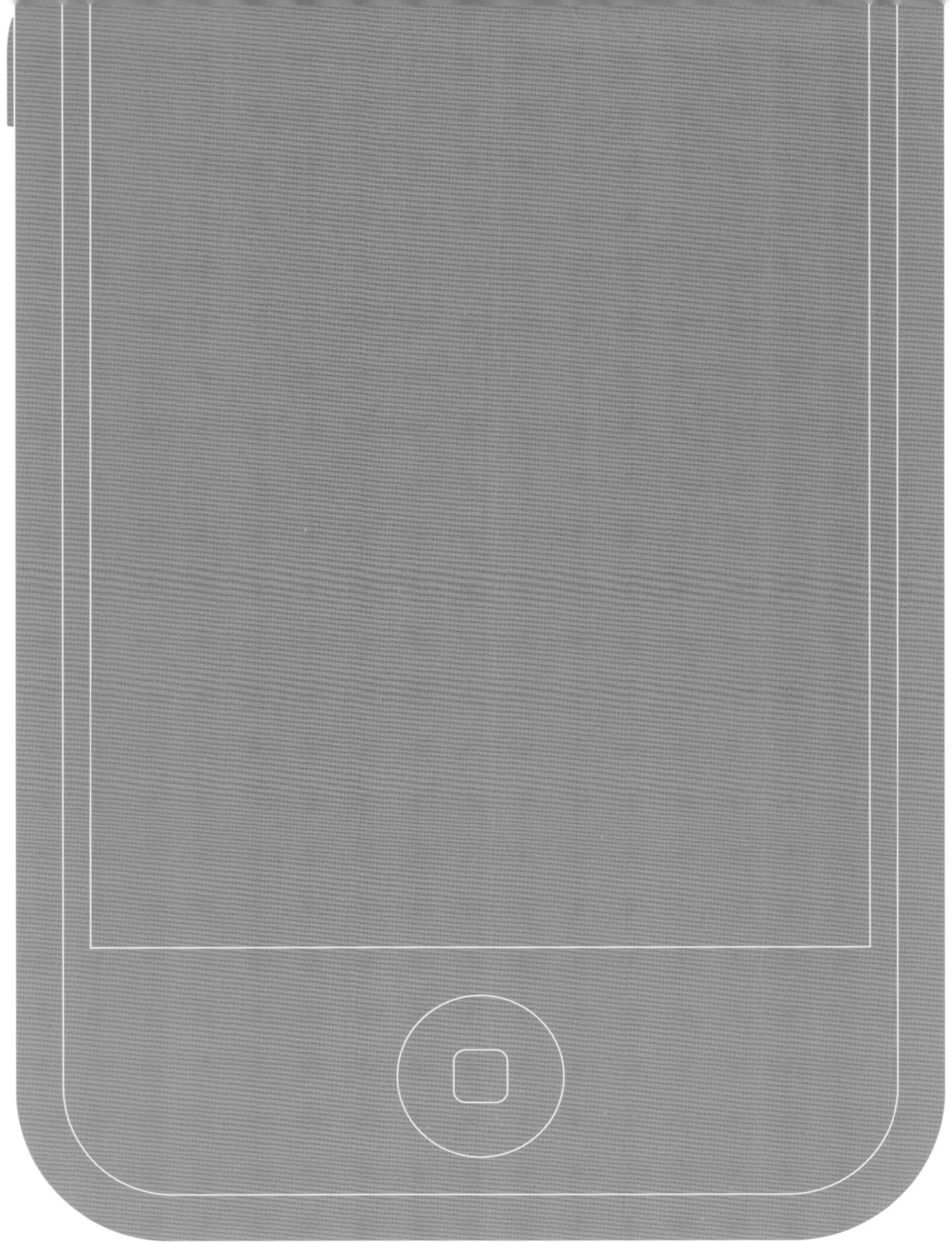

iPhones

20.34 million

causing the delay and cancellation of some products. Meanwhile, Apple's now notorious veil of secrecy would become even tighter for the project, with Jobs decreeing that team leaders could recruit anyone from within the company to work on the iPhone, but a ban would be placed on drafting in any talent from outside.

Alongside maintaining an active role in overseeing the iPhone's project, Jobs's focus was also being split with concerning new developments at Pixar. Having notched up blockbuster hits with *Monsters, Inc.*, and *Finding Nemo*, there remained two films still to go in the deal with Disney. Using the leverage of the success of the previous pair of films, Jobs once again tried to cut an improved deal for Pixar with Disney. The talks would eventually reach a stalemate, with Jobs threatening to take Pixar's movies to another studio. Disney CEO Michael Eisner retaliated by pressing ahead with development of sequels to *Monsters, Inc., Finding Nemo*, and even *Toy Story* without Pixar's involvement. The split and its potential repercussions left Pixar's chief creative officer John Lasseter devastated: 'I was worried about my children, what they would do with the characters we'd created,' he said.

The standoff would eventually end when Eisner was ousted as Disney CEO following a shareholder revolt that had seen him stripped of his chairman title a year earlier. His successor, Robert Iger, recognised how Pixar's expertise and the characters it had created had now become entwined into Disney's fabric. Not willing to risk losing them, Iger brought Jobs back to the table. Following lengthy discussions, Disney would eventually offer and then agree to buy Pixar for $7.4 billion in 2006. The deal saw Lasseter elevated to Disney's chief creative officer, while Pixar co-founder Ed Catmull, became president of Walt Disney Animation Studios. As part of the sale Jobs joined Disney's board of directors and would become Disney's largest single shareholder, with 7% of the stock, worth more than $3 billion. Following the announcement of the Pixar deal, speculation mounted that Jobs looked to take over as Disney's CEO, however to those at its Cupertino HQ, it was clear his attention remained focused solely on Apple.

In their earliest meetings, the iPhone design team had laid down a rule that nothing should detract from the handset's screen, with Ive using high-end 'infinity' swimming pools that feature an invisible edge as a major design inspiration. Like the iPod, no logo or branding would be allowed to appear on the front of the device, with its slick design the product's calling card.

Just a few months before its planned unveiling, it would be the centrepiece screen that would place the project into jeopardy. Jobs hated the plastic screens that were being used on the prototypes after badly scratching the screen on a test model when placing it into a jeans pocket that had his keys in it. Steve would order glass to be used similar to that featured on Motorola's RAZR flip phone. Finding a provider of a suitable type of reinforced glass for the phone would prove difficult, but Apple's operations team's search for material would eventually lead to Corning Incorporated in upstate New York, a company that had invented Pyrex glass for kitchenware. In the 1960s the company had developed a near unbreakable glass called Chemcor, but while it was used briefly by aviation and car firms, it never took off and production of the material was ended in the early seventies.

With the phone's launch less than two months away, Apple placed an order with the firm to create as much of the glass as possible within six weeks. Chemcor had never been made in large volume, or indeed for some years. 'None of our plants make the glass now,' Corning's CEO, Wendell Weeks, replied. But Jobs was insistent: 'Get your mind around it,' he cajoled. 'You can do it.' Such was Steve's persuasiveness, the company completely overhauled its manufacturing processes almost overnight, changing several of its LCD-making plants in Kentucky to make what had now been renamed Gorilla glass. By May 2007, Corning was making thousands of metres of the material to fulfil Apple's order.

As winter approached, Jobs gathered the management team working on the iPhone in the boardroom for a progress report. The iPhone was scheduled for launch at Macworld in San Francisco in early January 2007, but the feedback from all quarters painted a picture of a product that was nowhere close to being ready. The software was wildly unstable, the phone's antenna would persistently drop calls, the phone's battery couldn't hold charge, while the phone's proximity sensor didn't seem to work if the user had long dark hair. All those present in the boardroom expected a trademark tirade from the CEO, however Jobs was unusually calm, responding deadpan to the litany of problems: 'We don't have a product yet.'

While Jobs didn't raise his voice, his steely-eyed response indicated that a postponement wouldn't be an option. For those working on the iPhone at Apple, the next three months would be almost intolerably fraught. With so much of the technology within the iPhone breaking new ground, it was perhaps incredible that the project had even got to this stage. But just as it

# Jobs's final quarter revenue

Apple's record-breaking revenue figures from Q3 2011, the final financial quarter under Steve Jobs's stewardship, underline how mobile devices were now firmly established as the company's main source of income.

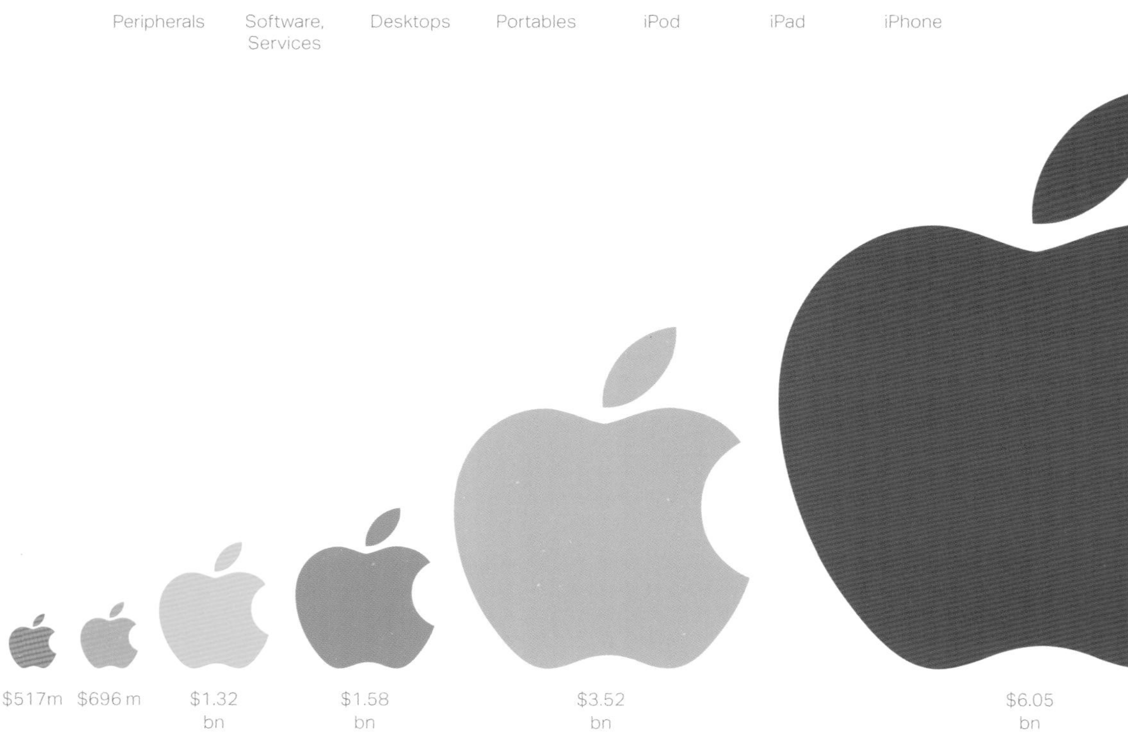

$13.3
bn

was looking like the device would be shelved, a prototype was completed that worked well enough to be shown off by Jobs for a planned December demo with AT&T's Stan Stigman. The mobile phone network's CEO was suitably impressed, calling the prototype 'the best device I have ever seen'. The iPhone was finally ready to be shown off to the world.

Secrecy had been maintained throughout the development process, and while there had been hints and educated guesses by the press and on discussion forums as to what was set to be unveiled, there was a palpable sense of anticipation and excitement among the gathered media prior to Jobs hitting the stage at the Moscone Center in San Francisco on the morning of 9 January 2007.

Dressed, as ever, in what had become his simplistic, self-imposed uniform of black turtleneck, Levi's and New Balance sneakers, Jobs's masterful presentation of the new device would go down as the watermark of what had by now become known as 'Stevenotes'. Conveying a genuine sense of excitement and enthusiasm for the product, the concise, yet impactful presentation was both playful and humorous throughout.

Teasing the crowd, Jobs said he had three products to introduce, and kept repeating the phrase: 'An iPod, a phone, and an internet communicator'. After stringing out the crowd, he followed up: 'Are you getting it? These are not three separate devices. This is one device, and we are calling it iPhone,' the quintessentially Jobsian theatrics earning waves of applause.

While the unveiling had been a barnstorming triumph, for the Apple engineers and programmers working on the actual product, the work was far from over. With six months until its announced release date, the truth was that the iPhone still barely existed. The prototypes used during the keynote were little more than glorified stage props rather than being anywhere near close to actual working versions ready for retail. There were hundreds of major and minor software bugs to iron out, and scores of seemingly unsolvable hardware issues still to be addressed.

Despite the intense deadline pressure, the iPhone somehow stayed on schedule for its 29 June launch. When it finally went on sale, news crews camped out at Apple stores across the US to witness the pandemonium as eager customers waited in line for hours, and sometimes even days before store openings – a phenomenon that would become a common feature of almost every major Apple launch from that point on.

Apple sold 270,000 iPhones in the first two days they were available. In the next six months the company would go on to sell a further 3.4 million iPhones. Just as Jobs had promised in his keynote to launch the handset, Apple had now changed the mobile phone industry forever in much the same way it had revolutionised the computer and music industries.

While some sections of the media dubbed it the 'Jesus phone', certain rivals were less effusive, with Microsoft CEO Steve Ballmer calling the iPhone a failed product because it didn't have a physical keyboard.

Jobs was initially keen to keep the iPhone within Apple's walled garden and wanted to restrict the software that could be used on the device. Following its launch, software developers began clamouring for permission to make programs for the device, but Jobs emphatically ruled out such a move. 'You don't want your phone to be like a PC,' he told John Markoff of *The New York Times* right after the announcement. 'The last thing you want is to have loaded three apps on your phone and then you go to make a call and it doesn't work anymore. These are more like iPods than they are like computers.'

Some commentators have suggested that Jobs was so focused on getting the device ready for sale that he didn't see the potential at first to open up the platform to developers. But amid pressure from within Apple, he eventually saw the light. Four months after shipping its first iPhone, Apple revealed that it would make available a software development kit for anyone who wanted to develop apps for its iOS operating system, a decision that would create something akin to a new gold rush within Silicon Valley and the venture capital community, with hundreds of small developers signed up alongside recognisable companies, to create software for the iPhone.

A common criticism of the original handset was that it felt incomplete – it only featured support for EDGE cellular connectivity rather than the faster 3G networks that most new phones could take advantage of. It was also unable to record video, nor were users able to cut and paste text and images. These omissions were largely due to the rush to get the iPhone to market – there simply wasn't enough time to fit the features in. All of these issues would be addressed with the iPhone 3G which shipped in July 2008. Arguably the biggest update would be the availability of the App Store for the device, allowing users to install software from non-Apple developers. At launch, the App Store had five hundred applications.

# Tim Cook in numbers

## $10,000

Total employee charitable contributions matched by Apple in a scheme introduced by Cook shortly after becoming CEO, addressing a criticism of a lack of public philanthropic activity during the Jobs era.

## 17 years

In 2012 Cook paid investors their first cash dividend since 1995, something the company never did during Jobs's reign as CEO.

## 45

Number of places Tim Cook dropped in Glassdoor's 2017 annual ranking of CEOs by employee approval.

## 560,000

Amount of Apple shares Cook will receive each year while CEO.

## 3.06 million

Cook's basic Apple salary in 2017 - Jobs famously took home just $1.

## 229 billion

Apple's revenue figure in 2017 - more than double the amount the company was posting when Cook first took over as CEO. By 2017, under his stewardship Apple had also doubled its profits and tripled the amount of cash it has in the bank.

## 200%

By 2017 the amount Apple's shares had increased since Cook became chief executive.

## 102 million

Cook's total 2017 payout: basic Apple salary $3.06m, cash bonus of $9.3m, plus share awards worth $89m.

## 48 billion

Apple's profits in 2017 – roughly as much as Microsoft and JP Morgan combined.

## 224,000 dollars

Annual cost of his personal security detail.

During the launch, famed venture investor John Doerr of Kleiner, Perkins, Caufield & Byers took to the stage to announce a $100 million iFund for app developers, kickstarting what would become known as the app economy. Prior to the App Store launch, none of that world existed. By 2014, the iOS App Store was distributing $10 billion to developers annually, with the ecosystem creating 627,000 jobs in the US in 2013 according to Apple's figures.

Meanwhile, a new race was just beginning – eighteen months after the iPhone had appeared, Google made its Android mobile operating system available free to hardware manufacturers, with scores of companies including Samsung, LG and HTC featuring the OS on its handsets. The move opened up a new line of competition for Apple, with a wave of new touchscreen smartphones, that were invariably cheaper than the iPhone, flooding the market.

There were far greater challenges closer to home, however. Never a big eater, by the beginning of 2008, Jobs was losing weight at a terrifying rate. This was partly because his appetite had been reduced due to his recent surgery and the morphine he was taking for pain relief, but the situation was being exacerbated by the restrictive diets and fasts Jobs had practised since his teenage years. Over the course of that spring, they would see him lose 18 kilos (40 lbs).

The changes in Jobs's appearance would soon become hard to ignore, with rumours beginning to foster over the state of his health. The unwanted focus on his gaunt look would continue further when, in August 2008, Bloomberg accidentally published a 2,500-word obituary on Jobs.

At a September 2008 keynote, Jobs poked fun at the embarrassing error, appearing on stage with the backdrop displaying the text: 'The reports of my death are greatly exaggerated', an adaptation of a famous Mark Twain quote. Despite the attempts at levity, his skeletal appearance was not particularly reassuring. Attempting to put aside his mounting health problems as best he could, Jobs continued to lead a now seemingly unstoppable Apple, which continued to roll out further great products including refined new iPods and iPhones, while its Mac range would be bolstered by the ultra-lightweight and portable MacBook Air. A stunning feat of industrial engineering, Jobs memorably unveiled the notebook by removing it from a standard manila envelope, highlighting its incredibly svelte profile, showing that he'd lost none of his flair for P.T. Barnum-style salesmanship.

Nevertheless, not all of Apple's output at this time would be unqualified successes. Apple TV, the company's set-top box which attempted to create a central hub for TV shows, movies, YouTube videos and home movies, never quite matched Jobs's wide-scale vision for the platform and failed to find a large audience, with Steve eventually compelled to describe the product as an ongoing 'hobby'.

Elsewhere, MobileMe, Apple's early attempt at a subscription-based cloud computing service, launched with a whole host of serious problems, resulting in irate customers losing emails. Furious with the way in which the product had fallen far below Apple's high standards, Jobs summoned the team to a meeting which ended in a brutal manner with the CEO yelling: 'You should hate each other for having let each other down!' In front of the whole group, he then proceeded to put someone new in charge of the product.

While the incident illustrated fire was still very much in Jobs's belly, his health continued to loom over Apple. In January 2009, Tim Cook took over as interim CEO while Jobs took a leave of absence. In a public statement released at the time, Steve attributed his weight loss to 'a hormone imbalance that has been robbing me of the proteins my body needs to be healthy. Sophisticated blood tests have confirmed this diagnosis. The remedy for this nutritional problem is relatively simple.'

While many tech and health experts speculated on the news, the hormone imbalance mentioned in the release was a result of his cancer spreading to his liver. Jobs had been placed on the waiting list for an organ transplant, with his need for a new liver quickly becoming desperate. Just as time was running out, a donor became available on 21 March 2009, with Jobs and Laurene immediately jetting out to Memphis for surgery. While the operation was successful, doctors found that there were tumours throughout his replaced organ that suggested the cancer had likely spread elsewhere. They also found spots on the thin membrane surrounding some of his other internal organs.

Jobs would once again go against his doctors wishes when he insisted that they not pump out his stomach when they needed to perform a routine procedure. It was a decision that led to him developing pneumonia. For a while it looked as though he may not recover, causing his family to rush to his bedside to be with him one more time. Somehow he managed to pull through, and would quickly show signs of his stubbornness, despite being deeply sedated. He decreed the oxygen monitor on his finger as being too 'ugly and too complex', and offered ideas for making the design simpler to hospital staff, while also frustrating his doctors by insisting on a diet of smoothies.

Just as he promised, Steve was ready to return to the fray at Apple in June and threw himself back into work to help orchestrate the launch of one final landmark product. As iPhone sales continued to soar, it was time to return to the unfinished business of the multi-touch tablet concept Jobs had green-lit years earlier.

Preparations for the launch coincided with the end of the noughties, an era on which Jobs and Apple had left an indelible imprint. Recognising his extraordinary achievements, *Fortune* named Jobs 'CEO of the Decade', saying, 'the past decade in business belongs to Jobs.' Calling him 'a showman, a born salesman, a magician who creates a famed reality-distortion field, [and] a tyrannical perfectionist', the magazine noted that in ten years, 'he has radically and lucratively reordered three markets – music, movies, and mobile telephones – and his impact on his original industry, computing, has only grown.' No wonder, it said, he was a worldwide celebrity.

While Ive's group of engineers and designers were secretly working on the iPad in tandem with new iPhone models, Jobs was throwing the press off the scent, telling the public and press that Apple had no intention of releasing a tablet. 'Tablets appeal to rich guys with plenty of other PCs and devices already,' he said publicly.

'Steve never lost his desire to do a tablet', Phil Schiller would later explain, with Jobs just waiting for the right time to bring the product to market. Mobile technology had evolved to such an extent that the bulky prototype tablets that Ive's team had produced in the early 2000s could now be worked up into elegant devices that matched the design of the iPhone and invited users to pick them up with one hand.

There was added incentive to move the project forward thanks to the emergence of netbooks, a new category of small, low-powered and ultimately cheap laptops that began to proliferate the market in 2007. Quickly cannibalising laptop sales, just two years later they would account for 20% of the laptop market. Jobs disliked the form factor immensely and vowed that Apple would never make a similar device. 'Netbooks aren't better than anything,' Steve Jobs said at the time. 'They're just cheap laptops.' The tablets Ive's team were working on would eventually be positioned as Apple's more satisfying alternative, with the device given the name iPad.

In January 2010, a still painfully thin Jobs returned to the stage to introduce the multi-touch-driven tablet. While some critics wondered whether the device would find a market, dismissing the iPad as just a giant iPhone, the new device would exceed sales expectations with Apple selling 7.5 million between its April launch and the end of September that year. The new product line saw Apple's sales reach $65 billion by its fiscal 2010 year end, a figure that had seen it grow 50% in one year, with profits reaching $14 billion.

An even more symbolic financial milestone was reached in May 2010 when Apple overtook Microsoft as the world's biggest tech company based on market value, with Apple's shares reaching $222 billion ahead of its long-time rival which had dipped to $219 billion. Apple's value would continue to race past Microsoft the following year, closing 2011 at $376 billion.

During some of the darker days of his battle with cancer, Jobs tearfully confided with Ive that he feared he wouldn't survive long enough to see his son Reed graduate from high school. It would be a moment of unbridled joy in June 2010, when the day of the ceremony arrived with Steve able to attend. 'Today is one of my happiest days,' he would recount in an email. A party that night saw Reed spend much of the night dancing with his father.

Sadly, by late 2010, the cancer reared up again, with his doctors finding evidence of new tumours. By Christmas his weight had plummeted to a mere 52 kilos (115 lbs). Concerns over his diet persisted. The family had a part-time cook who made him a variety of healthy meals, but he would refuse them after merely touching one or two to his tongue.

At the start of the new year, Jobs took what would be a third and final leave of absence with Cook once again ably taking on the day-to-day running of Apple. Around this time Jobs would be among the first people in the world to have a complete sequencing of all of the genes of his cancer tumour, and of his normal DNA. The sequencing would allow his medical team to deploy specific drugs targeted at the molecular pathways that were promoting the abnormal growth of cancer cells. The targeted new approach would see Jobs try out a string of new treatments, resulting in periods where he would improve before quickly relapsing.

He turned fifty-six in February and began eating again, improving enough to unveil the slimmer, updated iPad 2. He would return to the stage for one final keynote on 6 June to introduce Apple's iCloud service, which would allow users to sync and store their music, photos and other files.

# Apple vs Microsoft

## Market capital history

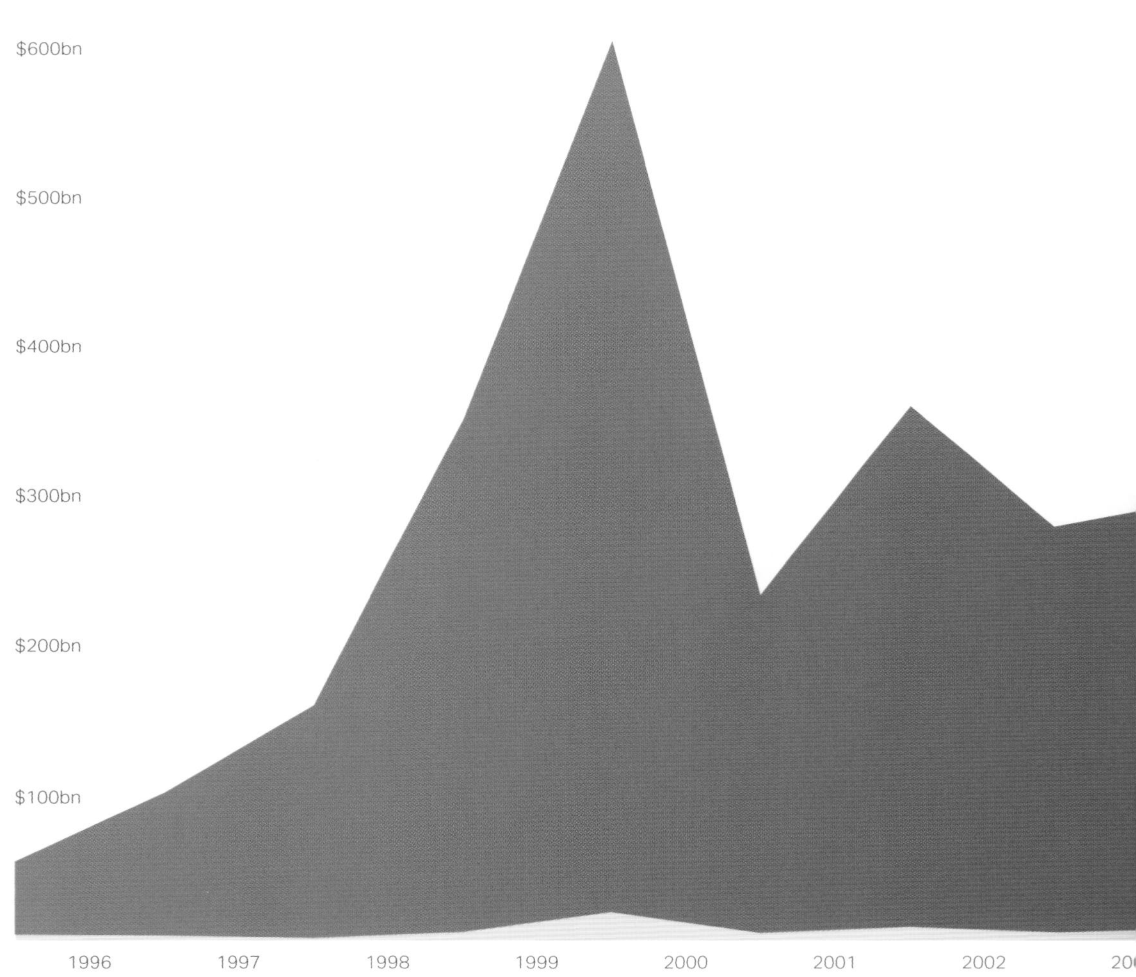

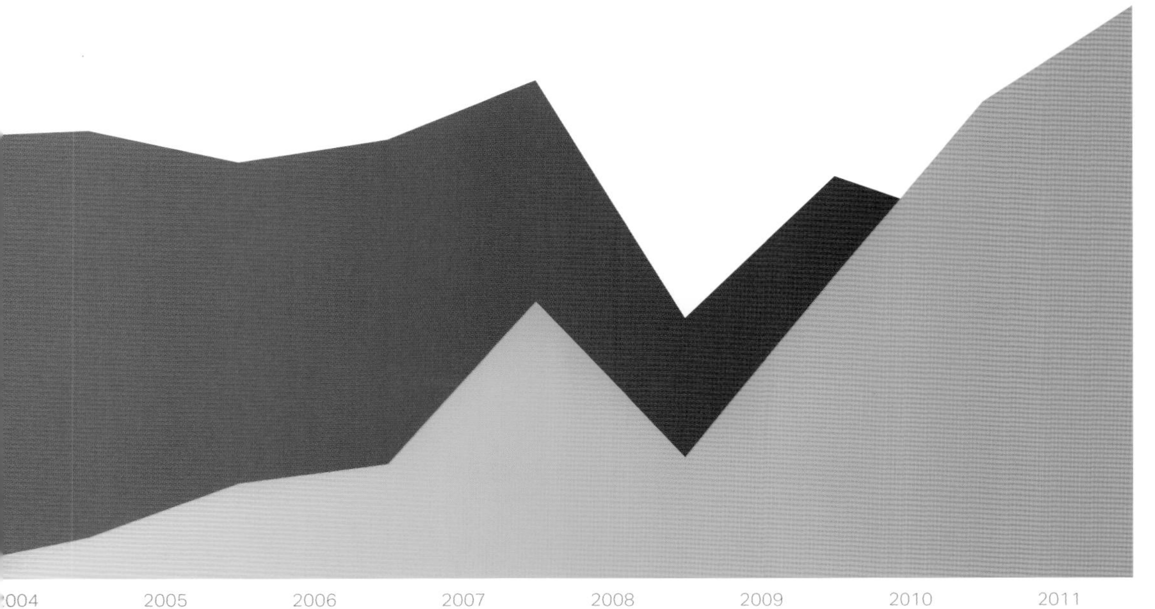
2004
2005
2006
2007
2008
2009
2010
2011
Apple
Microsoft

He continued to work from home, but eventually the pain he was experiencing became too much – the cancer had now spread to his bones, forcing him to concede that the end was close. Jobs decided that Tim Cook would be his eventual successor as CEO, a popular and unsurprising choice given how smoothly the company had been run during his spells as interim CEO. Jobs approached the subject in an August meeting, telling Cook he would soon take his role, while he would maintain the position of chairman of the board.

Upon hearing the news Cook was under the impression Jobs was likely to 'live a lot longer' and jokingly pondered what the arrangement would be like with the notoriously controlling Jobs. 'I tried to pick something that would incite him. So I said, "You mean that if I review an ad and I like it, it should just run without your okay?" And he laughed, and said, "Well, I hope you'd at least ask me!"'

Jobs reluctantly stepped down as Apple CEO on 24 August 2011. Intent on announcing the news in person, Jobs read out his statement to the board from a wheelchair.

His speech to the board announcing the end of his incredible era in charge would later be shared with the public: 'I have always said if there ever came a day when I could no longer meet my duties and expectations as Apple's CEO, I would be the first to let you know. Unfortunately, that day has come.'

Confirming Cook as his replacement, he added, 'I believe Apple's brightest and most innovative days are ahead of it. And I look forward to watching and contributing to its success in a new role.' As news of Steve's departure made headlines, Apple's share price fell by 5%.

Family and friends began to start visiting to say their goodbyes at the Jobs family home. Among those would be Bill Gates, with the pair spending three hours reminiscing and joking about how they had both managed to marry well to wives that had somehow kept them 'semi-sane'. Gates was now mainly focused on his charitable foundation rather than Microsoft, and Jobs noted that his former adversary looked 'happier than I've ever seen him'. Gates congratulated Jobs on 'the incredible stuff' he had created and for managing to somehow save Apple when it had reached rock bottom. He also admitted that Jobs's business approach of making both the software and hardware had worked. 'Your model worked, too,' Jobs countered. The pair hadn't always seen eye-to-eye, but the conversation would serve as a fitting close to a relationship that had fuelled the computer revolution and changed the world.

The Friday before he passed away, Cook spent the evening watching the sentimental American football movie *Remember the Titans* with Jobs. 'I was so surprised he wanted to watch that movie. I was like, Are you sure? Steve was not interested in sports at all. And we watched and we talked about a number of things and I left thinking that he was pretty happy.'

On 5 October 2011, with his wife, his children, and both of his sisters present, Steve Jobs passed away.

In her eulogy, which was reprinted in *The New York Times* a few weeks later, Mona Simpson drew attention to her brother's loyalty, his love of beauty and his hard work. The text would go on to detail Steve's final moments and words: 'He'd looked at his sister Patty, then for a long time at his children, then at his life's partner, Laurene, and then over their shoulders past them. 'Steve's final words were: "OH WOW. OH WOW. OH WOW."'

In Jobs's death, it seemed, the world came together to express its sorrow. Impromptu gatherings and ad hoc shrines quickly began to appear outside Apple stores across the globe. Twitter struggled to cope with the increased traffic as its users flooded the service with their own remembrances, while web users in China reportedly posted almost 35 million online tributes to the Apple founder.

In his statement, Bill Gates said: 'The world rarely sees someone who has had the profound impact Steve has had, the effects of which will be felt for many generations to come. For those of us lucky enough to get to work with him, it's been an insanely great honor.' The next generation of Silicon Valley pioneers were equally equivocal in their praise for the tech icon, with Facebook founder Mark Zuckerberg calling Jobs his 'mentor and friend'. Elsewhere, Apple's leading rivals such as Google and Sony all chipped in with glowing tributes.

Even world leaders as disparate as US President Barack Obama and his Russian counterpart Dmitry Medvedev were in agreement with their tributes, with both stating Jobs had changed the world. 'There may be no greater tribute to Steve's success than the fact that much of the world learned of his passing on a device he invented,' read Obama's official White House statement.

As a young man, Jobs had declared he wanted to 'put a ding in the universe', and no one could argue he had done just that.

Jobs was so closely identified with Apple that it was hard to imagine the company under any other CEO. While the understated Cook may not have the charismatic, showman-like charm that set his predecessor apart from so many of his peers and gained him an idol-like status among tech enthusiasts,

# #iSad

# How the world reacted online to Steve Jobs's death

15% of all tweets included the term 'Jobs'. #iSad was the highest trending Twitter hashtag, second was #ThankYouSteve

People sometimes have goals in life. Steve Jobs exceeded every goal he set himself.
**Steve Wozniak**

For those of us lucky enough to get to work with Steve, it's been an insanely great honor. I will miss Steve immensely.
**Bill Gates**

Steve, thank you for being a mentor and a friend. Thanks for showing that what you build can change the world. I will miss you.
**Mark Zuckerberg**

RIP Steve Jobs. A truly great businessman. Inspiration to so many. A real family man. He will be sorely missed.
**Richard Branson**

Steve lived the California Dream every day of his life and he changed the world and inspired all of us.
**Arnold Schwarzenegger**

Today the world lost a visionary leader, the technology industry lost an iconic legend and I lost a friend and fellow founder. The legacy of Steve Jobs will be remembered for generations to come.
**Michael Dell**

Rest in peace, Steve Jobs. From all of us at #Obama2012, thank you for the work you make possible every day - including ours.
**Barack Obama**

I have been in love with the world Steve Jobs made ever since my first Apple Mac. He was one of the great architects of the real. RIP.
**Salman Rushdie**

I feel honored to have known Steve Jobs. He was the most innovative entrepreneur of our generation. His legacy will live on for the ages.
**Steve Case**

Have the courage to follow your heart and intuition. They somehow already know what you truly want to become.
**Arianna Huffington**

Thank you, Steve.
**Jack Dorsey**

Woke to the news of Steve Jobs's death. He changed the world. I knew him a little and admired him entirely. Love to Apple and his family.
**Stephen Fry**

Just learned the terrible news of Steve Jobs' passing. What an incredible, inspiring life. Changed the world in so many ways. RiP Steve.
**Coldplay**

Today, we lost one of the most influential thinkers, creators and entrepreneurs of all time. Steve Jobs was simply the greatest CEO of his generation.
**Rupert Murdoch**

in the years that have passed most would concede that Cook has shown a similar ability to his predecessor in second guessing the market.

In 2014, the financial press giddily reported that Apple had more cash to spend than the United States government, with the company's most recent financial results at the time putting its reserves at $76.4bn in comparison to the US Treasury Department's operating cash balance of $73.7bn.

By the end of 2017, Apple's market capitalisation – the value ascribed to a company by investors – had more than doubled under Cook's tenure and was on course to inch toward a trillion dollars, cementing Apple's place as the world's most valuable public company.

Where the loss of Jobs has perhaps been most keenly felt by Apple is in the inspiration his innate sense for innovation and good design brought to the company. The two major new product lines introduced so far during Cook's stewardship, the Apple Watch and the Homepod smart speaker, have continued the company's tradition for well executed design, and strengthened the proposition of its ecosystem. But while both products have sold well, neither could be classed as a world-changing, disruptive product in the same way as the iPod, iPhone or indeed the iPad could.

However, one suspects he would be likely to have few qualms about Apple Park, the dream campus he helped to design with his great collaborator Jony Ive alongside British architect Norman Foster. In his last public appearance, weeks before his death, Jobs proudly showed off plans for the sprawling, space-age complex to the Cupertino City Council. On 12 September 2017, six years after his death, Apple opened its new home, realising the company founder's final big vision.

During its opening event, a previously unheard audio recording of Jobs talking about the soul of the company he had cofounded began to dissipate around the Park's cavernous auditorium bearing his name in tribute. During the moving prelude, Jobs's voice could be heard intoning how much can be told about the designer of a device by simply using the thing they had created – when people truly care about what they are working on, their thoughts, ideas and feelings get injected into their work and then transmitted to those who use it. As Apple CEO Tim Cook said in his opening remarks at the event, 'It was only fitting that Steve would open his theatre.'

Steve Jobs had earned his right to be regarded alongside the 'crazy ones' he had once celebrated. He'd been crazy enough to think he could change the world. And he did.

Endnotes:

Prologue

p. 5 'So we've got a plan that lets us stay in Cupertino.' – Steve Jobs Presents to the Cupertino City Council, 7 June 2011 https://www.youtube.com/watch?v=gtuz5OmOh_M

Chapter 1

p.12 'He had a workbench out in his garage' – Steve Jobs interview: One-on-one in 1995: https://www.computerworld.com/article/2498543/it-management/steve-jobs-interview--one-on-one-in-1995.html.

p.13 'It was really the most wonderful place in the world to grow up' – Steve Jobs interview, as above.

Chapter 2

p.21 'Lightning bolts went off in my head' – Isaacson, Walter. *Steve Jobs*, Simon & Schuster, New York, 2011.

p.23 'Things became much more clear' – Schlender, Brent and Tetzeli, Rick, *Becoming Steve Jobs: The Evolution of a Reckless Upstart into a Visionary Leader Crown,* New York, 2015.

p.24 'History of the 9100A desktop calculator, 1968', *HP.com*, ,2012 http://www.hp.com/hpinfo/abouthp/histnfacts/museum/personalsystems/0021/0021history.html

p.24 Data from http://www.willegal.net/appleii/apple1-originals.htm

p.28 'I saw my first desktop computer there' – Steve Jobs interview 1995 Smithsonian Institution Oral History Interview, http://americanhistory.si.edu/comphist/sj1.html.

p.28 'Recalling when Bill Hewlett himself had chatted' – 1984 Playboy Interview, http://reprints.longform.org/playboy-interview-steve-jobs.

p.28 'I remember my first day on the assembly line' – Denton, Bob, *"100 PC Moments",* Bob Dentonbself-published, 2014.

Chapter 3

p.35 'I was furious'– Young, Jeffrey S, *Steve Jobs – The Journey is the Reward*, Lynx Books, 1988.

p.38 'The Beatles' music was nice and good' – 'Steve Wozniak tells us one of his favorite stories about Steve Jobs', *Business Insider*, April 2017, http://uk.businessinsider.com/steve-wozniak-favorite-story-steve-jobs-bob-dylan-2017-4.

p.40 Data from http://www.hp.com/hpinfo/abouthp/histnfacts/museum/personalsystems/0021/0021history.html

p.41 'I got stoned for the first time;' – 'How blue box phone phreaking put Steve Jobs and Woz on the road to Apple', *Esquire.com*, October 2015, http://www.esquire.com/news-politics/a38878/steve-jobs-steve-wozniak-blue-box-phone-phreaking/.

p.43 'I was so grabbed by the article' – *The Making of Silicon Valley – A One Hundred Year Renaissance*, – Documentary, 1997 https://archive.org/details/XD1620_1_97MakingSiliconVlly_100yrRen.

p.43 Steve Wozniak interview with Dan Lyons, 2011 https://web.archive.org/web/20120615093253/http://realdanlyons.com/blog/2011/10/11/a-conversation-with-woz.

Chapter 4

p.47 'This was California' – 1984 Playboy Interview, http://reprints.longform.org/playboy-interview-steve-jobs.

p.48 'Steve said that Reed was the only college he wanted to go' – Young, Jeffrey S. and Simon, William L., *iCon: Steve Jobs, the greatest second act in the history of business*, Wiley, Hoboken, New Jersey, 1997.

p.48 'It's one of the things in life I really feel ashamed about' – Isaacson, Walter, *Steve Jobs*, Simon & Schuster, New York, 2011.

p.48 'I don't think he had any other friends' – Young, Jeffrey S. *Steve Jobs – The Journey is the Reward*, Lynx Books, 1988.

p.54 Data from statcounter.com.

p.56 'the power of intuition and experiential wisdom' – Isaacson, *Steve Jobs*, as above.

p.56 '[Chino] urged me to stay here.' – Isaacson, *Steve Jobs*, as above.

Chapter 5

p.62 'It's only one thing in life,' – How Steve Wozniak's breakout defined Apple's future, *Game Informer*, 2015 http://www.gameinformer.com/b/features/archive/2015/10/09/how-steve-wozniak-s-breakout-defined-apple-s-future.aspx.

p.63 Data from http://oldcomputers.net/appleii.html.

p.64 'It was as if my whole life had been leading up to this point' – Smith, Gina, *iWoz*, W. W. Norton, New York, 2006.

p.64 'I typed a few keys on the keyboard'– Smith, *iWoz*, as above.

p.68 'As far as I was concerned, it was "found money".' – 'Apple at 40: The forgotten founder who gave it all away', *BBC News*, 2016 http://www.bbc.co.uk/news/technology-35940300.

p.69 'That was the biggest single episode' – Moritz, Michael, *Return to the Little Kingdom*, Gerald Duckworth & Co Ltd, London, 2009.

Chapter 6

p.73 'It was clear to me' – Kunkel, Paul, *Apple Design: The Work of the Apple Industrial Design Group*, Graphis Inc., New York, 1997.

p.74 'He just conned me into working' – Moritz, Michael, *Return to the Little Kingdom*, Gerald Duckworth & Co, London, 2009.

p.74 '[Friedland] was charismatic and a bit of a con man' – Isaacson, Walter. *Steve Jobs*, Simon & Schuster, New York, 2011.

p.74 'It was a strange thing' – Isaacson, *Steve Jobs*, as above.

p.78 'weren't thinking anywhere near big enough' – Moritz, *Return to the Little Kingdom*, as above.

Chapter 8

p.102 'understood what we had a lot better than Xerox did' – 'The truth about Steve Jobs and Xerox PARC', LA Times, 2011 http://latimesblogs.latimes.com/technology/2011/10/steve-jobs-xerox-parc.html.

p.102 'They showed me really three things' – *Triumph of the Nerds*, PBS documentary, 1995.

Chapter 9

p.109 'Our friendship was all gone.' – Isaacson, Walter, *Steve Jobs*, Simon & Schuster, New York, 2011.

p.110 'I want to put a ding in the universe.' – 'The job Jobs did', The New York Times, 2011, https://tmagazine.blogs.nytimes.com/2011/08/25/the-job-jobs-did

p.110 'Design is not just what it looks like' – 'The guts of a new machine', The New York Times Magazine, 2003, https://www.nytimes.com/2003/11/30/magazine/the-guts-of-a-new-machine.html

p.110 'We hire people who want to make the best things' – 'The seed of Apple's innovation', Bloomberg, 2004, https://www.bloomberg.com/news/articles/2004-10-11/the-seed-of-apples-innovation

p.110 'Innovation distinguishes between a leader' - Callo, Carmine, *The Presentation Secrets of Steve Jobs*, McGraw-Hill Education, London, 2009.

p.111 'Your most unhappy customers are your greatest source of learning.' – Gates, Bill, and Collins Hemingway. Business @ the Speed of Thought: Using a Digital Nervous System, Warner Books, New York, 1999.

p.111 'Success is a lousy teacher.' – Gates, Bill, Nathan Myhrvold, and Peter Rinearson. The Road Ahead. Viking Press, New York, 1995.

p.111 'It's fine to celebrate success', - 'How Bill Gates became a leadership legend', Entrepreneur.com, 2016, https://www.entrepreneur.com/article/250607

p.111 'I never took a day off in my twenties' – Bill Gates interview, The Daily Mail, 2011, http://www.dailymail.co.uk/home/moslive/article-2001697/Microsofts-Bill-Gates-A-rare-remarkable-interview-worlds-second-richest-man.html

p.112 Data from https://www.networkworld.com/article/2236724/data-center/when-apple-flops--the-worst-apple-products-of-all-time.html.

Data from http://appleinsider.com/articles/11/05/08/fortunes_inside_apple_describes_a_furious_steve_jobs_after_mobileme_launch.

p.115 Data from http://oldcomputers.net/lisa.html

p.117 'In his presence, reality is malleable ...' – Isaacson, *Steve Jobs*, as above.

Chapter 10

p.123 'It was kind of a weird seduction visit' – Moritz, Michael, *Return to the Little Kingdom*, Gerald Duckworth & Co, 2009.

Chapter 11

p.146 'The Macintosh... is charting a simpler' – Linzmayer, Owen W., *Apple Confidential 2.0: The Definitive History of the World's Most Colorful Company*, No Starch Press, San Francisco, 2004.

p.158 'When the Macintosh Office was introduced in 1985' – Ex-Apple boss Sculley sets record straight on Jobs, BBC, 2012 http://www.bbc.co.uk/news/technology-16538745.
p.158 'I made my choice' – Schlender, Brent and Tetzeli, Rick, *Becoming Steve Jobs: The evolution of a reckless upstart into a visionary leader*, Sceptre, London, 2015.
p.159 'I hired the wrong guy, and he destroyed everything' – *Steve Jobs: The Lost Interview*, Magnolia Pictures, 2012.
p.159 'These guys were way ahead of us on graphics' – Schlender and Tetzeli, *Becoming Steve Jobs*, as above.

Chapter 13
p.169 'Texas billionaire Ross Perot immediately invested $20 million' *The Entrepreneurs*. PBS, 1986.
p.176 'I would have sucked at it on many levels' – Isaacson, Walter, *Steve Jobs*, Simon & Schuster, New York, 2011, p. 265.3
p.176 'I was in the parking lot with the key in the car' – Young, Jeffrey S. and Simon, William L., *iCon: Steve Jobs, the greatest second act in the history of business*, Wiley, Hoboken, New Jersey, 2005.
p.182 All data from imdb.com.
p.183 All data from imdb.com.
p.185 All data from statcounter.com.

Chapter 15
p.197 'You know, I've got a plan that could rescue Apple.' – Linzmayer, Owen W., *Apple Confidential 2.0: The Definitive History of the World's Most Colorful Company*, No Starch Press, San Francisco, 2004.
p.190 https://www.apple.com/newsroom/2011/07/19Apple-Reports-Third-Quarter-Results/
p.190 https://betanews.com/2011/07/19/apple-q3-2011-by-the-numbers-28-57b-revenue-and-7-31b-profit/
p.190 http://www.businessinsider.com/infographic-what-if-you-had-bought-apple-stock-in-1980-2011-10?pundits_only=0&get_all_comments=1&no_reply_filter=1&IR=T
p.201 'I'll advise Gil as much as I can' – Linzmayer, *Apple Confidential 2.0*, as above.
p.201 'I pretty much had given up hope' – Time interview, 12 August 1997.
p.201 'Steve Jobs meets Gil Amelio.' – Maclife, 6 Feb 2018.
p.202 http://www.willegal.net/appleii/apple1-originals.htm
p.208 http://www.businessinsider.com/infographic-what-if-you-had-bought-apple-stock-in-1980-2011-10?pundits_only=0&get_all_comments=1&no_reply_filter=1&IR=T
p.208 https://www.apple.com/newsroom/2011/07/19Apple-Reports-Third-Quarter-Results/
p.208 https://betanews.com/2011/07/19/apple-q3-2011-by-the-numbers-28-57b-revenue-and-7-31b-profit/

Chapter 16
p.216 'We already have a name we like a lot' – 'Steve Jobs Hated iMac, Wanted to Call it "MacMan"', 31 May 2012, https://mashable.com/2012/05/31/macman/#6Kw2f3ky6Zql.
p.217 'It was rough, really rough, the worst time in my life' – Isaacson, Walter, *Steve Jobs*, Simon & Schuster, New York, 2011.
p.221 'If you'd said, "Okay, we're going to change our microprocessor chip' – Isaacson, *Steve Jobs*, as above.
p.222 'I felt like a dope' – 'How big can Apple get?', Fortune, 21 Feb, 2005, https://web.archive.org/web/20050818025123/http://www.fortune.com:80/fortune/technology/articles/0,15114,1025093,00.html.
p.223 'The products stank' – iPod World, Newsweek,- 8 Jan 2004, http://www.newsweek.com/ipod-world-126245.
p.226 'They said they didn't know what to do with it.' – Straight dope on the iPod's birth, Wired, 17 October 2006, https://www.wired.com/2006/10/straight-dope-on-the-ipods-birth/.
p.226 'It's too big.' – Naughton, John, 'Steve Jobs: Stanford commencement address', The Observer, June 2005, - https://www.theguardian.com/technology/2011/oct/09/steve-jobs-stanford-commencement-address.
p.227 '1,000 songs in your pocket.' – Wired, as above.
p.231 'Steve made digital music fashionable.' – 'Seven ways iTunes changed the music industry', Billboard, 25 April 2013, https://www.billboard.com/biz/articles/news/1559622/seven-ways-itunes-changed-the-music-industry.
p.231 'You guys have your heads up your asses.' – 'The evolution of iTunes: The birth of a colossus', Billboard, 26 April 2013, https://www.billboard.com/biz/articles/news/branding/1559631/the-evolution-of-itunes-the-birth-of-a-colossus.
p.231 'It was going to be their storefront,' – 'iTunes' 10th anniversary: How Steve Jobs turned the industry upside down', Rolling Stone, 26 April 2013, https://www.rollingstone.com/music/news/itunes-10th-anniversary-how-steve-jobs-turned-the-industry-upside-down-20130426.
p.231 'When we told Steve, he looked at us like we just gave him a gift' – Billboard, as above.
p.234 'I thought, "Oh my God, it's starting to happen!' – Newsweek, as above.

Chapter 17
p.247 'This is going to change everything' – Isaacson, Walter, *Steve Jobs*, Simon & Schuster, New York 2011.
p.248 https://www.apple.com/newsroom/2011/07/19Apple-Reports-Third-Quarter-Results/
p.248 https://betanews.com/2011/07/19/apple-q3-2011-by-the-numbers-28-57b-revenue-and-7-31b-profit/
p.250 'I was worried about my children' – Isaacson, *Steve Jobs*, as above.
p.251 'None of our plants make the glass now' – Isaacson, *Steve Jobs*, as above.
p.251 'We don't have a product yet.' – The untold story: How the iPhone blew up the wireless industry', Wired, 1 Sept 2008, https://www.wired.com/2008/01/ff-iphone/.
p.252 https://www.apple.com/newsroom/2011/07/19Apple-Reports-Third-Quarter-Results/
p.252 https://betanews.com/2011/07/19/apple-q3-2011-by-the-numbers-28-57b-revenue-and-7-31b-profit/
p.255 'While some sections of the media dubbed it the 'Jesus phone' – 'Watch Steve Ballmer laugh at the original iPhone', Wired, September 2014, https://www.wired.com/2014/09/tech-time-warp-of-the-week-watch-steve-ballmer-laugh-at-the-original-iphone/.
p.255 'You don't want your phone to be like a PC' – Markoff, John, 'Phone shows Apple's impact on consumer products', New York Times, 11 January 2007, https://www.nytimes.com/2007/01/11/technology/11cnd-apple.html.
p.259 'You should hate each other' – Isaacson, *Steve Jobs*, as above.
p.260 'Tablets appeal to rich guys' – Isaacson, *Steve Jobs*, as above.
p.262 All data from https://ycharts.com.
p.264 'I tried to pick something that would incite him' – Schlender, Brent and Tetzeli, Rick, *Becoming Steve Jobs: The Evolution of a Reckless Upstart Into a Revolutionary Leader*, Crown Business, New York, 2015.
p.265 'I was so surprised he wanted to watch that movie.' – Schlender and Tetzeli, *Becoming Steve Jobs*, as above.
p.266 https://www.forbes.com/sites/jeffbercovici/2011/10/06/no-steve-jobss-death-did-not-set-a-twitter-record/#645e52db66fe
p.266 http://www.ask-kalena.com/social-media/death-of-steve-jobs-fails-to-break-twitter-record/
p.266 http://www.guinnessworldrecords.com/news/2016/3/10-years-of-twitter-five-key-tweets-that-made-record-breaking-history-421461

## Dedications

For Evie and Rory – Daddy's hope and inspiration
For my amazing wife and fellow adventurer Jen – we made it!
For Mum and the Brotherhood of Lynch – we are rock
For Des Lynch Snr – faraway, but always close


## Acknowledgments

Special thanks to Melissa Hookway for giving me the opportunity to tell this story and your encouragement amid the chaos, Charlotte Frost for helping keep things on track and the team at Founded for their excellent work in making my design briefs come to life.

Extra special thanks to Gerald Lynch, for being the catalyst and for all your help, even when things went nuclear, to Pat and Barry Langan – I'll never forgot all you've done for me and my incredible family during this time – and finally to the force of nature that is their daughter Jennifer – where would we all be without you.

Picture Credits:

p.8 Ralph Morse/Getty; p.10 SiliconValleyStock/Alamy Stock Photo; p.20 AF archive/Alamy Stock Photo; p.25 Tom Munnecke / Getty; p.26 Ted Thai/Getty; p.31 Lyn Alweis/Getty; p.34 AF archive/Alamy Stock Photo; p.39 Douglas Kirkland/ Getty; p.46 Science & Society Picture Library/Getty; p.57 John G. Mabanglo/Stringer/Getty; p.60 Future Publishing/ Getty; p.66 https://www.google.com/patents; p.72 Ted Thai/Getty; p.75 Ralph Morse/Getty; p.77 Kim Kulish/Getty; p.82 Science & Society Picture Library/Getty; p.85 Apic/Getty; p.87 Ted Thai/Getty; p.88 Bloomberg/Alamy; p.94 AF archive/ Alamy Stock Photo; p.96 Gilles Mingasson/Getty; p.106 Peter Da Silva/Getty; p.122 Hy Peskin/Getty; p.124 Myfreephotoshop.com; p.125 Pixeden.com; p.126-7 Wkimedia; p.133 Richard Lewisohn/Alamy Stock Photo; p.136 Chuck Nacke/ Alamy Stock Photo; p.138 New York Daily News/Getty; Stan Godlewski/Getty; William Stevens/Getty; Gabe Palacio/Getty; Kim Kulish/Getty; Kim Kulish/Getty; p.139 3 x Justin Sullivan/Getty; David Paul Morris/Getty; AFP/Getty; Justin Sullivan/ Getty; p.142 clockwise from top left (c) Levis; (c) Issy Miyake; (c) New-Balance; (c) Robert Marc; p.150 David Paul Morris/Getty; p.154 John G. Mabanglo/Getty; p.168 Justin Sullivan/Getty; p.180 AF archive / Alamy Stock Photo (c) FILM COMPANY WALT DISNEY / PIXAR; p.189 Bob Riha Jr/Getty; p.196 Justin Sullivan/Getty; p.199 Getty Images/Handout; p.205 https://www.reddit.com/r/apple/comments/5ah2ao/i_recently_acquired_several_original_think/; p.207 Ted Thai/ Getty; p.214 Taylor Hill/Getty; p.242 VCG/Getty; p.257 Justin Sullivan/Getty; p.269 Justin Sullivan/Getty

First published in 2018 by White Lion Publishing,

an imprint of The Quarto Group.
The Old Brewery, 6 Blundell Street
London N7 9BH,
United Kingdom
T (0)20 7700 6700 F (0)20 7700 8066
www.QuartoKnows.com



A catalogue record for this book is available from the British Library.

ISBN 978 1 78131 722 8

10 9 8 7 6 5 4 3 2 1

Design by Founded Design Ltd

Printed in China